MSM

MATHEMATICS

GW00632704

BOOK 5^x

Graham Newman
Head of Mathematics, Prestwich High School, Bury
and Chief Examiner in GCSE Mathematics

Jim Miller
Deputy Head, Redewood School,
Newcastle upon Tyne and Assistant Chief
Examiner in GCSE Mathematics

MSM Series Editor:
Dr Charles Plumpton

Nelson

Published by
Thomas Nelson and Sons Ltd
Nelson House Mayfield Road
Walton-on-Thames Surrey
KT12 5PL UK

51 York Place
Edinburgh
EH1 3JD UK

Thomas Nelson (Hong Kong) Ltd
Toppan Building 10/F
22a Westlands Road
Quarry Bay Hong Kong

Thomas Nelson Australia
102 Dodds Street
South Melbourne
Victoria 3205 Australia

Nelson Canada
1120 Birchmount Road
Scarborough Ontario
M1K 5G4 Canada

First published 1992
ISBN 0-17-438450-5
NPN 9 8 7 6 5 4 3

Printed in Italy

The author and publishers wish to thank the following for permission
to use copyright material.

Barclays Bank Plc, Girobank Plc, Lloyds Bank Plc, Midland Bank Plc, National
Westminster Bank Plc and TSB Bank Plc for the reproduction of their logos;

British Railways Board for the figure and timetable from 'Section K-Solent
and Wessex/West of England Line';

Casio Computer Company, Tokyo, Japan, for reproduction of the FX45IM Calculator;

National Express for material from their timetable leaflet;

Wickes Building Supplies Ltd for material from their catalogue.

Photographic material:

British Aircraft Corporation, p. 230; Camera Press (Globe) London, pp 119, 125, 228;
Eurocamp, p. 116; Ford Motor Company Ltd, p. 167; Glyn Genin, Camera Press (F/T)
London, p. 123; John Laing Plc, p. 50; New York Convention and Visitors Bureau,
p. 117 bottom; Olympia Business Machines Co. Ltd, p. 30; Renault, p. 165; and
Thomson Holidays, p. 117 top.

Cover picture copyright The Photo Source

Every effort has been made to trace all the copyright holders, but if any have been
inadvertently overlooked the publishers will be pleased to make the necessary
arrangements at the first opportunity.

Contents

Preface

This book forms part of the MSM Series which has been written to correspond to the National Criteria for GCSE Mathematics examinations, and to the Mathematics National Curriculum assessment and testing framework. In particular the X-stream of books are for use of pupils who are intending going on to the intermediate and lower levels of the GCSE Mathematics examination.

Book 5X further extends the skills which have already been used in Books 3X and 4X, provides necessary revision of topics, and places a greater emphasis on the use and application of mathematics in everyday life and the world of work. As such, Book 5X supports the series but can also stand alone as a revision textbook for those students who are either re-taking or revising GCSE. It may also appeal to mature students, and indeed to others taking non-GCSE courses in Mathematics and Numeracy, such as City & Guilds, RSA or courses certified by other means.

In terms of the National Curriculum, the work covered in Book 5X revises the work covered in both the previous books. Book 5X covers all the Attainment Targets, and several extension topics, up to level 8.

1. Personal finance

Income

Soon you may be in employment, earning money. You will therefore need to be aware of some factors which affect a regular income. A primary consideration is likely to be the rate of pay – how much an hour or week or month or year you can earn. There are other items which directly affect the money you receive; for example, overtime, income tax, national insurance, pension contributions. Also, you must be aware of how a bank or building society account is operated. Further, you may want to save some of your earnings by investing in life assurance or a regular payments scheme.

In this chapter we shall look at some of the principal factors which affect income.

Fancy Fashions

Shop Assistant Required

£1.85 per hour   9.00 - 5.00

Tel: 037-2916

Rates of pay

Example 1

'Part-time receptionist/telephonist required – 20 hours per week – actual times negotiable – £2.64 per hour.'

Jenny is thinking of applying for the job.

(*a*) How much will she be paid for 3 hours' work?

(*b*) On a Wednesday she could work from 9.00 a.m. until 12 noon, and then from 1.30 p.m. to 5.30 p.m. How much would she be paid for Wednesday?

(c) If she could work from 9.00 a.m. until 11.30 a.m. on a Friday, how much would she be paid for that day?

(d) What would be her weekly pay for 20 hours?

Answer:

(a) For 3 hours the pay will be $3 \times £2.64 = £7.92$.

(b) She could work for 7 hours, so her pay would be $7 \times £2.64 = £18.48$.

(c) For $2\frac{1}{2}$ hours she would be paid $2\frac{1}{2} \times £2.64 = £6.60$.

(d) The weekly pay for 20 hours would be $20 \times £2.64 = £52.80$.

Example 2

'Manufacturing assistant required – up to £4.36 per hour (depending upon qualifications) for a 35 hour week.'

Assuming that Peter has the necessary qualifications, how much will he be paid for

(a) a day in which he works for 7 hours

(b) a week in which he works 35 hours

(c) working during a month in which he works $7\frac{1}{2}$ hours on each of 23 days

(d) a day when he starts at 8.30 a.m., stops for lunch at 12 noon, starts work again at 1.00 p.m. and finishes at 5.00 p.m.?

Answer:

(a) Peter will be paid $7 \times £4.36 = £30.52$.

(b) He will be paid $35 \times £4.36 = £152.60$ (remember that 152.6 on your calculator means £152.60).

(c) He will be paid $23 \times 7\frac{1}{2} \times £4.36 = £752.10$.

(d) He works for $3\frac{1}{2}$ hours in the morning, and 4 hours in the afternoon. He will be paid $7\frac{1}{2} \times £4.36 = £32.70$.

EXERCISE 1.1

1 Alison works for two hours in the evening at a local shop. If she is paid £1.15 per hour, how much will she be paid for working (*a*) one evening (*b*) three evenings (*c*) five evenings?

2 Andrew starts a job in a supermarket; he is paid £1.40 an hour.

(*a*) On his first day he works for six hours. How much will he be paid?

(*b*) During the next four days he works for seven hours a day. How much will he be paid for these four days?

(*c*) How much will he be paid altogether for these five days?

3 Jill can work for $7\frac{1}{2}$ hours a day from Monday to Thursday, but can only do 3 hours on a Friday. How much will she be paid for the week, if her rate of pay is £2.30 per hour?

4 Megan has been offered two jobs. One is for 30 hours a week, at a rate of £2.40 an hour. The other is for 36 hours a week, at £1.90 an hour.

(*a*) Work out which job pays more in a week, the first or the second.

(*b*) The second job changes its rate of pay. If both jobs now pay the same amount weekly, what is this new rate of pay?

5 Julia is paid £2.88 an hour. If she expects to be paid at least £20 a day, for how many complete hours a day will she need to work?

6 My pay is going up from £1.80 to £1.98 per hour.

(*a*) What percentage increase is this?

(*b*) How much more will I be paid for a 32-hour week?

4

Example 3

Robert begins a job in advertising, for which the rate of pay is £650 per month. How much will Robert be paid for (*a*) three months' work (*b*) a year's work (12 months) (*c*) a week's work?

(*a*) For three months he will be paid $3 \times £650 = £1950$.

(*b*) For a year he will be paid $12 \times £650 = £7800$.

(*c*) Weekly pay $= \dfrac{\text{annual pay}}{52} = \dfrac{£7800}{52} = £150$.

Because the number of days in a month varies, it is only an approximation to divide monthly pay by 4 to obtain weekly pay. In Robert's case we would obtain a value of $£650 \div 4 = £162.50$ a week by this method. To work out the weekly pay, we need to divide the annual pay by 52, as there are 52 weeks in a year.

$$\text{Weekly pay} = \frac{\text{monthly pay} \times 12}{52}$$

Example 4

Zara is appointed to a post in an insurance company at a salary of £10 452 a year.

(*a*) How much will she be paid in her first five months?

(*b*) John joins the company on the same salary as Zara, but leaves after seven weeks. How much will he be paid?

(*c*) After a year, Zara's salary rises by 6.5%. What is her new salary?

(*a*) Monthly pay $= \dfrac{£10\,452}{12} = £871$.

After five months, Zara will be paid $5 \times £871 = £4355$.

(b) Weekly pay $= \dfrac{£10\,452}{52} = £201.$

   For seven weeks, John will receive $7 \times £201 = £1407.$

(c) Increase is 6.5% of £10 452 $= \dfrac{6.5 \times 10\,452}{100}$

$$= £679.38$$

   Zara's new salary $= £10\,452 + £679.38$

$$= £11\,131.38$$

We can do the calculation more quickly, by realising that the new figure is 106.5% of the old figure.

$$\text{New salary} = \dfrac{106.5 \times 10\,452}{100}$$

$$= £11\,131.38, \text{ in one step}$$

If increase is 8%, then new value = 1·08 × old value

EXERCISE 1.2

1 How much a week is £8000 per year, to the nearest £?

2 How much a week is £675 per month, to the nearest £?

3 'Starting pay £570 a month. After working for three months, your monthly pay rises to £610.'

   Joan works for seven months before leaving the job.

   (a) How much will she be paid altogether?

   (b) What is the percentage rise after three months, to the nearest whole number?

4 Susan and Tracy each work for £185 per week. When both girls are due for a rise, Susan's new wage will be £202.50, while Tracy's rise is 9%.

(a) How much extra pay does Susan get?

(b) Who will be earning more after both girls receive their rises?

5 If you could have either £9000 a year, £750 a month, or £180 a week, which would you choose?

6 Mike is paid £830 per month. A rise of £720 per *year* is agreed. What is Mike's new monthly pay?

7 At present Ivan earns £910.75 per month. He sees a job advertised at £11 000 annually. What percentage increase would this job pay compared with his present one?

8 Harry is paid £175.50 a week, and Surea works for £738.25 a month. How much a year do they earn together?

9 Steven's basic pay is £8320 a year, but he earns commission on any sales he makes. How much commission will he need to make in order to increase his monthly income to £900?

10 Neil's pay for this month is £828.94, a rise of 9.5% compared with last month. What was Neil's pay last month?

Overtime

```
┌─────────────────────────────────────────┐
│                                           │
│         SUPERSTORE                        │
│      ─────────────────────                │
│   Assistant Manager Required              │
│       Overtime available                  │
│        Apply: 396-4127                    │
│                                           │
└─────────────────────────────────────────┘
```

Some jobs, by their nature, allow opportunities to work for more hours than is normal. For instance, a supermarket may stay open until 8.00 p.m. on two or three nights during a week. The till operator may therefore work longer than normal on those days. In order to encourage the till operator to work longer hours, the rate of pay for the extra hours is usually higher than the normal rate of pay. Some common phrases describing overtime rates are 'time-and-a-half' or 'time-and-a-third' or 'double time on Sundays'.

'Time-and-a-half' means that the rate of pay is half as much again as the normal rate. If the normal pay is £3.00 per hour, then the overtime rate, at 'time-and-a-half', is £3.00 + £1.50 = £4.50 per hour.

Similarly, **'time-and-a-third'** means £3.00 + $\frac{1}{3}$ of £3.00, which is a total of £4.00 per hour.

'Double time' would be £6.00 per hour.

EXERCISE 1.3

Calculate the overtime rate (*a*) at time-and-a-half (*b*) at time-and-a-third, for each of these hourly rates. Give your answers correct to the nearest penny.

1	£2.00	*2*	£4.50
3	£3.30	*4*	£2.43
5	£5.40	*6*	£2.50
7	£3.57	*8*	£4.99
9	£5.17	*10*	£7.77

Example 5

'Assistant required in market garden – £2.52 per hour for a 35-hour week – overtime available at time-and-a-half.'

Mike takes the job. How much will he earn if he works for 40 hours in one week?

For the regular 35 hours he will earn 35 × £2.52 = £88.20.

The overtime rate is £2.52 + $\frac{1}{2}$ of £2.52 = £2.52 + £1.26 = £3.78 per hour.

For five hours of overtime Mike will earn 5 × £3.78 = £18.90.

Therefore he will earn £88.20 + £18.90 = £107.10 for his 40 hours.

EXERCISE 1.4

1   Marie, who works on the till, is paid at a rate of £2.70 an hour. All hours worked on a Saturday are paid at 'time-and-a-half'. How much will Marie earn for working seven hours on a Saturday?

2   Kevin, from the paint department, is paid £3.42 an hour. If he works for more than seven hours in one day, then he is paid 'time-and-a-third' for any extra hours. How much will he be paid if he works for ten hours on one day?

3   Kath, the gardening section manager, is paid £3.80 an hour for whatever hours she works. If she works for the same ten hours as Kevin, will she be paid more or less than Kevin?

4 During the next bank holiday weekend, the supermarket will stay open on Sunday and Monday, from 9.00 a.m. until 5.00 p.m. Workers will be paid 'double time' for all hours worked on Sunday or Monday. Pete intends to work on both days. His normal pay is £3.42 an hour. He takes an hour off (unpaid) for lunch on both days. How much will he earn for working these two days?

Income tax

If you are working, then the Government takes from you some of your earnings in order to help to pay for the running of the country. The money taken from you is called **Income Tax** (i.e. a tax, or contribution, from your income), and is usually deducted from your pay by your employer, under the Pay-As-You-Earn (PAYE) scheme.

The actual amount that you pay depends upon a number of factors, and can be complicated to work out. First we look at the more usual items which affect income tax.

(The figures below refer to the tax year 1988-89, i.e. from 6th April 1988 to 5th April 1989).

Personal allowance A single person can earn up to £2605 a year, £217.42 a month or £50.18 a week without having to pay any income tax. For a married man the figure is £4095 a year, £341.59 a month or £78.83 a week.

Rate of income tax If earnings are greater than these personal allowances, then income tax must be paid at the **basic** tax rate of 25% on taxable income (total income less personal allowance). For high earners, the **higher** tax rate of 40% is paid on taxable income greater than £19 300 a year.

Example 6

Dulip, who is unmarried, earned £307.42 last month. How much income tax will he pay?

Firstly, he will pay no tax on £217.42. This leaves £307.42 − £217.42 = £90 of *taxable* income.

His income tax is therefore 25% of £90 which is £22.50.

Example 7

Helen is single and her annual salary is £7500. How much income tax will she expect to pay each month, throughout the year?

Helen's taxable income is £7500 − £2605 = £4895.

Her income tax is therefore 25% of £4895 = £1223.75.

Each month she will pay $\dfrac{£1223.75}{12}$ = £101.98 in income tax.

So she will expect to pay about £102 per month in income tax.

National Insurance

To pay towards the state pension, **National Insurance contributions (NICs)** are deducted from your earnings, rather like income tax. During the 1988-89 tax year they were calculated in a fairly complicated way, like this:

P. ANDERSON	14.10.89 - 21.10.89
Gross Pay 689.23	**Net Pay** 519.39
Income Tax 107.81	
N.I. 62.03	

Weekly earnings	NIC
up to £40.99	nothing
£41.00 up to £69.99	5% of earnings
£70.00 up to £104.99	7% of earnings
£105.00 up to £304.99	9% of earnings
£305.00 and over	9% of £305 (= £27.45)

Example 8

Calculate the NIC for weekly earnings of (*a*) £50 (*b*) £100 (*c*) £150 (*d*) £320 (*e*) £520.

(*a*) NIC is 5% of £50 = £2.50

(*b*) NIC is 7% of £100 = £7.00

(*c*) NIC is 9% of £150 = £13.50

(*d*) NIC is 9% of £305 = £27.45

(*e*) NIC is 9% of £305 = £27.45

'Take-home' pay

When you start work, you will be particularly interested in how much you will actually receive from your employer to take home with you each week, or month.

Let us look at some examples of how 'take-home' pay can be calculated. We will need to refer to the Income Tax and National Insurance sections above, in order to work out how much money has to be deducted in the examples.

Example 9

Clive is paid £750 per month as a plant manager in the paper factory where he works. He is married, and pays only income tax and national insurance. What is his take-home pay?

As he is married, Clive will pay no income tax on £341.59 (the married man's personal allowance – see Income Tax section above).

This means that his taxable income is £750 – £341.59 = £408.41.

At the basic tax rate of 25%, Clive will pay 25% of £408.41 = £102.10 in income tax.

His weekly rate of pay will be about $\frac{1}{4}$ of £750 which is £187.50.

This means that his NI contribution will be 9% of his earnings (see NI section above). So he will pay 9% of £750 = £67.50 per month in NICs.

Clive's take-home pay is therefore £750 – (£102.10 + £67.50)

$$= £750 - £169.60$$

$$= £580.40 \text{ per month.}$$

(£750 per month is actually £750 × 12 ÷ 52 = £173.08 per week. This means that Clive still has to pay 9% of £750 as NICs.)

Example 10

Jim applies for a job as a worker in the paper factory, where the wages are advertised as £155 per week. He is single, paying only income tax and NI. Work out his take-home pay.

Because Jim's personal allowance is £50.18, his weekly taxable income is £155 − £50.18 = £104.82.

He will therefore pay 25% of £104.82 = £26.21 in income tax.

His NICs will be 9% of £155 = £13.95.

Jim's take-home pay will be £155 − (£26.21 + £13.95)

$$= £155 − £40.16$$
$$= £114.84 \text{ per week}$$

Example 11

Edward, having just left school, starts at the factory earning a weekly wage of £75.00. Assuming only income tax and NI as deductions, how much will Edward take home weekly?

Edward's taxable income is £75 − £50.18 = £24.82.

He will pay 25% of £24.82 = £6.21 in income tax.

His NICs will be 7% of £75.00 = £5.25.

Edward's weekly take-home pay is £75.00 − (£6.21 + £5.25)

$$= £75.00 − £11.46$$
$$= £63.54 \text{ per week}$$

EXERCISE 1.5

In this exercise, assume that income tax and NI are the only deductions and use these figures:

Income tax − Personal allowances 1988-89 (amount earned before tax is payable)

	Weekly	Monthly	Annually
Single	£50.18	£217.42	£2605
Married man	£78.83	£341.59	£4095

(Take the rate of income tax as 25% of taxable income.)

National Insurance Contributions (1988-89)

Weekly earnings	NIC
up to £40.99	nothing
£41.00 up to £69.99	5% of earnings
£70.00 up to £104.99	7% of earnings
£105.00 up to £304.99	9% of earnings
£305.00 and over	9% of £305 (= £27.45)

Work out the 'take-home' pay for these weekly wages:

1 £88.00 **2** £100

3 £200 **4** £150

5 £142.50 **6** £63.78

7 £91.56 **8** £360.20

9 £115.00 **10** £275.94

11 George has a salary of £13 000 a year.

(*a*) How much per week is this?

(*b*) Work out his take-home pay, per week.

(*c*) How much will he take home in a year?

12 Marie is paid £17 400 a year. By working out her weekly wage and weekly take-home pay, calculate her take-home pay for the year.

13 Leslie's salary is £9340 a year. Using the method of questions 11 and 12 above, work out (*a*) his take-home pay for the year (*b*) the percentage of his salary which is taken in NICs and income tax.

14 Jeanette is paid £837 per month. Work out (*a*) her pay for a year (*b*) her weekly pay (*c*) her weekly take-home pay (*d*) her annual take-home pay (*e*) her monthly take-home pay.

15 If Jeanette, in question 14, is given a rise of 8% in monthly pay, work out her new monthly take-home pay.

Is this a rise of more than, or less than, 8% of her previous take-home pay?

Life assurance

Although there are many life assurance companies, each with a number of schemes, there are essentially two types of life assurance.

(i) **Term assurance,** in which you pay a small premium (i.e. monthly payment) to be assured a large sum of money, payable on death.

(ii) **Endowment assurance,** where the premiums are higher, and the sum assured smaller than for term assurance: if you die, then the sum assured is paid, but if you are still living after an agreed date (typically 15, 20 or 25 years after starting the scheme) then you receive the sum of money assured.

With term assurance there is no final payment to you, as it is paid to your dependents only on your death. Endowment assurance, however, can be used as a method of saving for your future.

A typical table enables you to work out various premiums, depending on the type of life assurance, the length of an endowment assurance and the sum of money assured.

Example 12

The table lists the annual premiums payable for each £1000 of term assurance.

(*a*) Why are the premiums higher for older people?

(*b*) What annual premium would a 35-year-old person pay, for a £10 000 assurance?

(*c*) Noel is 43, and wishes to have £35 000 term assurance. What will be his *monthly* payment?

(*d*) Hilary, who is 27, can afford to pay £10 a month on term assurance. What is the maximum amount for which she can be insured?

Term assurance – cost per £1000	
Age	Annual premium
under 21	£7.80
under 26	£9.40
under 31	£11.30
under 36	£13.90
under 41	£17.40
under 46	£22.00
under 51	£28.10
under 56	£36.50

(a) The older you are, the fewer payments you are likely to make before you die. Hence the older you are, the higher the premiums for each £1000.

(b) A 35-year-old person is under 36. The table gives the premium of £13.90 for £1000. For £10 000 of term assurance, the premium will be $10 \times £13.90 = £139$.

(c) Noel is under 46. His annual premium for £1000 will be £22; for £35 000 his premium will be $35 \times £22 = £770$. Hence, his *monthly* payment will be $£770 \div 12 = £64.17$.

(d) Hilary can afford to pay an annual premium of $12 \times £10 = £120$. From the table, a premium of £11.30 will cover her for £1000. So a premium of £120 will enable her to obtain $120 \div 11.30 \times £1000$ of term assurance. This is £10 619.

Example 13

The table shows the monthly premiums for each £1000 of endowment assurance for 15, 20 or 25 years.

Endowment assurance – monthly premiums per £1000, excluding bonuses				
Age next birthday		Period of time during which premiums are paid		
Man	Woman	15 years	20 years	25 years
20	25	£5.91	£4.43	£3.53
25	30	£5.96	£4.47	£3.56
30	35	£6.02	£4.52	£3.63
35	40	£6.09	£4.59	£3.71
40	45	£6.19	£4.70	£3.88
45	50	£6.37	£4.94	£4.17
50	55	£6.66	£5.29	£4.62
55		£7.09	£5.78	–

(a) How much is the monthly premium for endowment assurance of £1000, for Parveen, who is a 29 year old woman who wishes to be paid in 15 years' time?

(b) Denis takes out a 20-year endowment assurance for £10 000. He is 36 years old. How much will be the premium?

(*c*) Pauline, who is nearly 35, decides to take out an endowment assurance, to be paid to her when she retires in 25 years' time. If she can afford to pay £15 per month, what sum of money (excluding bonuses) will she be due to receive when she retires?

(*a*) From the table, Parveen's monthly premium is £5.96.

(*b*) Denis will pay £4.70 for each £1000. His monthly premium for £10 000 will be $10 \times £4.70 = £47$.

(*c*) For a monthly premium of £3.63, Pauline would receive £1000 in 25 years' time. If she pays a premium of £15, then in 25 years' time she will receive $15 \div 3.63 \times £1000$, which comes to £4132.23.

EXERCISE 1.6

Using the table on page 14 for term assurance, work out the annual premium for these people:

1 Wendy, aged 22, who would like £10 000 insurance.

2 Jill, aged 43, wishing to have £20 000 insurance.

3 Brian, aged 28, who would like to have £45 000 of insurance cover.

4 Janice, aged 30, requiring £33 000 of insurance cover.

5 Steve, aged 47, who would prefer to have an insurance of £25 000.

Work out the amount of term assurance payable on death to the following people:

6 James, paying a premium of £240 per year. He is 40 years old.

7 Amanda, aged 24, whose premium for the year is £600.

8 Dilip, who is 42 years old, and who pays £540 in a year.

9 Jennifer, who begins on her eighteenth birthday to pay £12 a *month*.

10 Allan, aged 28, who pays £55 per *month*.

Use the endowment assurance table on page 15 to complete the missing figures below for women:

	Age	Period of assurance	Assurance required	Premium payable
11	27	20 years	£1000	*
12	53	15 years	£8000	*
13	21	25 years	£12 500	*
14	33	20 years	£6000	*
15	39	25 years	*	£37.10
16	28	20 years	*	£22.35
17	41	15 years	£7500	*
18	49	15 years	*	£63.70
19	19	25 years	*	£52.95
20	23	20 years	*	£45.00

Bank accounts

The majority of people who earn wages or salaries are nowadays paid by cheque, often directly into their bank account. How can they get at their money, so that they can buy food, clothes, etc., and pay other bills?

Let us see how to open a bank account, and how it operates.

(i) Select your bank, go in and tell the counter clerk that you wish to open a *current* account (i.e. an account for day-to-day use). You will usually need to take with you some money, either cash or a cheque payable to you from someone else, so that you can deposit the money in your new account.

(ii) After giving details (name, address, typical signature, etc.) you are likely to be given a temporary cheque book, and possibly a deposit book, to use until such time as the bank has processed your request. This enables you to **withdraw** from (take money or cheques out of) or **deposit** into (pay money or cheques into) your account until your personal cheque book and deposit book arrive.

(iii) Now you can pay for goods (a coat, say) by writing a cheque.
You need to remember to write *five* things on your cheque:
(a) the date,
(b) whom you are paying,
(c) the amount in words,
(d) the amount in figures,
(e) your signature.

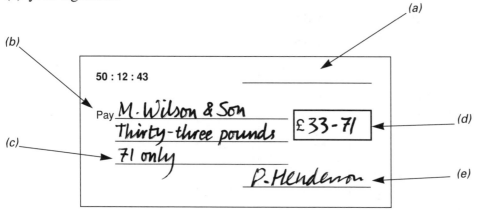

It is also helpful to make a copy on the cheque book stub or
counterfoil. You then give the cheque to the shop assistant, in return
for the goods (i.e. the coat). What happens after that is intricate, but
basically your account will be *debited* (reduced) by an amount equal
to the price of the coat, in about three or four days' time.

(iv) If you need some actual cash, then you can write a cheque to
yourself (for £25.00, say), take it to your bank, hand it over, and the
bank clerk will give you £25 in cash (two £10 notes and a £5 note, or
250 10p pieces, if you wish!).

(v) You can deposit cash, or cheques payable to you, into your
account in a similar manner.

(vi) You can arrange for the bank to send you a **statement** of your
account at regular intervals, say every month. This tells you how
much you have withdrawn or deposited during the month, and tells
you your current **balance** (how much money is in the account).

Date	Code	Reference	Debit	Credit	Balance
20SEP91				Brought forward	240.26
20SEP91	SPB	B'STOKE.TOWN CNTRE	40.00		200.26
23SEP91	TC		72.62		127.64
25SEP91	VIS	OUR PRICE RECORDS	18.99		108.65
26SEP91	CHQ	B'STOKE.,WOTE ST.		22.28	130.93
27SEP91	SPB	B'STOKE.TOWN CNTRE	70.00		60.93
30SEP91	CHQ	001771	44.55		
30SEP91	SPB	B'STOKE.,WOTE ST.	20.00		3.62 DR
10CT91	DD	NUJ CONTRIBUTIONS	8.00		
10CT91	CHG	MANAGEMENT FEE	4.00		15.62 DR
20CT91	CHQ	001773	21.55		
20CT91	VIS	CORKS RESTAURANT	28.30		65.47 DR
30CT91	DD	TSB-TRUST-CO-LTD	30.75		96.22 DR
40CT91		FUNDS TRANSFER		500.00	
40CT91	SPB	B'STOKE.TOWN CNTRE	35.00		368.78
70CT91	DD	LIBERTY LIFE D/D	18.00		

Example 14

Here is part of Ann's bank statement.

Date	Details	Withdrawals	Deposits	Balance
20APR				374.92
24APR	000474	35.73		339.19
25APR	000475	19.99		319.20
28APR	000476	114.55		204.65
30APR	Salary		785.60	990.25
03MAY	SO	235.42		754.83
05MAY	000477	79.41		675.42
05MAY			12.50	687.92
05MAY			23.66	711.58
09MAY	000478	100.00		611.58

The amount of money Ann had·in the bank on 20th April (her 'balance') was £374.92.

   She wrote a cheque for £35.73 at a supermarket, which was *withdrawn* from her account on 24th April, leaving a balance of £339.19.

   Two further cheques, for £19.99 (pair of slippers) and £114.55 (clothes) left Ann with £204.65 by 28th April.

   Then her salary of £785.60 was paid in (*deposited*), increasing her balance to £990.25.

   Her mortgage of £235.42 was paid by **standing order,** SO (an arrangement with the bank to pay a fixed amount every month), followed by a further cheque for £79.41 (car bill).

   She received two cheques, for £12.50 and £23.66, for some dresses she had made for other people. She deposited these on 5th May, and on 9th May she withdrew £100 cash.

EXERCISE 1.7

1 Continue Ann's bank statement in Example 14, starting with
the balance of £611.58, with these headings:

Date	Details	Withdrawals	Deposits	Balance
09MAY				611.58

On 10th May, Ann's cheque, number 000479, for £89.35
at the supermarket was deducted.

Three standing orders were paid on 15th May: £68.50 to
British Gas, £50.40 to the Electricity Board and £42.75 to
British Telecom for her telephone.

She bought train tickets, paying £53.50 by cheque, which
was deducted on 17th May.

She received two cheques on 20th May, one for £10.00
and one for £18.50, for some dresses she had made.

What was her balance on 21st May?

2 Complete the balance column on Hubert's bank statement.

Date	Details	Withdrawals	Deposits	Balance
11AUG				43.67
12AUG	024353	28.36		
15AUG	024354	12.86		
15AUG			350.00	
18AUG	SO	110.00		
20AUG	SO	69.50		
20AUG			8.50	
21AUG	024355	45.00		
21AUG			53.93	
25AUG	024356	100.00		
26AUG	SO	37.50		
28AUG	024357	60.00		

Why should Hubert be concerned about his bank account?

3 Brenda has found a mistake on her bank statement.

Date	Details	Withdrawals	Deposits	Balance
08NOV				59.38
09NOV			32.93	92.31
09NOV	103224	75.72		16.59
13NOV	103225	12.39		14.20
14NOV			24.35	38.55

(*a*) Find the mistake.

(*b*) What should her balance be on 14th November?

4 Peter's bank balance is £24.85. He receives two cheques, for £16.89 and £43.71, as well as £25.00 in cash, which he deposits in the bank. Peter then writes a cheque for £52.49 for shoes and a shirt. Can he now write a cheque for £34.99 for a jacket, without being 'overdrawn'?

5 David's bank statement shows that he is overdrawn (o/d). This means that he has paid more money out of his account than he has put into it, and he is therefore in debt to the bank.

Date	Details	Withdrawals	Deposits	Balance
23FEB				18.50
26FEB	295002	32.71		14.21 o/d
27FEB	SO	53.69		67.90 o/d

If he has two more standing orders to pay, one for £20.00 and one for £61.31, will he exceed his allowed overdraft of £150?

In recent years banks, and some building societies, have installed automatic cash machines, usually just beside the entrance, on an outside wall. With a 'cash card', issued to you by the bank, and with your own personal number (PIN), you can obtain money from the machine, in £5, £10 or £20 notes. Your account is automatically debited with the amount that you withdraw; the main advantage is that you can obtain cash at times when the bank is closed, for example, in the evenings, at weekends or during bank holidays.

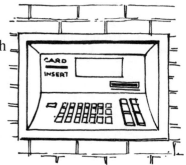

Credit cards

Most banks and large shopping chains offer a system of payment which enables you to buy goods and services using a personal **credit card.** You do not pay cash at the time of purchase, but show your card and sign a credit slip. Once a month you receive a statement which itemises the purchases made using your credit card, states the balance that you owe, and then asks for a minimum repayment (typically 5% of the balance owing).

You can pay the total balance, which means you owe nothing, or you can repay a smaller sum, so long as it is at least the minimum.

However, you are charged a fairly high rate of interest on the balance remaining (about 2% per month, or about 25% per year).

If you are careful, a credit card can simplify your budgeting, since you have only one cheque to write each month. It is very easy and costly, however, to allow your balance to accumulate, incurring high interest payments.

Bank PLC

Card Services Department
Telephone: Account Enquiries
Lost/Stolen Cards
Cardline – For details of our 24 hour telephone service, please see over.

STATEMENT OF ACCOUNT

Please quote your account number in all correspondence

MRS X. TRAVAGANT
10, SPENDTHRIFT ST,
LONDON

Statement Date
04/01/90

12345
A minus sign indicates a credit

Date	Reference Number	Description	Previous Balance
			221.40
271289	3545MD	PAYMENT – THANK YOU	21.00 –
		INTEREST	4.87
		* * * * * * * * * * * *	
		CURRENT INTEREST RATE 2.2% PER MONTH	
		(APR 29.84%)	

* * *   AIR MILES SCHEME   * * *
WE ARE PLEASED TO ANNOUNCE THAT AIR MILES POINTS
WILL CONTINUE TO BE AVAILABLE ON ACCOUNTS IN 1990.
SO PAY THE SMART WAY AND FLY THE FREE WAY

MINIMUM PAYMENT SHOULD REACH US BY 29/01/90

Please use the attached slip to make your payment, EITHER by Bank Giro, or direct and ALLOW AT LEAST 4 WORKING DAYS FOR THE PAYMENT TO REACH YOUR ACCOUNT. See overleaf for explanation of interest charges and other details.

DETACH HERE AND RETAIN STATEMENT

New Balance
205.27

Your Credit Limit
£250

Minimum Payment
10.00

EXERCISE 1.8

1 Michael's credit card statement is shown.

(*a*) What is the total amount owing?

(*b*) How much is the minimum payment?

(*c*) How many days does Michael have before his payment is overdue?

(*d*) If Michael pays £40.00, how much will he owe?

(*e*) How much can he then spend, without exceeding his limit?

		Bank PLC	

Card Services Department
Telephone: Account Enquiries
      Lost/Stolen Cards
      Cardline – For details of our 24 hour telephone service, please see over.

STATEMENT OF ACCOUNT

Please quote your account number in all correspondence

MICHAEL HARRIS,
ROSE COTTAGE, SWINBY
YORKS

Statement Date
04/01/89

12345

A minus sign indicates a credit

Date	Reference Number	Description	Previous Balance
			28.73
171288	8542MT	PAYMENT – THANK YOU	10.00 –
		INTEREST	0.63
		* * * * * * * * * * *	
		CURRENT INTEREST RATE 2.2% PER MONTH (APR 29.84%)	
191288	2914XV	GREEN LANE GARAGE	15.00
201288	9162AT	SAVASTORE	39.88
201288	1086BD	PAYMORE DIY	89.37

        * * *   AIR MILES SCHEME   * * *
WE ARE PLEASED TO ANNOUNCE THAT AIR MILES POINTS
WILL CONTINUE TO BE AVAILABLE ON ACCOUNTS IN 1989.
SO PAY THE SMART WAY AND FLY THE FREE WAY

New Balance
163.61

Your Credit Limit
£250

MINIMUM PAYMENT SHOULD REACH US BY 29/01/89

Please use the attached slip to make your payment, EITHER by Bank Giro, or direct and
ALLOW AT LEAST 4 WORKING DAYS FOR THE PAYMENT TO REACH YOUR ACCOUNT.
See overleaf for explanation of interest charges and other details.

DETACH HERE AND RETAIN STATEMENT

Minimum Payment
8.00

2 On Saturday I used my credit card to buy a coat for £68.99 and a pair of shoes for £34.50. If I also bought £12.00 of petrol using my credit card, how much will my credit card account be debited for these three purchases?

3 The minimum payment is 5% of the amount owing on my credit card. How much is the minimum payment if I owe £147.20?

4 Steven's credit card statement shows that he owes £265.72. His credit limit is £350. If he uses his card to buy a cricket bat costing £68.75, can he also buy a pair of batting gloves which cost £19.98 without exceeding his credit limit?

5 John owes £83.58 on his credit card. He decides to pay half now, and the rest next month. If next month he is charged 2% on the unpaid balance, how much will he then have to pay to clear his account?

6 Work out the missing figures (*a*), (*b*), and (*c*) on this credit card statement.

Bank PLC

Card Services Department
Telephone: Account Enquiries
    Lost/Stolen Cards
    Cardline – For details of our 24 hour telephone service, please see over.

STATEMENT OF ACCOUNT

MS M. MITCHELL,
17, KING ST.,
NEWTOWN

Please quote your account number in all correspondence

Statement Date
04/03/89

12345
A minus sign indicates a credit

Date	Reference Number	Description	Previous Balance
			42.09
070290	3075CD	PAYMENT – THANK YOU	5.00 –
		INTEREST	(*a*)
		* * * * * * * * * * *	
		CURRENT INTEREST RATE 2.2% PER MONTH (APR 29.84%)	
120290	1713XO	CITY CLEANERS	7.29
170290	1086BD	D.I.Y. SHOPS	39.71

* * * AIR MILES SCHEME * * *
WE ARE PLEASED TO ANNOUNCE THAT AIR MILES POINTS WILL CONTINUE TO BE AVAILABLE ON ACCOUNTS IN 1989. SO PAY THE SMART WAY AND FLY THE FREE WAY

MINIMUM PAYMENT SHOULD REACH US BY 29/03/89.

Please use the attached slip to make your payment, EITHER by Bank Giro, or direct and ALLOW AT LEAST 4 WORKING DAYS FOR THE PAYMENT TO REACH YOUR ACCOUNT. See overleaf for explanation of interest charges and other details.

DETACH HERE AND RETAIN STATEMENT

New Balance
(*b*)

Your Credit Limit
£400

Minimum Payment
(5% of balance)
(*c*)

How much would the payment need to be to reduce the balance owing to £60?

In Chapter 11 there are examples of budgeting over a wide range of items, where other credit systems are investigated.

2. Maths at work

The use of mathematics in the world of work is often hidden, or unrecognised as such. Many people's work involves them in using mathematics without realising it. It is, therefore, useful to examine some of the mathematics which is used at work.

Bookkeeping

Clerks and office workers are required to keep accounts in order, and to occasionally 'balance the books'. Cross-casting is done to check totals in accounts:

	£	£	£	Totals
	2.50	9.50	8.73	20.73
	3.45	2.22	2.34	8.01
	1.25	8.47	1.37	11.09
Totals	7.20	20.19	12.44	39.83

Addition of the column totals should give the same grand total as adding the row totals.

EXERCISE **2.1**

Use your calculator to find both the row and column totals,
ensuring the grand total is the same by both methods.

1

£	£	£	Totals
5.23	3.45	1.05	
9.23	2.44	6.47	
2.65	9.50	2.41	
Totals			

2

£	£	£	Totals
264.93	236.83	126.39	
392.84	128.39	204.13	
832.94	843.92	100.01	
Totals			

3

£	£	£	Totals
248.92	361.91	421.91	
117.94	42.28	155.23	
148.84	145.07	91.87	
Totals			

4

£	£	£	£	Totals
184.28	214.28	194.52	421.87	
147.29	176.49	94.87	842.91	
139.80	82.36	491.93	491.76	
Totals				

5

£	£	£	£	Totals
28.29	109.07	297.23	187.52	
37.46	84.26	184.91	93.94	
104.91	93.94	91.07	72.91	
39.47	47.85	85.55	84.72	
Totals				

6

£	£	£	£	Totals
78.91	181.54	213.91	49.28	
46.07	271.29	47.92	275.07	
93.91	85.05	317.72	45.92	
7.59	471.09	56.95	72.87	
Totals				

Investigation A

You might like to see whether you can use a computer spreadsheet to insert your own cross-checking accounts, or an account from Exercise 2.1.

Formulas

If a calculation has to be done many times at work, usually there is a formula to help workers remember how to find the answer. There may be several formulas for a particular situation. Some workers are expected to substitute numbers into a formula to obtain a numerical result. As some products are still manufactured to imperial specifications, for export, or parts for old equipment, some formulas are used with imperial measurements.

Example 1

The circumference of a circle is given by the formula $C = \pi D$.

Find the circumference of a circular machined tool of radius 4 cm.

Radius = 4 cm, so diameter = 8 cm, $C = \pi D = 3.14 \times 8 = 25.12$ cm.

EXERCISE 2.2

1 The speed of rotation of a machine lathe is given by the

formula $N = \dfrac{12S}{\pi D}$, where

S = speed at which the metal can be cut (ft/min),
D = diameter of the tool (inches).

Find N, to the nearest whole number of rev/min, when

(*a*) $S = 100$ ft/min, $D = 2$ inches
(*b*) $S = 230$ ft/min, $D = 3$ inches
(*c*) $S = 100$ ft/min, $D = 1\frac{1}{2}$ inches
(*d*) $S = 50$ ft/min, $D = \frac{1}{2}$ inch.

2 In plumbing, a pipe may have to be bent.

$$\text{Bending allowance (mm)} = \frac{2R \times \text{bend angle}}{360°}$$

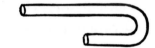

where R is in mm.

Calculate the bending allowance when (*a*) $R = 45$ mm,
angle = 80° (*b*) $R = 57$ mm, angle = 120° (*c*) $R = 60$ mm,
angle = 180°.

3 The volume of a cylindrical container is

$\pi \times (\text{radius})^2 \times \text{height}.$

Find the volume of such a container, to the nearest whole
number, when

(*a*) radius = 5 cm, height = 10 cm
(*b*) radius = 3 cm, height = 8 cm
(*c*) radius = 10 mm, height = 15 mm
(*d*) radius = 1.5 m, height = 2 m.

4 Typists might use this formula for setting up tab positions and margins:

$$\text{width of margin} = \frac{\text{width of page} - \text{width of tabulation}}{2}$$

Calculate the width of the margins when (*a*) page width = 30 cm, tabulation width = 20 cm (*b*) page width = 20 cm, tabulation width = 15 cm (*c*) page width = 25 cm, tabulation width = 20 cm.

5 The total surface area of a cylindrical drum is given by the formula:

$$\text{surface area} = 2 \times \pi \times \text{radius} \times (\text{height} + \text{radius}).$$

Find the surface area, to the nearest whole number, when (*a*) radius = 5 cm, height = 10 cm (*b*) radius = 3 cm, height = 8 cm (*c*) radius = 10 mm, height = 15 mm (*d*) radius = 0.5 m, height = 1 m.

6 To change °C into °F we can use the formula: $°C = \dfrac{5\,(°F - 32)}{9}$

Change the following temperatures into °C:

(*a*) 80°F (*b*) 120°F (*c*) 55°F (*d*) 25°F (*e*) 45°F.

Flow charts

Flow charts are used to show a series of instructions diagrammatically. For example, in using the formula $C = \pi D$ in Example 1, we could also have shown the series of calculations necessary on a flow chart:

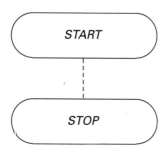

START

STOP

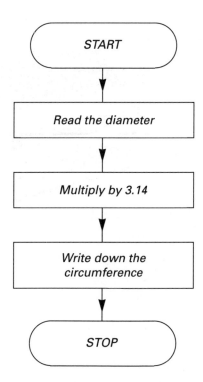

Alternatively, to find the diameter when we know the circumference, we could reverse the flow chart:

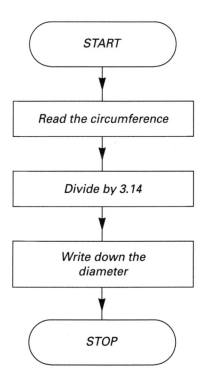

EXERCISE 2.3

1 This flow chart is for finding the perimeter of a rectangle

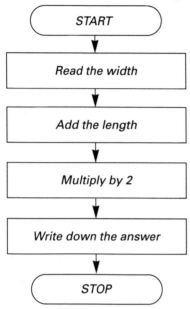

Find the perimeter of the following rectangles: (*a*) width = 5 cm, length = 8 cm (*b*) width = 2.5 m, length = 4.5 m (*c*) width = 16 mm, length = 22 mm (*b*) width = 3.25 cm, length = 4.74 cm.

2 This flow chart is for finding the perimeter of a circle.

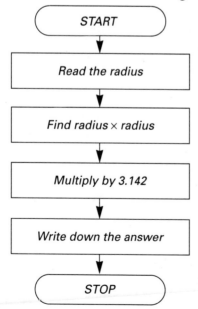

Find the area of a circle when the radius is (*a*) 4 cm
(*b*) 3.5 cm (*c*) 10.7 mm (*d*) 3.45 m.

3 This flow chart is for changing temperatures from °C into °F.

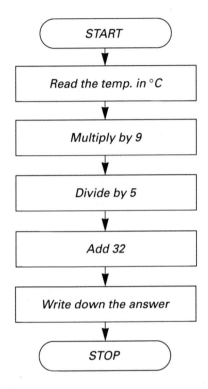

Change the following temperatures into °F: (*a*) 100°C
(*b*) 20°C (*c*) 10°C (*d*) –3°C (*e*) 12.5°C.

4 Rewrite the flow chart in question 3 in reverse so it could be
used to change temperatures from °F into °C.

5 The flow chart overleaf is used to find the area of a triangle
given the height and the length of the base.

Find the area of the following triangles: (*a*) height = 2 cm,
base = 3 cm (*b*) height = 2.5 cm, base = 3.5 cm (*c*) height
= 15 mm, base = 20 mm (*d*) height = 1.3 m, base = 1.7 m.

6 Rewrite the flow chart in question 5 in reverse so it could be
used to find the base of a triangle given the area and the
height.

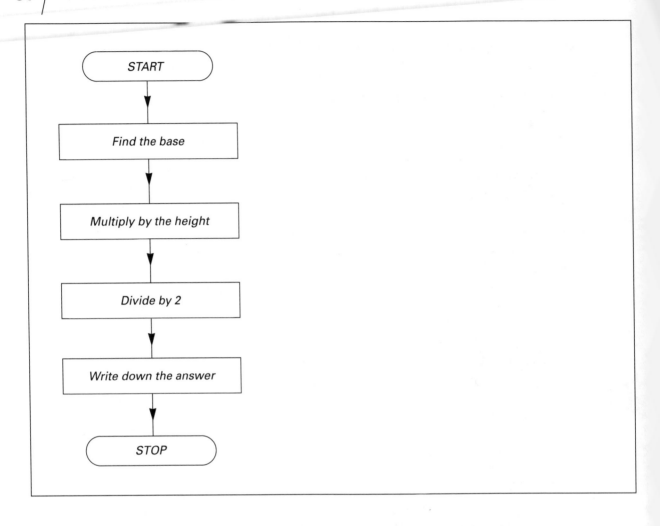

Investigation B

Is it possible to write all flow charts in reverse? Try to think of a flow chart which might not have a reverse.

Decisions in flow charts

A decision box in a flow chart helps us to use it for a variety of situations and can represent comprehensive sets of instructions which sometimes require us to make a decision or ask a question.

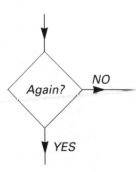

Example 2

Draw a flow chart to give instructions for using a telephone.

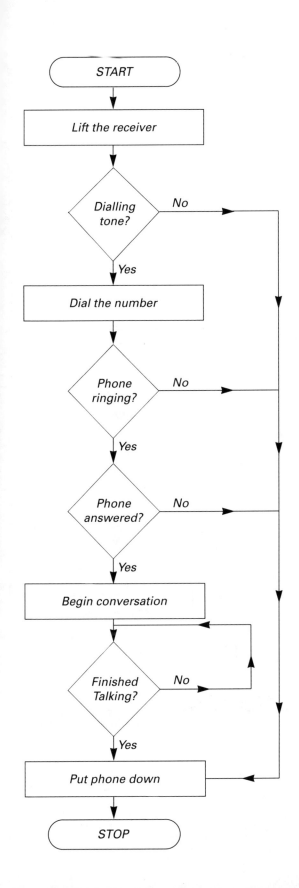

EXERCISE 2.4

Draw flow charts to give instructions for the following:

1 Using a pelican crossing.

2 Making a cup of tea.

3 Finding a tune on a cassette tape.

4 Starting a car and moving off.

5 Running a bath.

Follow the instructions in these flow charts:

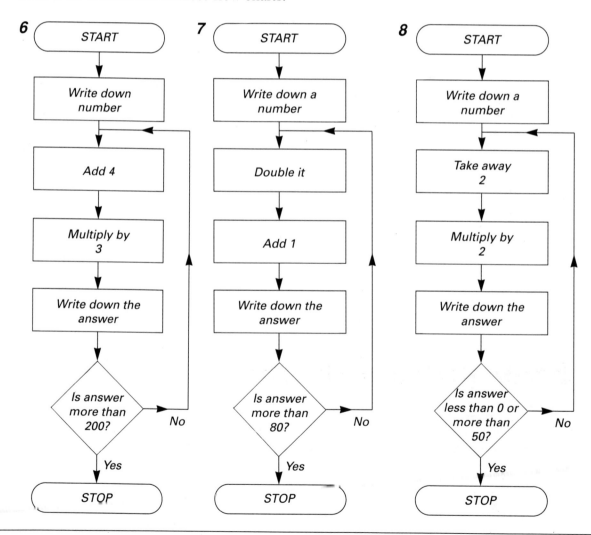

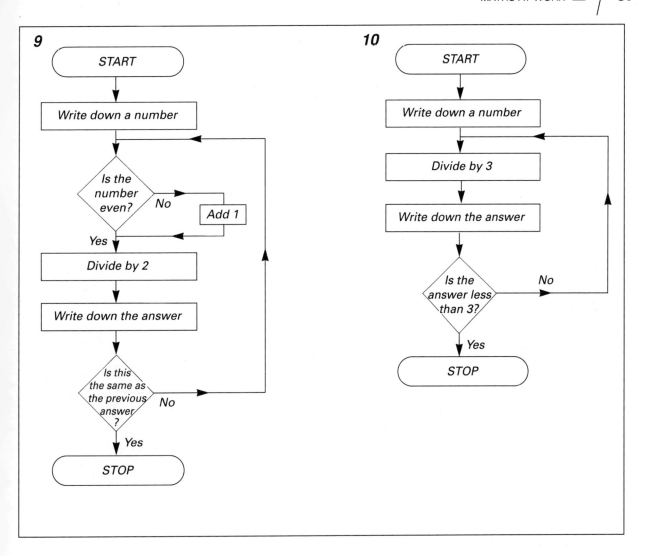

Error and accuracy

In handling figures we must always be aware of possible error. Sometimes we cause this error by rounding. The two most common methods of rounding are rounding to a specific number of decimal places (d.p.), or significant figures (s.f.).

Example 3

Round 3.417 to (a) 2 decimal places (b) 2 significant figures.

(a) 3.417 = 3.42 to 2 d.p., rounding up since the 7 is '5 or more'. The 4 is the first decimal place, and the 2 is the second decimal place.

(b) 3.417 = 3.4 to 2 s.f. The 3 is the first significant figure, the 4 the second.

EXERCISE 2.5

Round off each decimal to the given number of decimal places.

1 3.421   (a) 1 d.p. (b) 2 d.p.   **2** 13.402   (a) 2 d.p. (b) 3 d.p.

3 9.471 89   (a) 3 d.p. (b) 4 d.p.   **4** 0.0143   (a) 2 d.p. (b) 3 d.p.

5 0.0082   (a) 1 d.p. (b) 2 d.p.

Round off each number to the required number of significant figures.

6 100.51   (a) 3 s.f. (b) 4 s.f.   **7** 83.27   (a) 2 s.f. (b) 3 s.f.

8 0.0042   (a) 1 s.f. (b) 2 s.f.

9 1530   (a) 1 s.f. (b) 2 s.f. (c) 3 s.f.

10 55 555   (a) 3 s.f. (b) 4 s.f. (c) 5 s.f.

Investigation C

Some of the numbers in Exercise 2.5 did not change when you rounded them to a given number of decimal places, or significant figures. Write down some more numbers like these, and try to explain why they remain unchanged after rounding.

Example 4

Find the error induced in the number 3.417 in Example 3.

(a) Accurate number = 3.417, rounded number = 3.42

Error is $3.42 - 3.417 = 0.003$ or $\dfrac{3}{1000}$

(b) Accurate number = 3.417, rounded number = 3.4

Error is $3.4 - 3.417 = -0.017$ or $\dfrac{-17}{1000}$

EXERCISE 2.6

Round off each decimal to the given number of decimal places
and find the error after rounding.

1 34.213   (*a*) 1 d.p. (*b*) 2 d.p.   **2** 10.678   (*a*) 1 d.p. (*b*) 2 d.p.

3 9.9999   (*a*) 1 d.p. (*b*) 3 d.p.   **4** 2.909   (*a*) 2 d.p. (*b*) 3 d.p.

5 2.285 13   (*a*) 2 d.p. (*b*) 4 d.p.

Round off each number to the required number of significant figures, and
find the error after rounding.

6 230.9   (*a*) 2 s.f. (*b*) 3 s.f.   **7** 3003   (*a*) 2 s.f. (*b*) 3 s.f.

8 20.20   (*a*) 1 s.f. (*b*) 2 s.f.   **9** 9.999   (*a*) 2 s.f. (*b*) 3 s.f.

10 0.0553   (*a*) 1 s.f. (*b*) 2 s.f.

Metric measurement of length

Today, in measuring and producing diagrams, metric measurement is
normally used: the **millimetre** (**mm**) is the unit used most frequently
in industry. We need to be able to convert between all units of metric
measurement.

Example 5

Write 20.4 cm in mm.

1 cm = 10 mm, so 20.4 cm = 20.4 × 10 = 204 mm

EXERCISE **2.7**

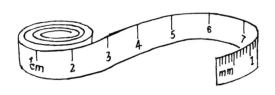

1 cm = 10 mm	1 mm = $\frac{1}{10}$ cm
1 m = 100 cm	1 cm = $\frac{1}{100}$ m
1 m = 1000 mm	1 mm = $\frac{1}{1000}$ m

Change the following measurements as indicated:

1 2.9 cm into mm   **2** 4 m into mm   **3** 4.2 cm into m   **4** 4 mm into cm

5 0.4 m into mm   **6** 12.9 cm into m   **7** 327 mm into cm   **8** 52.7 cm into m

9 500 mm into m   **10** 0.03 m into cm   **11** 400 mm into cm **12** 7.29 cm into mm

13 0.08 m into mm   **14** 15.01 m into cm **15** 7000 mm into m

16 What length, in mm, would 83 cm be if reduced by a scale of $\frac{1}{10}$?

17 A diagram requires a reduction by a scale of $\frac{1}{5}$ .What length
would 14 cm become when written in mm?

18 A diagram is drawn to a scale of 1 : 100. What would be the
actual length, in metres, of a line which is of length 12.8 cm in
the diagram?

19 A length of 14 m is represented in a drawing to the scale of $\frac{1}{25}$.
How long would be the corresponding line, in mm, in the
drawing?

20 A diagram represents part of a building to a scale of $\frac{1}{100}$.
What would be the actual length of the building,
in metres, if it is of length 108.3 mm in the diagram?

Imperial measurement of length

Imperial measurements, such as the inch, are still used in industry, and we should be prepared to perform calculations involving them.

Example 6

Two rods, of lengths $\frac{7}{16}$" and $\frac{5}{8}$", are joined, together.

(The symbol " means inches.) What is the total length?

$$\frac{7}{16}" + \frac{5}{8}" = \frac{7}{16}" + \frac{10}{16}" = \frac{17}{16}" = 1\frac{1}{16}"$$

EXERCISE 2.8

Find the total length, in inches, of the following:

1 $\frac{1}{4}" + \frac{1}{8}"$ **2** $\frac{1}{16}" + \frac{1}{8}"$ **3** $\frac{3}{8}" + \frac{3}{4}"$ **4** $\frac{1}{16}" + \frac{1}{4}"$

5 $1\frac{1}{2}" + \frac{3}{8}"$ **6** $\frac{3}{4}" + 2\frac{7}{8}"$ **7** $\frac{1}{2}" + 1\frac{13}{16}"$ **8** $\frac{5}{8}" + \frac{1}{2}"$

9 $2\frac{1}{4}" + \frac{5}{16}"$ **10** $\frac{7}{8}" - \frac{7}{16}"$ **11** $\frac{1}{2}" + 2\frac{3}{8}"$ **12** $\frac{3}{8}" - \frac{5}{16}"$

13 $4" - 3\frac{5}{16}"$ **14** $2\frac{1}{2}" + \frac{7}{8}" - \frac{3}{16}"$ **15** $\frac{3}{4}" + \frac{3}{8}" + \frac{3}{16}"$ **16** $5\frac{7}{8}" - \frac{1}{4}" + \frac{1}{2}"$

Change the following into inches, given that 12 inches = 1 ft (12" = 1'):

17 1' 3" **18** 3' 4" **19** 2' 8$\frac{1}{2}$" **20** 1' 2$\frac{3}{8}$" **21** 2' 10$\frac{3}{4}$"

22 3' 7$\frac{5}{8}$" **23** 4' 10$\frac{1}{8}$"

Change the following into feet and inches:

24 40" **25** 28" **26** 56$\frac{1}{8}$" **27** 37$\frac{3}{4}$" **28** 72"

29 19$\frac{5}{8}$" **30** 49$\frac{7}{8}$"

Investigation D

Using the conversions already calculated, draw a conversion graph, and make up a conversion table, to help you change metric to imperial units of length.

Investigation E

What other imperial units might industry use? Remember some quantities are measured in both imperial and metric units. Investigate ways of converting between these units. Illustrate the conversions using graphs and tables.

Scale diagrams

Frequently, accurate or scale diagrams are produced by draughtsmen or designers of parts to be machined, or of templates to help the cutting of a part.

EXERCISE 2.9

Produce accurate diagrams of the following parts.

1

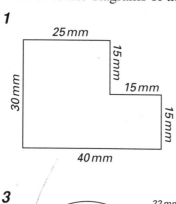

2

3

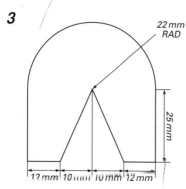

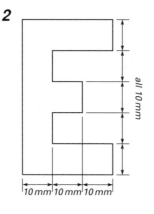

4

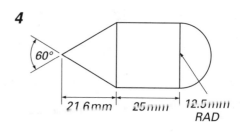

5

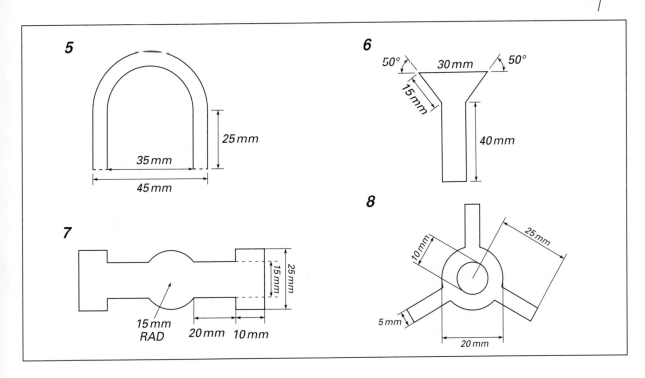

6

50° 30mm 50°

15mm

40mm

8

10mm 25mm

5mm

20mm

7

25mm
15mm

15mm
RAD 20mm 10mm

EXERCISE **2.10**

The actual measurements of an object are shown in each diagram. Draw a diagram for each object to the scale indicated.

1 Produce an accurate drawing to a scale of $\frac{1}{10}$.

2 Use a scale of 1 cm to 2".

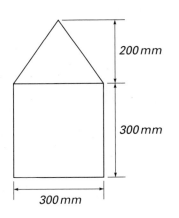

200mm

300mm

300mm

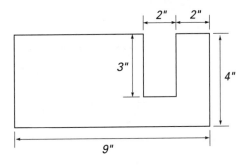

2" 2"

3"

4"

9"

3 Use a scale of 1 mm to 2.5 cm.

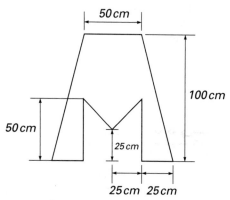

4 Produce an accurate diagram to $\frac{1}{5}$ scale.

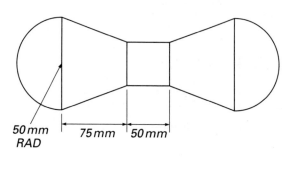

5 Produce an accurate diagram to a scale of $\frac{1}{10}$.

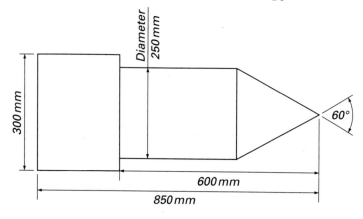

6 Use a scale of 2 cm to 3".

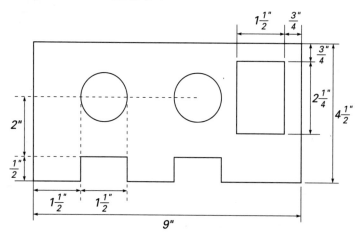

Vectors and translation

Vectors are used to describe movement, particularly when we need to give both direction and a measure of movement. Bold type is used to represent vectors in print: **a**. When handwritten, a vector is shown by underlining with a wavy line: $\underset{\sim}{a}$.

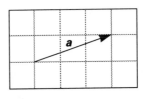

Example 7

A vector can be represented either diagrammatically

or in numerical form: Vector $\mathbf{a} = \begin{pmatrix} 3 \\ 1 \end{pmatrix}$

This vector represents a movement of *three* units across from left to right and *one* unit vertically *upwards*.

Example 8

Vector $\mathbf{AB} = \begin{pmatrix} 4 \\ -2 \end{pmatrix}$

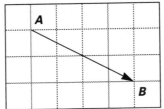

This vector represents a movement of *four* units across from left to right, and *two* units vertically *downwards*.

Example 9

Vectors can also be used to describe some movements of shapes or templates, applied to either drawing diagrams or moving parts in a manufacturing process. Such movements are called **translations.**

The translation in the diagram is $\begin{pmatrix} 3 \\ 2 \end{pmatrix}$.

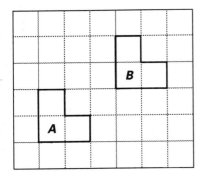

EXERCISE 2.11

1 Represent each of the vectors in the diagram in numerical form.

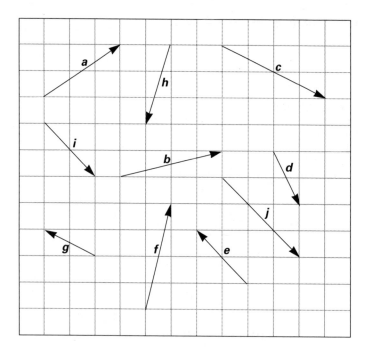

2 Draw the following vectors:

$$AB = \begin{pmatrix} 3 \\ 4 \end{pmatrix} \qquad CD = \begin{pmatrix} 3 \\ -2 \end{pmatrix} \qquad PQ = \begin{pmatrix} -3 \\ 4 \end{pmatrix} \qquad EF = \begin{pmatrix} 4 \\ -5 \end{pmatrix}$$

$$ST = \begin{pmatrix} -2 \\ -3 \end{pmatrix} \qquad MN = \begin{pmatrix} 2 \\ -5 \end{pmatrix} \qquad XY = \begin{pmatrix} -1 \\ -4 \end{pmatrix} \qquad GH = \begin{pmatrix} -3 \\ 3 \end{pmatrix}$$

3 Write down the vectors of the translations which map
(a) A on to B (b) B on to E (c) C on to D (d) D on to E
(e) B on to E (f) A on to D (g) E on to C (h) B on to D

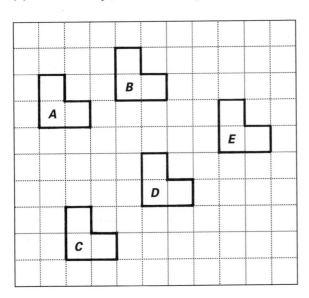

4 Write down the vectors of the translations which map
(a) C on to B (b) B on to D (c) F on to E (d) A on to E
(e) E on to F (f) D on to C (g) A on to C (h) C on to D

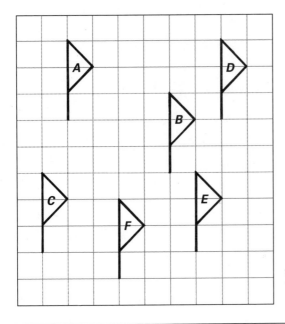

The picture shows an automatic stacking system in a warehouse. The robot stacker is located in its loading position, and can be directed to any of the pallets by means of a vector instruction.

Example 10

What instruction would be given to move the pallet in C7 to A3, and return the stacker to its loading position?

Loading position to C7: $\begin{pmatrix} -3 \\ 2 \end{pmatrix}$ C7 to A3: $\begin{pmatrix} -4 \\ 2 \end{pmatrix}$ A3 to loading: $\begin{pmatrix} 7 \\ -4 \end{pmatrix}$

Complete movement is: $\begin{pmatrix} -3 \\ 2 \end{pmatrix} + \begin{pmatrix} -4 \\ 2 \end{pmatrix} + \begin{pmatrix} 7 \\ -4 \end{pmatrix}$

EXERCISE **2.12**

Write down the instructions which would be given to move the
following pallets and return the stacker to its loading position at
the end of each action.

1 E6 to C6   **2** E2 to C5   **3** E5 to B3   **4** B2 to D7

5 A5 to E9   **6** B8 to D1   **7** C7 to A3   **8** D3 to C9

9 D3 to C5 followed by C7 to A7   **10** E5 to D7 followed by B8 to B3

11 B2 to D8 followed by E2 to A9   **12** E6 to C1 followed by A5 to B9

EXERCISE **2.13**

An inexperienced operator gave the stacker these instructions
from D1:

$\begin{pmatrix} 3 \\ 2 \end{pmatrix} + \begin{pmatrix} 4 \\ 1 \end{pmatrix}$, which could have been replaced by a single vector $\begin{pmatrix} 7 \\ 3 \end{pmatrix}$,

that took the stacker to A8.

    For each of the following, write down (*a*) the
destination of the stacker (*b*) the single vector to
replace those given.

1 From B2: $\begin{pmatrix} 2 \\ -2 \end{pmatrix} + \begin{pmatrix} 4 \\ 3 \end{pmatrix}$ **2** From D3: $\begin{pmatrix} 3 \\ 3 \end{pmatrix} + \begin{pmatrix} 3 \\ -4 \end{pmatrix}$

3 From A5: $\begin{pmatrix} 2 \\ -3 \end{pmatrix} + \begin{pmatrix} 2 \\ 2 \end{pmatrix}$ **4** From C7: $\begin{pmatrix} -3 \\ 2 \end{pmatrix} + \begin{pmatrix} -3 \\ 0 \end{pmatrix}$

5 From B8: $\begin{pmatrix} 0 \\ -2 \end{pmatrix} + \begin{pmatrix} 0 \\ -5 \end{pmatrix}$ **6** From E5: $\begin{pmatrix} -1 \\ 0 \end{pmatrix} + \begin{pmatrix} 0 \\ 3 \end{pmatrix} + \begin{pmatrix} 2 \\ -2 \end{pmatrix}$

7 From D5: $\begin{pmatrix} -2 \\ 2 \end{pmatrix} + \begin{pmatrix} 4 \\ 1 \end{pmatrix} + \begin{pmatrix} 2 \\ -2 \end{pmatrix}$ **8** From E2: $\begin{pmatrix} 4 \\ 4 \end{pmatrix} + \begin{pmatrix} 1 \\ -3 \end{pmatrix} + \begin{pmatrix} 2 \\ 2 \end{pmatrix}$

Investigation F

Write down a vector. Draw its translation, and also its opposite translation. Can you find a quicker way to write down the opposite of any translation in vector form?

Write down and draw another vector and its translation. Extend this translation to twice its length. Write down the vector for the translation of twice the length. What has happened to the numbers in the vector?

Extension: use a computer

Many of the exercises above can also be completed on a computer. Use either LOGO, or the MOVE & DRAW instructions on some computers, and see whether you can complete some of the vector problems. You will have to use a different scale of movement.

Uses of trigonometry

Trigonometry is used in some situations where it is difficult to measure a particular length or angle. We can sometimes use alternative measurements to help us find the ones we want.

The three trigonometrical ratios are

$$\sin x = \frac{\text{opposite side}}{\text{hypotenuse}}$$

$$\cos x = \frac{\text{adjacent side}}{\text{hypotenuse}}$$

$$\tan x = \frac{\text{opposite side}}{\text{adjacent side}}$$

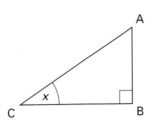

Example 11

A piece of wood needs a V-groove cut in it as shown. To what depth should it be cut?

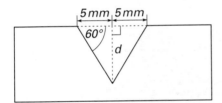

We need to find the opposite side; the adjacent side is 5 mm. We therefore need the tan ratio:

$$\tan 60° = \frac{d}{5} \quad \text{so } d = 5 \times \tan 60° = 8.66 \text{ mm, to 3 sig. figs.}$$

Example 12

A ramp for the disabled is to be built as shown. At what angle will it need to be inclined?

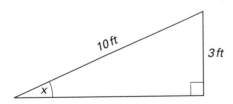

$$\text{Sin } x = \frac{3}{10} = 0.3 \quad \text{so } x = 17.458° = 17.5°, \text{ to 1 dec. pl.}$$

EXERCISE **2.14**

Calculate x in each diagram, writing lengths correct to
3 significant figures, and angles correct to 1 decimal place.

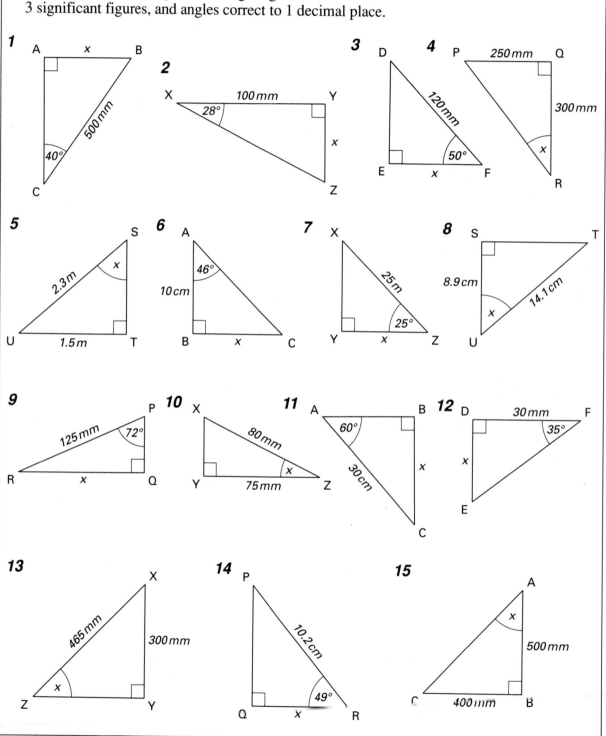

16 A hole is to be drilled through the block as shown. At what angle should the drill bit be inclined?

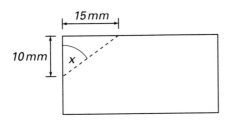

17 A children's slide of length 5 m is to be built at an angle of 35° to the horizontal. What will be the height of the highest point?

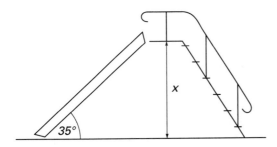

18 A new staircase is planned alongside the wall of a room going up to a loft conversion. At what angle should it be inclined?

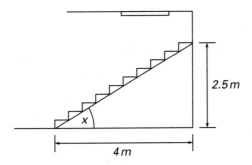

19 A 15 ft ladder is inclined at an angle of 65° against the side wall of a house. How high is the top of the ladder above the ground?

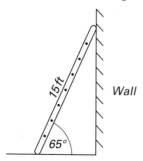

20 Mark stands at a point which is 1000 m horizontally from the top of a hill as measured on a map. The top of the hill is inclined at 18° from where he stands. How high will he have to climb to reach the top?

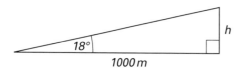

Investigation G

Explain how you might use trigonometry to find the height of a tree, or a building, when it is not possible to measure the height directly. If possible, carry out the exercise yourself on a tree or a building.

Surveys

One primary concern of companies is the sale of their products. Companies carry out surveys to predict sales figures of new products, or to discover how successful existing products have been. In conducting a survey we must decide:

(*a*) how the survey will be carried out,

(*b*) how many people will canvass (the size of the survey),

(*c*) what questions we will ask.

However, there are important points to consider for each of these aspects.

(*a*) *How?*

Frequently surveys are carried out in the street, perhaps in shopping precincts where people congregate. Other methods available are telephone surveys, postal questionnaires, or surveys viewed in popular newspapers and magazines.

(*b*) *How many?*

A very small sample is unlikely to be representative of the population, but a very large sample can be too costly to examine. We may need to survey a particular section of the population only, or in a certain area, but we must be sure that we have a representative sample which is not biased.

(*c*) *What questions?*

The questions asked should be clear and to the point, should not be leading questions, and should only require the information we need.

EXERCISE 2.15

For each survey describe (a) how many people you would ask, and (b) how you would carry out the survey.

A number of surveys are designed to obtain the following information:

1 The most popular political party.

2 The most popular flavour of crisp.

3 The make of car which is most popular.

4 The make of tights which is most run-resistant.

5 The number of people owning National Savings Bonds for the retired.

6 How many teenage smokers there are in England.

7 The proportion of passengers who have had to stand on the 0830 train from Euston station.

8 The most popular method of transport to school.

EXERCISE 2.16

List any advantages, disadvantages and any improvements you would suggest for the following proposals:

1 To find the proportion of people who have had difficulty using payphones, a telephone survey asks 'How many people in your house have had difficulty using payphones?'

2 To find the number of people who regularly use mail-order catalogues, a survey is carried out in the local precinct which asks 'Can you tell me your name? Have you ever bought things through the post?'

3 A survey to find the favourite chocolate bar eaten by children is to be conducted. A postal questionnaire carried in a well-known woman's magazine asks 'Is the Mars bar your children's favourite chocolate bar?'

4 A survey to decide people's preference for driving saloon or estate cars is proposed. The survey is to be carried out in a bus station to attract many responses. The survey asks 'Of all the styles of car, do you like a saloon-type body best?' and 'What is your star sign?'

5 A survey is to be carried out to find people's preference for disposable or terry nappies. The survey is to be conducted by telephone throughout the central area of a city and asks 'Do you consider terry nappies to be the best choice for babies due to their softness and durability?'

A survey has been carried out by a chocolate manufacturer involving a new chocolate bar called 'Yummy', aimed at the younger end of the market. The manufacturer has commissioned the survey to find whether it is worth marketing the new chocolate bar. The following question was asked of youngsters shopping in a precinct during their school holidays:

(i) 'Do you eat chocolate bars more than once a week?'

A small sample of Yummy was then offered for a taste, followed by this question:

(ii) 'Having tried a sample, would you want to buy a bar of Yummy?'

These are the answers given (Y=yes, N=no):

(i) Y N N Y N Y Y Y N N N Y N Y Y N Y N Y N Y N Y Y
    Y Y N Y N N Y Y N Y Y Y Y Y N N Y N Y N Y N Y Y Y
    Y Y N Y Y N

(ii) Y Y N Y N Y N N Y N N Y Y Y Y N N Y N Y N Y Y N Y
     N Y Y Y N N Y Y N N Y N N N Y Y N Y N N N Y N
     Y Y N Y N N

EXERCISE 2.17

In the survey on the Yummy chocolate bar

1 how many people answered (*a*) yes (*b*) no to question (i)?

2 how many people answered (*a*) yes (*b*) no to question (ii)?

3 what percentage of people ate chocolate more than once a week?

4 how many chocolate eaters would want to try Yummy?

5 how many of those who do not eat chocolate regularly would try Yummy?

6 based on the results of the survey, what recommendations would you make to the manufacturers of Yummy?

EXERCISE 2.18

Yes/no answers are the easiest to analyse. Go back to Exercise 2.16 and write a series of yes/no questions for each survey.

Investigation H

Choose a particular topic in which you are interested, and design a questionnaire to obtain people's views on this topic. Carry out the questionnaire, and present your results. Were the results what you expected? Do you think your results are biased in any way? If you were to repeat the exercise, would you do it any differently?

Extension

Many computers are provided with **database** packages which we can use to store information. Once you have conducted your survey, use a computer database package to load your information into a computer. You can then use some of the facilities of the database package to *investigate* the information, which will help you to interpret the data.

Mathematics industry test

Some employers set their own mathematics test for job applicants. The test below is typical of many of the tests which are given to potential employees for training in industry. The test is to be completed without the aid of a calculator.

1 43 + 89 + 163

2 593 + 482

3 £23 + £127 + £2.35 + £1.80

4 86 − 27

5 £3.27 − £1.50

6 372 × 8

7 182 × 9

8 48 ÷ 8

9 204 ÷ 6

10 Find the cost of 7 articles at 26p each.

11 Find the cost of 8 articles at £53 each.

12 How many articles can be bought for £1.26 when each costs 9p?

13 If I spend 68p out of £1.00, what change do I get?

14 If I buy 52 articles at 20p each, which of these amounts is nearest to the correct answer: £2, £10 or £50?

15 Find the total cost of 4 articles at £3.45 each.

16 2.30 + 18.51

17 9.54 + 4.7

18 584 − 338

19 4.38 − 2.29

20 527 × 34

21 298 × 45

22 3.91 × 6

23 3.91 × 100

24 446 ÷ 8

25 $\dfrac{3}{4} + \dfrac{5}{8}$ **26** $\dfrac{3}{4} - \dfrac{5}{8}$

27 Find three quarters of 40.   **28** Find 12% of £20.00.

29 £2.00 – £1.12   **30** 12p × 5   **31** $3\dfrac{1}{2} - 1\dfrac{3}{4}$

32 $\dfrac{5}{8} + \dfrac{3}{4} + \dfrac{3}{16}$ **33** $2\dfrac{1}{2} \times 1\dfrac{1}{2}$ **34** Express $\dfrac{5}{8}$ as a decimal.

35 Express $\dfrac{3}{5}$ as a percentage.   **36** Express 35% as a fraction.

37 If $T = \dfrac{3a + b - c}{2}$, and $a = 3$, $b = 5$ and $c = 7$, find T.

38 If $C = 2\pi r$ and $\pi = 3.14$, find C when $r = 3$.

39 Find the cost of an article when its price of £3 is decreased by 20%.

40 Find the total cost of a radio costing £18 + VAT, when VAT is 15%.

3. Buying and shopping

Buying and shopping is something we have to do almost every day. There are many situations while buying and shopping in which we use mathematics, in different ways. A popular way of shopping today is in a supermarket.

Estimation

When shopping in a supermarket we like to have an idea of how much we are spending as we walk around the store. It would be rather difficult to add up all the prices in our heads to the exact penny, so we *estimate* the cost of the goods, without the aid of a calculator, rounding them off to the nearest 10p to make them easily managed prices.

We buy the following:

A box of cereals £1.12	A jar of coffee £2.98
A tinned pie 95p	Washing-up liquid £1.04
3 tins of carrots at 18p each	Custard powder 54p

Can you add all these prices up in your head? How long will it take you?

Compare the list against this list with rounded prices:

A box of cereals £1.10	A jar of coffee £3
A tinned pie £1	Washing-up liquid £1
3 tins of carrots at 20p each	Custard powder 50p

It is much easier to add the rounded prices. Compare the totals:

Original total amount £7.17   Rounded total amount £7.20

Our estimate is 3p above the correct amount. Is this important? By estimating, it is possible to have some idea of the amount you are spending as you go around the supermarket.

EXERCISE 3.1

Estimate the total cost of these goods, by rounding off and finding the total, without using a calculator.

1   Steak pie filling 95p
  A packet of biscuits 39p
  Mashed potatoes 99p
  Soap flakes 96p

  3 tins of potatoes at 31p each
  Paella mix £1.29
  Sponge pudding 52p

2   2 tins of peas at 24p each
  Car wash £2.52
  Light bulbs 99p
  A box of Indian rice 99p

  2 tins of mushrooms at 49p each
  A box of cereals £1.04
  Stain remover 89p
  Beef chow mein 96p

3   A tin of sardines 28p
  Freezer bags 79p
  Tin of paint £6.49
  White spirit £1.03

  4 tins of beans at 19p each
  Large tin of salmon £1.69
  Window cleaner 99p

4   3 sardine spreads at 29p each
  Packet of biscuits 48p
  Jar of coffee £2.79
  4 tins of cat food at 31p each

  Jar of jam 53p
  Beef risotto £1.09
  Kitchen towels 79p
  Frozen sausages £1.39

5   Large washing powder £4.49
  Batteries £2.04
  Air freshener 53p
  Tea bags £3.02
  1 kg spaghetti 87p

  Weedkiller £1.53
  3 boxes of tissues at 69p
  Tomato ketchup 52p
  2 packs of butter at 58p each

6   Madras curry sauce 59p
  Orange cordial £1.49
  Light bulb 79p

  Chick pea dhal 79p
  Car de-icer 42p
  Antifreeze £5.99

7   Drinking chocolate £1.54
  Naan bread mix 89p
  Box of drinking straws 54p
  Beef curry and rice 98p

  2 tins of tomatoes at 18p
  Chili sauce 79p
  Frozen pizza £1.48

EXERCISE **3.2**

Go back and work out the totals for Exercise 3.1 with your calculator.
Compare your answers. Do you think estimation gives you totals
which are too inaccurate?

Till receipts

While estimation gives us an approximation for the total cost of items
as we buy them, many shops advise us to check the till receipt for
errors, which do occasionally happen at supermarkets. It is important
to use your calculator in checking the receipts to obtain accurate
answers.

EXERCISE **3.3**

Use your calculator to find the total of these supermarket
receipts:

1	**2**	**3**	**4**	**5**	**6**
0.27	0.31	0.29	0.37	0.21	0.34
0.53	0.31	0.19	5.99	0.18	12.99
0.54	0.27	0.19	6.12	0.18	0.14
0.54	0.27	0.58	0.14	0.18	0.29
0.18	0.27	0.58	0.14	11.48	0.36
0.18	1.03	0.58	0.23	0.53	3.27
0.18	3.05	0.58	0.23	2.79	0.36
0.18	0.98	1.09	0.79	0.31	0.36
1.32	0.62	0.79	2.83	0.31	0.36
3.37	1.27	0.79	2.83	0.31	0.36
2.52	0.89	1.39	0.99	0.31	0.36
0.19	0.54	0.39	0.97	0.31	0.99
0.19	1.09	1.04	0.99	6.49	12.17
0.19	2.93	1.29	2.27	1.02	0.77
0.99	0.33	0.77	0.19	2.22	0.64
0.17	0.33	0.23	0.33	0.93	0.64
0.17	0.19	1.03	0.33	0.43	0.64
1.57	2.99	14.17	6.59	0.43	0.64
0.89	0.22	0.62	0.87	0.50	0.64
0.51	0.22	1.01	0.80	0.53	0.27
0.51	0.22	0.22	0.99	0.99	0.73

Investigation A

A computer fault in the supermarket means that all the tills will read sevens incorrectly as nines. Calculate the increase in each of the till receipts in Exercise 3.3. Will you have to add all the figures up again? Can you think of a quicker way to find the increased amounts?

Calculating change

PLEASE CHECK YOUR CHANGE BEFORE LEAVING THE STORE

EXERCISE 3.4

Calculate the change you would receive from a £10 note after buying the following:

1 4 tins of baked beans at 18p each
4 tins of peas at 20p each
3 tins of soup at 32p each
1 meat pie at 40p

2 2 tins of carrots at 25p each
3 tins of ham at 90p each
1 bottle of orange juice at 73p

3 3 ties at £1.99 each
4 pairs of socks at 80p each

4 2 packets of tea bags at £1.40 each
3 jars of coffee at £1.28 each
2 packets of milk powder at 95p each

5 6 tins of dog food at 35p each
3 meat pies at 60p each
4 tins of luncheon meat at 80p each
1 tin of new potatoes at 28p

6 2 air fresheners at 55p each
1 fly spray at 69p
3 paperback books at £1.30 each

7 7 boxes of tissues at 68p each
2 packets of soap powder at £1.05 each
4 boxes of matches at 19p each
250 g egg noodles 39p

8 6 tins of baked beans at 18p each
5 tins of peas at 20p each
5 tins of cat food at 35p each
1 packet of tea bags at £1.40

9 500 g macaroni 41p
Moglai curry sauce 59p
3 Naan bread mixes at 89p each
2 jars of coffee at £2.85 each

10 1 packet of tea bags at £1.40
3 packets of Poppadums at 49p each
1 tin of chick pea dhal at 79p
1 box beef chow mein at 95p

Buying in quantity

If we go to the grocer we see signs such as:

Grocers use both lb (pounds weight) and kg (kilograms).

Example 1
Carrots are 16p/lb. How much will $\frac{1}{2}$ lb cost?

1 lb costs 16p, so $\frac{1}{2}$ lb is half of 16p, which is 8p.

Example 2
Potatoes are 70p for 5 kg. How much will 2 kg cost?

First find the cost of 1kg: 5 kg costs 70p so 1 kg costs 70p ÷ 5 = 14p.

Now find the cost of 2 kg: 2 kg will cost 2 × 14p = 28p.

EXERCISE 3.5

Find how much just one of each of the following products would cost.

1 A packet of 3 Mars bars for 57p.

2 4 kitchen rolls together for £2.08

3 6 ice lollies at 72p a box

4 3 'cod in butter sauce' for £1.11

5 A packet of 80 chews for 80p

6 A box of 12 cloths for £1.32

7 24 stock cubes for 72p

8 A box of 12 Biro pens for 84p

9 A box of 48 packets of crisps for £9.12

10 A packet of 8 beef stock cubes at 96p a packet

EXERCISE **3.6**

1 Carrots are 30p for 3 lb. How much is 1 lb?

2 Onions are advertised at 28p for 2 lb. How much is this per lb?

3 A 5 lb bag of new potatoes costs £1.20. How much will a 3 lb bag cost?

4 Tomatoes are sold at 52p per lb. How much will 2 lb of tomatoes cost?

5 A large crate of sugar is sold at £3 for 5 kg. How much will a 1 kg bag of sugar cost?

6 The price of carrots rises to 12p per lb. How much will 3lb cost?

7 If a bag of 6 oranges costs 72p how much is the cost of one orange?

8 5 razor blades cost 45p. Find the cost of 15 razor blades.

9 3 bananas cost 36p. What will 5 bananas cost?

10 A packet of 16 bolts costs 64p. How much would 12 bolts cost?

11 200 g of sweets cost 56p. What would 500 g cost?

12 5 video tapes cost £21.75. How much will 8 tapes cost?

13 What will be the cost of 5 lemonade bottles if 6 cost £1.38?

14 9 tins of cat food came to £3.24. What would just 5 tins cost?

15 How much would 8 pairs of socks cost, if 5 pairs came to £4.10?

'The best buy'

Whenever we go shopping we try to spend money carefully, and try to get the 'best buy' we can.

Example 3

Corn flakes are sold in boxes of 500 g costing 90p, or 750 g for £1.27. Which is the best buy?

500 g for 90p is $\dfrac{90}{500}$ pence/gram = 0.18p per gram.

750 g for £1.27 is $\dfrac{127}{750}$ pence/gram = 0.169p per gram.

As 0.169p/g is cheaper than 0.18p/g, the larger box will give the better value.

EXERCISE 3.7

Find out which of these is the best buy:

1 A packet of 6 stock cubes for 24p, or a box of 24 cubes for 87p.

2 A 1-litre bottle of cooking oil for 81p, or a 5-litre can of oil for £3.90.

3 A pack of 2 kitchen rolls for £1.20, or a pack of 4 kitchen rolls for £2.40.

4 A packet of 12 cloths for 74p, or bought individually for 6p each.

5 4 cans of lemonade for 45p, or a crate of 24 for £2.55.

6 A 400 g box of washing powder for 60p, or a large box of 2 kg for £2.80.

7 A packet of 5 felt-tip pens for 32p, or a packet of 30 pens for £1.50.

8 A $\frac{1}{2}$-litre bottle of orange cordial for 28p, or a 2-litre bottle for £1.08.

9 Pencils advertised as follows:

3p each   a packet of a dozen for 34p

a box of two dozen for 73p   a box of 4 dozen for £1.40

10 Table salt packaged in three sizes of container:

1000 g for 50p,   500 g for 24p,   250 g for 14p

11 10 litres of paint for £12.95, or 6 litres for £7.99.

12 3 litres of gloss paint for £7.99 or 1 litre for £3.79.

13 Brilliant white emulsion: 10 litres for £11.95, 6 litres for £7.49, 3 litres for £3.79.

14 A 500 g packet of breakfast cereal for £1.02, or a 750 g packet for £1.48.

15 200 g of coffee for £2.79, or 300 g of coffee for £3.92.

Packets and tins

Packets and tins come in various sizes. Packets are cut from flat pieces of card, while tins are cut from tin plate. The plan of the box drawn on card before cutting out and assembly is called a **net.**

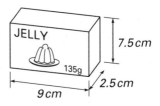

Example 4

(*a*) Draw a net for the box of jelly. Calculate (*b*) the volume of the box (*c*) the total area of card used to make the box.

(*a*)

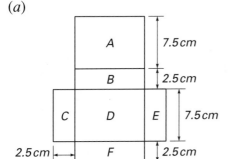

(b) The volume of the box is $9 \times 2.5 \times 7.5 = 168.75$ cm³.

(c) The surface area is calculated by finding the area of each of the rectangles in the net:

$$\begin{array}{ccccccccccc}
A & + & B & + & C & + & D & + & E & + & F \\
67.5 & + & 22.5 & + & 18.75 & + & 67.5 & + & 18.75 & + & 22.5 & = 217.5 \text{ cm}^2
\end{array}$$

EXERCISE 3.8

For each box, (a) draw a net and calculate (b) the volume of the box and (c) the surface area of the box.

1

CUP
A
SOUP

13 cm

4.5 cm

10 cm

2

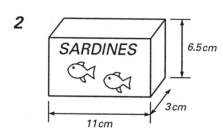

SARDINES

6.5 cm

3 cm

11 cm

3

BREAKY
POPS

27 cm

6 cm

17.5 cm

4

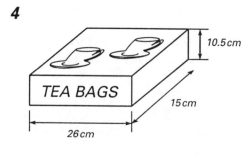

TEA BAGS

10.5 cm

15 cm

26 cm

5

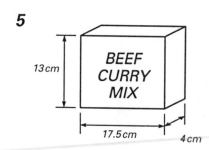

BEEF
CURRY
MIX

13 cm

17.5 cm

4 cm

Investigation B

Double the size of each of the dimensions of the jelly box in Example 4, and calculate the new surface area and volume. Were they doubled also? By what factor have they increased? Repeat the exercise with some other different shapes of boxes, increasing the dimensions 3 or 4 times. How does the surface area and the volume increase in each case? Can you find a relationship between the length, area and volume of these boxes when they are increased in this way?

Example 5

A new brand of chocolates is to be packaged in a triangular-shaped box.

Calculate (*a*) the area of the label on the front of the box (*b*) the volume of the box.

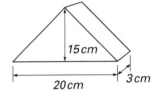

(*a*) The area of the label = area of the triangle

$$= \tfrac{1}{2} \text{ base} \times \text{height} = \tfrac{1}{2} \times 20 \times 15 = 150 \text{ cm}^2.$$

(*b*) Volume of box = area of cross-section × depth of box = 150 × 3
$$= 450 \text{ cm}^3.$$

EXERCISE 3.9

Calculate for each box (*a*) the area of the triangular label (*b*) the volume.

1
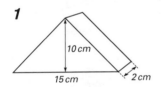

2
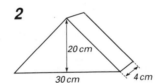

3
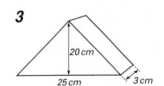

4
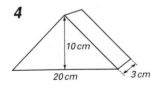

5
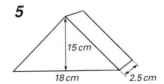

6
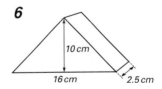

7
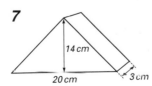

8
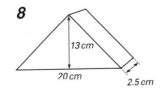

Example 6

Calculate (*a*) the volume of the tin (*b*) the area of the label on the curved surface given that the volume of the tin is given by the formula $\pi r^2 h$ and the area of the curved surface is $2\pi rh$.

r = radius of the tin, h = height of the tin, and π = 3.142.

(*a*) Volume $= \pi r^2 h = \pi \times 3.25 \times 3.25 \times 10 = 331.8 \text{ cm}^3$.

(*b*) Area $= 2\pi rh = 2 \times \pi \times 3.25 \times 10 = 204.2 \text{ cm}^2$.

EXERCISE 3.10

Calculate for each tin (*a*) the volume (*b*) the curved surface area of the label, writing your answer to the nearest whole number in each case.

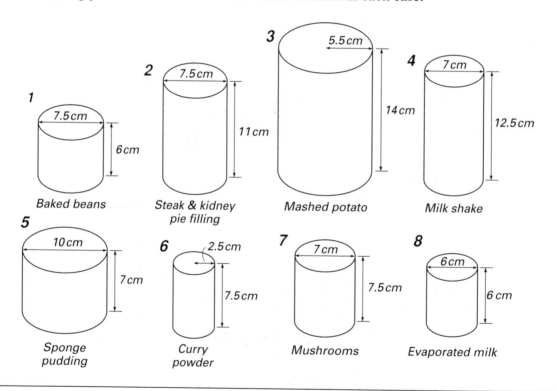

Investigation C

The length of the tin in Example 6 is increased by 10% to 11 cm. What is the new volume? Has the volume increased by 10%?

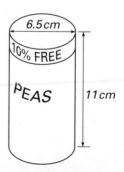

VAT

Some articles you buy may be advertised exclusive of VAT, that is, requiring VAT to be added to the price. The percentage rate of VAT in the past has most commonly been 15%.

Example 7

The television is advertised at £230 + VAT. Calculate the full price to be paid.

$$\text{VAT} = £230 \times \frac{15}{100} = £34.50, \text{ so the full price is } £230 + £34.50$$
$$= £264.50.$$

EXERCISE 3.11

1 Calculate the total cost of having (*a*) 7 (*b*) 5 double glazed windows.

2 Find the cost, inclusive of VAT, of the starting price of (*a*) a
40-point service (*b*) an exhaust system (*c*) a car battery.

Calculate the cost of the following (remember VAT is to be
calculated at 15% for these problems):

3 A calculator priced at £13.99 + VAT

4 A television priced at £169 + VAT

5 A meal costing £24.50 + VAT

6 Video rental of £8.50 + VAT

7 A camera for £149.99 + VAT

8 A telescope for £49.99 + VAT

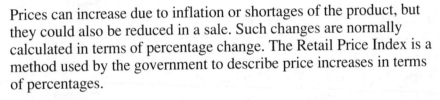

9 A three-piece suite for £599.99 + VAT **10** A bed for £159.99 + VAT

11 A satellite system advertised at £199 + VAT

12 A set of photographs priced at £5.20 + VAT

13 A haircut costing £2.50 + VAT **14** A lawnmower for £49.95 + VAT

15 A washing machine advertised at £239.99 + VAT

Percentage increase and decrease

Prices can increase due to inflation or shortages of the product, but they could also be reduced in a sale. Such changes are normally calculated in terms of percentage change. The Retail Price Index is a method used by the government to describe price increases in terms of percentages.

Example 8

A coat priced at £35 is to be increased in price by 5%. What will be its new price?

The price increase is 5% of £35 = $\frac{5}{100} \times 35 = £1.75$

The new price is therefore £35 + £1.75 = £36.75

EXERCISE 3.12

1   The price of a £7500 car is to be increased by 6%. What will be its new price?

2   House prices have risen by 17% in a year. What will be the present value of a house originally valued at £30 000 a year ago?

3   A £43 gold chain has its price increased by $5\frac{1}{2}$%. What will be its new price?

4   An antique teapot has increased in price by 235% since it was bought for £40. What is its present value?

5   A suit advertised at £120 is to be reduced by 20% in a sale. What will it now cost to buy?

6   An end-of-line shirt for £10.99 is to be reduced by 30%. What will be its new price?

7   A damaged fridge normally priced at £205 will be sold at a 15% discount. What will it cost to buy?

8   A house rental of £65 is to be increased by $4\frac{1}{2}$%. What will be the revised rental?

9   A set of golf clubs for £253.90 is sold with $12\frac{1}{2}$% off its price in a closing down sale. What is the sale price?

10 How much would it cost to buy this calculator?

CASIO.
Scientific with
132 Functions
Ideal for GCSE or
'A' Level Maths

▲ 10-digit LCD with touch sensor keys
▲ Solar powered-no batteries to replace!
▲ 16 metric/imperial conversions
▲ Ultra slim style with wallet.
   Model: fx-451.
   Was £19.99

Percentage change

Example 9

A large box of washing powder has increased in price from £2.50 to £2.70. What is the percentage change?

The actual change in price is £2.70 − £2.50 = 20p

The percentage change in price is $\frac{20p}{£2.50} \times \frac{100}{1} = 8\%$ increase

Note that it is important to state that the change is an increase, and not a decrease.

EXERCISE 3.13

1 A telephone is reduced from £25 to £20. What is the percentage reduction?

2 A bedroom unit is increased from £60 to £80. What is the percentage increase?

3 A flat originally bought for £50 000 is sold for £55 000. What is the percentage gain?

4 A car bought for £3000 is sold for £2400 a year later. What is the percentage loss?

5 A lawn mower has been increased in price from £200 to £220. What is the percentage change?

6 What are the percentage changes in the prices of these calculators?

7 A cooker advertised at a sale price of £450 was increased to £465 once the sale had finished. What is the percentage increase?

8 A gold watch bought for £65 is now worth £140. What is the percentage increase?

9 The price of a text book has changed from £4.95 to £5.20. What is the percentage increase?

10 A coat normally priced at £65 has been reduced to £60 in a sale. What is the percentage reduction?

Hire purchase

If you need to buy something and you do not have enough money to pay for it at once, an alternative is to pay for it *on credit*, that is, to owe some of the money, and pay it back over a period of time. A common form of credit is **Hire Purchase (HP)**: you put a deposit down, and pay the remainder as a series of instalments. You will end up paying more this way because you are charged interest on the money you owe.

Example 10

Calculate the additional cost of buying this bike on HP.

6 payments of £27.80	=	£27.80 × 6	=	£166.80
		+ deposit	=	£17.50
		HP cost		£184.30

The additional cost is therefore £184.30 − £160 = £24.30

BMX £160

Deposit £17·50 and 6 Payments of £27·80

EXERCISE **3.14**

Calculate the additional cost if the following items were bought by hire purchase:

1 A video camera for a cash price of £640, or on HP with a 10% deposit and 26 payments of £26.00.

2 A car is advertised for £7000, or paid for with a 20% deposit plus 24 monthly payments of £291.60.

3 A new £360 television can be paid for in cash, or by an HP agreement which specifies a £50 deposit and 36 monthly payments of £11.55.

4 A microwave oven would normally cost £199.99. A 10% deposit can secure an HP agreement requiring 100 weekly payments of £2.25.

5 A bicycle can be bought for £159.99 cash, or with a deposit of £16 and 99 payments of £1.80.

6 An HP agreement for the purchase of a home computer specifies a deposit of £60 plus monthly payments of £14 over a period of 2 years. The cash price is £360.

7 A deposit of £96 would secure a second-hand car, followed by 12 monthly payments of £59.25. The alternative is £650 cash.

8 A carpet would normally cost £870, but could be paid for over a year at £20 per week.

9

£100

OR
Deposit of 15%
12 Payments
of £8.25

10 A washing machine has a cash price of £260. The alternative HP cost is a 25% deposit with 12 monthly payments of £18.15.

Loans

An alternative to HP is to take out a loan to cover the cost of a purchase. You must be sure you can afford the repayments, otherwise you will get yourself into debt. It is also good advice to shop around for the cheapest loan.

Example 11

For a loan of £4000 repayable over 84 months find (*a*) the monthly repayment (*b*) the total payable.

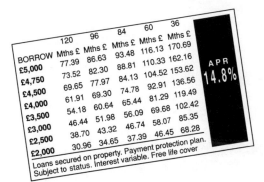

BORROW	120 Mths £	96 Mths £	84 Mths £	60 Mths £	36 Mths £
£5,000	77.39	86.63	93.48	116.13	170.69
£4,750	73.52	82.30	88.81	110.33	162.16
£4,500	69.65	77.97	84.13	104.52	153.62
£4,000	61.91	69.30	74.78	92.91	136.56
£3,500	54.18	60.64	65.44	81.29	119.49
£3,000	46.44	51.98	56.09	69.68	102.42
£2,500	38.70	43.32	46.74	58.07	85.35
£2,000	30.96	34.65	37.39	46.45	68.28

APR 14.8%

Loans secured on property. Payment protection plan. Subject to status. Interest variable. Free life cover

From the table, £4000 over 84 months gives a monthly repayment of £74.78.

The total payable is 84 × £74.78 = £6281.52

EXERCISE *3.15*

Use the table in Example 11 to find for each loan
(*a*) the monthly repayment (*b*) the total payable.

1 £2500 over 60 months

2 £4500 over 96 months

3 £3000 over 36 months

4 £5000 over 120 months

5 £2000 over 60 months

Continued overleaf

For each loan find (*a*) the monthly repayment (*b*) the total payable.

6 £2000 over 60 months

7 £8000 over 120 months

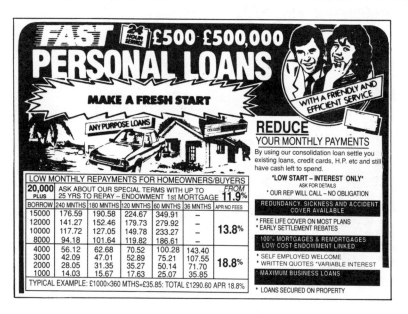

8 £12 000 over 180 months

9 £2000 over 36 months

10 £15 000 over 240 months.

Home insurance

HOME CONTENTS INSURANCE TABLE				
Cover Required	**AREA A** All Postal Districts not listed under Areas B/C/D	**AREA B** Birmingham B1 to B44, B47, B66, B67, B90 Bradford BD1 to BD10 Leeds LS1 to LS14 Newcastle NE1 to NE6 Sheffield S1 to S14	**AREA C** Former London GLC Areas – Excluding Harrow and London Postal Districts (See Area D) Glasgow G1 to G62, G73 G76, G77, G81 Manchester M1 to M23, M32 Paisley PA1 to PA5	**AREA D** Harrow HA0 to HA9 London E1 to E18, EC1 to EC4 N1 to N22, NW1 to NW11 SE1 to SE28, SW1 to SW20 W1 to W14, WC2 Liverpool/Birkenhead L1 to L30, L32 to L36, L41 to L45
£8,000	£44.00 p.a.	£68.00 p.a.	£76.00 p.a.	Min Insurance Cover in This Area is £9,000
£9,000	£49.50 p.a.	£76.50 p.a.	£85.50 p.a.	£135.00 p.a.
£10,000	£55.00 p.a.	£85.00 p.a.	£95.00 p.a.	£150.00 p.a.
£12,000	£66.00 p.a.	£102.00 p.a.	£114.00 p.a.	£180.00 p.a.
£14,000	£77.00 p.a.	£119.00 p.a.	£133.00 p.a.	£210.00 p.a.
£16,000	£88.00 p.a.	£136.00 p.a.	£152.00 p.a.	£240.00 p.a.
£18,000	£99.00 p.a.	£153.00 p.a.	£171.00 p.a.	£270.00 p.a.

Example 12

Calculate the annual cost of £12 000 insurance cover in the postal district of Sheffield S4.

From the table: Sheffield S4 is in Area B: £102.00 p.a.

EXERCISE 3.16

Using the table on page 80, calculate the annual cost of house insurance for the following:

1 £14 000 insurance for a house in Manchester M20.

2 £18 000 insurance for a house in London N4.

3 £10 000 insurance for a house in Glasgow G30.

4 £8000 insurance for a house in Liverpool L15.

5 £14 000 insurance for a house in Leeds LS9.

6 £14 000 insurance for a house in Manchester M28.

7 £9000 insurance for a house in Newcastle NE7.

8 £18 000 insurance for a house in Basingstoke.

9 £12 000 insurance for a house in Cambridge.

10 £16 000 insurance for a house in Paisley PA4.

Mortgages

After deciding to buy a house the next step is to apply for a mortgage. The maximum amount granted depends on the salary of those applying.

Example 13

Tony and Sally apply for a 90% mortgage on a £30 000 house from a building society. Tony's wage is £7100 and Sally's is £6000. The

building society is prepared to lend a maximum amount based on the formula: (3 × main earnings) + secondary earnings. Can they afford to buy the house?

The amount they need to borrow is 90% of the value of the house:

$$90\% \text{ of } £30\,000 = \frac{90}{100} \times 30\,000 = £27\,000$$

$$\text{Maximum mortgage} = (3 \times £7100) + £6000 = £27\,300$$

As the maximum mortgage £27 300 available is greater than the £27 000 they need, they can therefore afford to buy the house.

EXERCISE 3.17

Find out whether the following people can afford to buy the house of their choice:

1 Jeremy earns £12 000 and his wife Jane earns £11 000. They want to buy a house advertised at £48 000, and have applied for a 90% mortgage. The loan is calculated using the formula (3 × main earnings) + secondary earnings.

2 Newtown Building Society uses the formula (3 × main earnings) + secondary earnings to calculate maximum loans for 90% mortgages. Bobby and Sandra have earnings of £4300 and £9500 respectively, and have applied for a mortgage against a £36 000 house.

3 Remi earns £5300 p.a., and would like a 100% mortgage for a £14 000 house. A building society will consider a loan using the formula 3 × single earnings.

4 Peter and Mark would like to buy a £31 000 house jointly, and have applied for a 85% mortgage which is calculated using the formula (2 × joint earnings). Their earnings are £7200 and £6000.

5 Irshad earns £12 400 p.a., and Shaheen £7000. They would like to buy a £52 800 house. Their bank calculate 90% mortgages using the formula (3 × main earnings) + secondary earnings.

6 A husband and wife earn £9000 and £8800 respectively. Their 90% mortgage application for a £39 500 house will depend on the formula (2 × joint earnings).

7 A house valued at £64 000 is being bought by Colin and Susan who earn £15 000 and £15 400 respectively. They have applied for a 95% mortgage, which will be calculated using the formula ($2\frac{1}{2}$ × main earnings) + ($1\frac{1}{2}$ × secondary earnings).

8 An offer on a house of £46 950 from Vivek (who earns £9400 p.a.) and Sheila (who earns £9000 p.a.) has been accepted. They apply to a building society for an 80% mortgage. The formula used is (3 × main earnings) + secondary earnings.

9 A husband and wife each have a salary of £19 000 p.a. They would like to buy an £85 400 house with a mortgage of 90%. The formula their bank uses is (3 × main earnings) + secondary earnings.

10 A 70% mortgage application has been received by a building society which uses the formula (2 × joint earnings) to calculate maximum mortgages. The application, from Mr Shah, is against a house valued at £140 000. His earnings are £28 800 p.a., and his wife earns £21 900.

4. Enterprises

Running a mail-order catalogue

Many people either run, or buy from, mail-order catalogues. Some of the advantages are:

(i)   the ability to browse through the brochure (which is usually large, bright and colourful) at any time of day or night which suits you, whether or not the shops are open;

(ii)   the brochure contains a very wide range of goods - you have no need to visit different kinds of shops if, for example, you are looking for shoes, chair covers or a microwave oven;

(iii) 'free trial' at home of clothes, for size and colour, or of a lampshade in the actual room for which it is intended;

(iv) payment by instalments, either weekly, fortnightly or monthly, to a friend rather than to a shop;

(v)   details of quality, style, etc. from the person running the catalogue;

(vi) commission, if you are running the catalogue yourself. This means that your are paid a percentage of the value of your sales (typically 10% or 12.5%).

Imagine that you wish to buy a bicycle from a catalogue (see opposite) run by your aunt. These are the main stages in the process.

(i)   Select a bicycle from the brochure, and inform your aunt.

(ii)   Your bicycle should arrive a few days later for you to inspect. If you decide that you do not want it, you can return it, and that is the end of the matter.

(iii) If you decide to keep the bicycle, your aunt will give you a payment card on which she will write the cost of the bicycle (say £119.99) and the amount of the weekly payment required (usually 5p in the £, which is £6.00 a week in this case).

PHILLIPS PHASER BY RALEIGH

ADJUSTABLE RACING STYLE SADDLE

ALLOY STEM

DUAL LEVER BRAKES

[A]

REAR REFLECTOR

FROM
£99.99
50 WEEKS £2.00

REFLECTOR PEDALS

5 SPEED 19½ and 21½ ins FRAMES
10 SPEED 21½ · 23½ and 25 ins FRAMES

ALL THESE BIKES CONFORM TO BS6102 SAFETY STANDARDS

A Raleigh Phillips Phaser 5-speed cycle with 73 degree parallel frame, alloy handlebar stem, Huret derailleur gears, alloy hubs and water bottle. Wheel size 26ins. Frame size 19½ins. inside leg 27-30ins.
★R3870R Cycle   £99.99
          20 wks £5.00; 38 wks £2.65
                         50 wks £2.00

Raleigh Phillips Phaser 5-speed cycle. Wheel size 27ins. Frame size 21½ins. Inside leg 29-32ins.
★R3871M Cycle   £99.99
          20 wks £5.00 38 wks £2.65
                         50 wks £2.00

Raleigh Phillips Phaser 10-speed cycle with cotterless chain set. Wheel size 27ins. Frame size 21½ins. inside leg 29-32ins.
★R3872F Cycle   £106.99
          20 wks £5.35 38 wks £2.85
                         50 wks £2.14

Raleigh Phillips Phaser 10-speed cycle with cotterless chain set. Wheel size 27in. Frame size 23½ins. Inside leg 32-35ins.
★R3873C Cycle   £106.99
          20 wks £5.35 38 wks £2.85
                         50 wks £2.14

Raleigh Phillips Phaser 10-speed cycle with cotterless chain set. Wheel size 27ins. Frame size 25ins. Inside leg 33-36ins.
★R3874U Cycle   £106.99
          20 wks £5.35 38 wks £2.85
                         50 wks £2.14

ALL AVAILABLE ON 50 WEEKS TERMS

ALL AVAILABLE ON 50 WEEKS TERMS

RALEIGH Quasar

B Raleigh Quasar 12-speed cycle. Unique Aerospace Contour frame with Reynolds 501 double butted main tubes, derailleur gears, Weinmann concave eyeletted narrow section rims, quick release hubs and brake levers. Aero style handlebars with concealed brake cables, alloy detachable chain set, toe clips and straps. Complete with waterbottle. Wheel size 700c (Equivalent 27½" wheel). Frame size 21½ins. Inside leg 29-32ins.
★R3864F Cycle   £179.99
          20 wks £9.00 38 wks £4.75 50 wks £3.60

EXTENDED CREDIT TERMS To order this item on extended terms quote catalogue no. ★R5947T. Full details see page 998/9

Raleigh Quasar 12-speed cycle. Frame size 25ins. Inside leg 33-36ins.
★R3866U Cycle   £179.99
          20 wks £9.00 38 wks £4.75 50 wks £3.60

EXTENDED CREDIT TERMS To quote this item on extended terms quote catalogue no. ★R3949K. Full details see page 998/9

Extended Credit Terms

REYNOLDS 501 TUBING

[B]

Raleigh Quasar 12-speed cycle. Frame size 23½ins. Inside leg 32-35ins.
★R3865C Cycle   £179.99
          20 wks £9.00 38 wks £4.75 50 wks £3.50

RALEIGH Winner

C Raleigh Winner 10-speed cycle with 73 degree parallel frame, cotterless chain set with alloy cranks and disc, alloy side-pull brakes with extension levers. Simplex derailleur gear. Wheel size 27ins. Frame size 21½ins., inside leg 29-32ins.
★R3867T Cycle   £134.99
          20 wks £6.75 38 wks £3.60
                         50 wks £2.70

Raleigh Winner 10-speed cycle. Frame size 23½ins. inside leg 32-35ins.
★R3868P Cycle   £134.99
          20 wks £6.75 38 wks £3.60
                         50 wks £2.70

Raleigh Winner 10-speed cycle. Frame size 25ins. Inside leg 33-36ins.
★R3869K Cycle   £134.99
          20 wks £6.75 38 wks £3.60
                         50 wks £2.70

COTTERLESS CHAIN SET

[C]

£179.99
50 WEEKS £3.60

12 SPEED 3 FRAME SIZES

£134.99
50 WEEKS £2.70

10 SPEED 3 FRAME SIZES

912

(iv) You now pay your aunt £6.00 a week, and she makes a note on your payment card of your payment, and of how much you still need to pay (the balance owing). After three weeks your card could look like this:

Name	B. PASCOE

WEEKLY PAYMENTS (continued)

Date	CASH PAID		BALANCE OWING Add Purchases Subtract Returns		AGENTS INITIALS
	£	p	£	p	
			119	99	
17/3	6	00	113	99	AS
24/3	6	00	107	99	AS
31/3	6	00	101	99	AS

(v)   After 19 weeks you will have paid £114, so your final payment will be £5.99 instead of £6.00. The bicycle is now officially yours!

Example 1

Mike decides to buy a lawnmower, costing £74.49, from his mother's catalogue. Assuming that he pays 20 weekly instalments, at 5p in the £, (*a*) how much is each instalment (to the nearest penny)

(*b*) how much will he still owe after five payments

(*c*) how much will be the last payment?

(*a*) Each instalment will be £74.49 ÷ 20 = £3.72 (to the nearest penny).

(*b*) Five instalments = 5 × £3.72 = £18.60.

Mike will still owe £74.49 – £18.60 = £55.89.

(*c*) 19 payments will be 19 × £3.72 = £70.68. The last payment will therefore be £74.49 – £70.68 = £3.81.

EXERCISE **4.1**

Work out the missing amounts in the table. Assume 20 weekly payments, at 5p in the £ (to the nearest 10p), with the last payment being different, possibly, in order to complete the purchase exactly.

	Cost of purchases	Weekly payment	Amount paid after 19 weeks	Final payment
1	£25.99	£1.30	*	*
2	£73.40	£3.70	*	*
3	£48.95	*	*	*
4	£126.29	*	*	*
5	£9.70	*	*	*

6 Betty decides to buy a dress, costing £32.99 from a catalogue. She already owes £16.82. What will be her new weekly payment (5% of the total amount she now owes), to the nearest 10p?

7 Mandy calculates her weekly payment as £1.40 for a pair of shoes from her catalogue. (*a*) How much do the shoes cost? (*b*) How many weeks will she need to pay before the amount owing is less than £15.00?

8 Mr Holmes buys a coal bunker, costing £43.99, a wheel barrow costing £25.99 and some step ladders for £23.99, from a catalogue.

    (*a*) How much do these three items cost altogether?

    (*b*) He agrees to pay £5 a week. Is this more, or is it less, than the minimum payment?

    (*c*) For how many weeks will he need to pay £5?

    (*d*) What will be his final payment?

9 A dining room suite costs £649.00. If you are allowed to pay over 38 weeks instead of 20, what will be the weekly payment, correct to the nearest penny?
    How much will be the final payment?

10 Although she still owes £59.52 on her catalogue, Margery decides to buy a microwave oven, costing £159.99.

    (*a*) If she can spread the total outstanding over 38 weeks, what will be the weekly payment?

    (*b*) If instead, Margery pays £6 per week, how many weeks will she need to pay £6, and what will be her final payment?

If you decide to run a catalogue yourself, you will need to do some arithmetic, keep accurate records, collect and send off payments regularly, keep track of your commission, as well as dealing with returns of unwanted goods and informing your customers of any special offers and reduced prices.

After writing to the mail-order firm asking to become an agent, you will be given an agent's reference number and receive your agent's stationery. Three of the more important items of stationery are (i) customer payment cards (ii) order forms and (iii) agent's ledger.

(i)   Earlier you saw a **customer payment card** – here is another
one, showing that Mrs Parker owes £6.88.

Name	T. PARKER

WEEKLY PAYMENTS (continued)

Date	CASH PAID		BALANCE OWING Add Purchases Subtract Returns		AGENTS INITIALS
	£	p	£	p	
13-6	Bt. forward		48	88	AS
20-6	10	00	38	88	AS
27-6	10	00	28	88	AS
4-7	5	50	23	38	AS
11-7	5	50	17	88	AS
18-7	5	50	12	38	AS
25-7	5	50	6	88	AS

(ii)   On an **order form** you need to enter the catalogue reference
number of the item, its description, colour and size if appropriate,
how many you wish to order, the price and the name of the customer
who is ordering the item. Here is a typical order form; there is usually
one for you to send off to the mail-order firm, and a carbon copy to
keep as your reference. (With many mail-order catalogues there is
often a telephone ordering system; you must keep a record of any
order placed over the telephone.)

John Moores
Kershaw Avenue Crosby
Liverpool X L70 2TT

ORDER FORM

Please ensure your Agent's Number is correct.

Mark this box with a large 'X' if you have recently changed your address.

| Agent's Number | | | | | | | | | — | |

Agent's Name _____

Address _____

Postcode _____

Telephone Number _____   Date _____

Orders

CREDIT TERMS: State 20, 38 or 100 weeks according to choice available

Page no. if known	Catalogue Item Nos.	How many	Colour	Size or Size No.	Description	Price each £	p	Total value £	p	Credit terms	Customer number	If this order is yourself or an your househo please tick th

Items for DIRECT DELIVERY to a customer

CREDIT TERMS: State 20, 38 or 100 weeks according to choice available

Page no. if known	Catalogue Item Nos.	How many	Colour	Size or Size No.	Description	Price each £	p	Total value £	p	Credit terms	Customer number	Mr Mrs Miss

Address _____

Postcode _____   Tel No. _____

(iii) Orders and payments are transferred to your **agent's ledger,** which you update weekly or fortnightly. A record of all your dealings is usually kept in your ledger, and a copy sent off, together with payments you have received, to the mail-order firm at regular intervals (usually monthly). An example of a ledger sheet is shown opposite. Although it looks complicated, it is fairly straightforward to complete if you follow the instructions given with your initial supply of stationery.

LEDGER SHEET

CUSTOMER NAME

| Date from | 22nd June |
| Date to | 20th July |

Sales and Returns — Add sales, Subtract returns | Payments

Customer	No	Balance brought forward £ p	Week 1 £ p	Week 2 £ p	Week 3 £ p	Week 4 £ p	Week 5 £ p	Total sales less returns	Week 1 £ p	Week 2 £ p	Week 3 £ p	Week 4 £ p	Week 5 £ p	Total cash paid	Balance brought forward
Mrs. T. Brown	1	17 82							1 30	1 30	1 30	1 30		5 20	12 62
Mary Knight	2	23 13				15 99		15 99	2 50	2 50	2 50	2 50		10 00	29 12
Julie Knight	3	4 51		3 50		7 99		11 49	1 00	1 00	1 00	1 00		4 00	12 00
Mr. Hall	4	86 81							5 40	5 40	5 40	5 40		21 60	65 21
Sally James	5	3 60							1 00	1 00	1 00	0 60		3 60	
		163 35 C				Total sales this month £		27 48 A				Total cash paid this month £ Send this amount to us by the date shown on your payment slip		44 40 B	

Example 2

Mary, a new customer, wants to order two dresses from your catalogue.

(*a*) Complete the order form.

John Moores
Kershaw Avenue Crosby Liverpool X L70 2TT

ORDER FORM
Please ensure your Agent's Number is correct.

Mark this box with a large 'X' if you have recently changed your address.

| Agent's Number | 1 9 2 3 7 6 4 – 3 |

Agent's Name: Ann Scott
Address: 49, Green Lane Newtown   Postcode:
Telephone Number: 37152   Date: 20th July

Orders

CREDIT TERMS: State 20, 38 or 100 weeks according to choice available

Page no. if known	Catalogue Item Nos.	How many	Colour	Size or Size No.	Description	Price each £ p	Total value £ p	Credit terms	Customer number	If this order is not for yourself or anyone in your household please tick this box
157	GB 2741	1	—	12	Dress	24 99	24 99	20	7	✓
160	GK 4031	1	Black	12	Jersey dress	32 99	32 99	20	7	✓

Items for DIRECT DELIVERY to a customer

CREDIT TERMS: State 20, 38 or 100 weeks according to choice available

Page no. if known	Catalogue Item Nos.	How many	Colour	Size or Size No.	Description	Price each £ p	Total value £ p	Credit terms	Customer number	Mr Mrs Miss
									Address	
									Postcode	Tel No.

(b) She decides to keep both dresses Make out a customer payment
card for her.

Name	MARY CHARLTON

GOODS PURCHASED

Date	Description	Cost £	p
27.7	Dress	24	99
27.7	Jersey Dress	32	99

GOODS RETURNED

Date	Description	Cost £	p

WEEKLY PAYMENTS

Date	CASH PAID £	p	BALANCE OWING Add Purchases Subtract Returns £	p	AGENTS INITIALS
27.7	3	00	54	98	A S
3.8	3	00	51	98	A S

(c) You are due to send in a copy of your agent's ledger after Mary
has made two payments. Update her customer payment card, and
complete your ledger.

LEDGER SHEET

Date from **20th July**
Date to **24th August**

Sales and Returns — Add sales, Subtract returns
Payments

Customer	No	Balance brought forward	Week 1	Week 2	Week 3	Week 4	Week 5	Total sales less returns	Week 1	Week 2	Week 3	Week 4	Week 5	Total cash paid	Balance brought forward
Mrs. T. Brown	1	12 62							1 30	1 30					
Mary Knight	2	29 12							2 50	2 50					
Julie Knight	3	12 00							1 00	1 00					
Mr. Hall	4	65 21							5 40	5 40					
Sally James	5	—							—	—					
Tom James	6	7 80							- 80	- 80					
Mary Charlton	7		57 98					57 98	3 00	3 00					
		126 75 C		Total sales this month £ 57 98 A									Total cash paid this month £		

Send this amount to us by the date shown on your payment slip _____ B

(*d*) Complete the next ledger sheet after three more weeks, and update Mary's payment card.

LEDGER SHEET

Date from **20th July**
Date to **24th August**

Sales and Returns — Add sales, Subtract returns
Payments

Customer	No	Balance brought forward	Week 1	Week 2	Week 3	Week 4	Week 5	Total sales less returns	Week 1	Week 2	Week 3	Week 4	Week 5	Total cash paid	Balance brought forward
Mrs. T. Brown	1	12 62							1 30	1 30	1 30	1 30	1 30	6 50	6 12
Mary Knight	2	29 12							2 50	2 50	2 50	2 50	2 50	12 50	16 62
Julie Knight	3	12 00							1 00	1 00	1 00	1 00	1 00	5 00	7 00
Mr. Hall	4	65 21							5 40	5 40	5 40	5 40	5 40	27 00	38 21
Sally James	5	—							—	—	—	—	—	—	—
Tom James	6	7 80							- 80	- 80	- 80	- 80	- 80	4 00	3 80
Mary Charlton	7		57 98					57 98	3 00	3 00	3 00	3 00	3 00	15 00	42 98
		126 75 C		Total sales this month £ 57 98 A									Total cash paid this month £	70 00 B	114 73

Send this amount to us by the date shown on your payment slip _____ B

Name	MARY CHARLTON

GOODS PURCHASED

Date	Description	Cost £	p
27.7	Dress	24	99
27.7	Jersey Dress	32	99

GOODS RETURNED

Date	Description	Cost £	p

WEEKLY PAYMENTS

Date	CASH PAID £	p	BALANCE OWING Add Purchases Subtract Returns £	p	AGENTS INITIALS
27.7	3	00	54	98	AS
3.8	3	00	51	98	AS
10.8	3	00	48	98	AS
17.8	3	00	45	98	AS
24.8	3	00	42	98	AS

Example 3

Mary now orders a pair of shoes. When they come, she likes them and decides to keep them.

(*a*) Complete the order form.

John Moores
Kershaw Avenue Crosby
Liverpool X L70 2TT

ORDER FORM

Please ensure your Agent's Number is correct.

Mark this box with a large 'X' if you have recently changed your address.

Agent's Name	Ann Scott
Address	49 Green Lane
	Newtown
Telephone Number	37152

Postcode

Date 24th August

Agent's Number: | 1 | 9 | 2 | 3 | 7 | 6 | 4 | – | 3 |

Orders

CREDIT TERMS: State 20, 38 or 100 weeks according to choice available

Page no. if known	Catalogue Item Nos.	How many	Colour	Size or Size No.	Description	Price each £	p	Total value £	p	Credit terms	Customer number	If this order is not for yourself or anyone in your household please tick this box
297	LW 7661	1	Black	6	Court Shoes	23	99	23	99	20	7	✓

Items for DIRECT DELIVERY to a customer

CREDIT TERMS: State 20, 38 or 100 weeks according to choice available

Page no. if known	Catalogue Item Nos.	How many	Colour	Size or Size No.	Description	Price each £	p	Total value £	p	Credit terms	Customer number	Mr Mrs Miss
												Address
												Postcode / Tel No.

(*b*) What is the total balance that Mary owes, including the shoes?
Mary now owes £42.98 + £23.99 = £66.97

(*c*) Work out her new weekly payment on this new total balance.

New payment $= \dfrac{£66.97}{20} = £3.35$

(*d*) After four of these new payments, the ledger is due to be sent off.
Complete the payment card and ledger sheet overleaf.

LEDGER SHEET

CUSTOMER NAME

Date from: **24th August**
Sales and Returns
Add sales, Subtract returns

Date to: **21st September**
Payments

Customer	No	Balance brought forward	Week 1 £ p	Week 2 £ p	Week 3 £ p	Week 4 £ p	Week 5 £ p	Total sales less returns	Week 1 £ p	Week 2 £ p	Week 3 £ p	Week 4 £ p	Week 5 £ p	Total cash paid	Balance brought forward
Mrs. T. Brown	1	6 12							1 30	1 30	1 30	1 30		5 20	- 92
Mary Knight	2	16 62		19 99	52 99			72 98	4 50	4 50	4 50	4 50		18 00	71 60
Julie Knight	3	7 00							1 00	1 00	1 00	1 00		4 00	3 00
Mr. Hall	4	38 21			10 99			10 99	2 50	2 50	2 50	2 50		10 00	39 20
Sally James	5														
Tom James	6	3 80							- 80	- 80	- 80	- 80		3 20	0 60
Mary Charlton	7	42 98	23 99					23 99	3 35	3 35	3 35	3 35		13 40	53 57

114 73 C

Total sales this month £ **107 96** A

Total cash paid this month £ **53 80** **168 89** B
Send this amount to us by the date shown on your payment slip

(Check: A + C - B = £168.89)

Name: **MARY CHARLTON**

GOODS PURCHASED

Date	Description	Cost £ p
27.7	Dress	24 99
27.7	Jersey Dress	32 99
24.8	Court shoes	23 99

GOODS RETURNED

Date	Description	Cost £ p

WEEKLY PAYMENTS

Date	CASH PAID £ p	BALANCE OWING Add Purchases Subtract Returns £ p	AGENTS INITIALS
27.7	3 00	54 98	AS
3.8	3 00	51 98	AS
10.8	3 00	48 98	AS
17.8	3 00	45 98	AS
24.8	3 00	42 98	AS
31.8	Add	23 99	

WEEKLY PAYMENTS

Date	CASH PAID £ p	BALANCE OWING Add Purchases Subtract Returns £ p	AGENTS INITIALS
31.8		66 97	AS
31.8	3 35	63 62	AS
7.9	3 35	60 27	AS
14.9	3 35	56 92	AS
21.9	3 35	53 57	AS

Enterprises

Many teenagers have a hobby, by which they can develop an interest outside of school. For example, the hobby may be gardening, decorating pebbles, knitting soft toys, or making model ships. Occasionally the products of a hobby can be sold to friends and relations, the money being used to extend the hobby. For example, the gardener might sell bedding plants, or tomatoes, while the model maker could paint the ships and sell them to friends to use as gifts. From these small beginnings, it may be possible to develop the profit-making side more fully, so expanding the hobby into a **small business** or **enterprise.**

Example 4

Sara collects pebbles from a beach, paints them, and sells them for 35p each. Originally her paints were a Christmas present, but some of the colours will soon need replacing, at a cost of 80p per tube.

(*a*) How many pebbles will she need to sell if she will soon be needing three new tubes of paint?

(*b*) She has enough paint for 12 pebbles. How much will she receive if she sells them all?

(*c*) Sara would dearly love to have the set of paints that she has seen in a catalogue. It costs £14.50. How many pebbles will she have to sell in order to have enough money to buy these paints?

(*a*) Three tubes of paint will cost $3 \times 80p = £2.40$.

As each pebble brings in 35p, she will need to sell $\dfrac{£2.40}{35p}$ pebbles.

(Take care, you will need to work either in £s or in pence.)

$$\frac{2.40}{0.35} \text{ or } \frac{240}{35} = 6.857 \ldots$$

This means that she will need to sell 7 pebbles if she is to have at least £2.40.

(*b*) 12 pebbles will earn her $12 \times 35p = £4.20$.

(*c*) Again, we can work either in £s or pence, not both at once!

$$\frac{14.50}{0.35} \text{ or } \frac{1450}{35} = 41.4 \dots$$

Sara will have to sell 42 pebbles if she is to have enough money for the paints.

EXERCISE 4.2

1 Beth and Saleem decide to make sandwiches, and sell them at break times. They can make 20 sandwiches from a loaf of bread costing 55p and enough sandwich mix, costing 68p, to fill the 20 sandwiches. If they sell the sandwiches for 10p each,

(*a*) how much profit will they make on 20 sandwiches

(*b*) what percentage profit is this

(*c*) how many sandwiches will they have to sell in a week if they wish to have a profit of at least £6 each, by the end of the week?

2 Arthur and his brother Jeff use their father's small greenhouse to grow bedding plants from seed. Packets of seed cost 65p each and potting compost costs £4.72 for a bag which will fill 30 seed boxes. They can grow about 50 plants in one seed box, and they use one packet of seed for each box. They sell the plants for 3p each.

(*a*) How much will it cost to buy a box of plants from Arthur and Jeff?

(*b*) How much does it cost Arthur and Jeff to grow 30 boxes of plants?

(*c*) How much profit will they make if they sell all 30 boxes?

3 Three girls decide to offer a children's party service. They will supply food, drinks, party novelties and prizes, in addition to providing music and organising games. The cost to the girls of buying various items is given below. Using this information, what would be a reasonable fee to charge for a party of ten children, if the three girls wish to make a profit of £2.00 each?

Food (sandwiches, sausage rolls, cakes, etc.)	30p each child
Drinks (two bottles of juice)	85p a bottle
Paper plates	48p for ten
Paper cups	48p for ten
Prizes (one per child)	35p each

4 Judith likes using her mum's knitting machine, and decides to make and sell garments. A ball of wool costs her 80p. She makes plain and patterned garments to sell at the prices in the table.

Garment	Number of balls of wool	Price	
		plain	patterned
Jumper	6	£8.00	£10.00
Hat	$1\frac{1}{2}$	£2.50	£3.00
Pair of gloves	1	£2.50	£3.00
Scarf	3	£3.50	£4.50
Sweater	8	£10.00	£12.50

(*a*) How much will Judith charge for two plain jumpers and a patterned sweater?

(*b*) Her aunt wants a plain hat, pair of gloves and a scarf. How much will she have to pay Judith?

(*c*) How much profit will Judith make on a patterned jumper?

(*d*) Work out the profit in (*c*) as a percentage.

(*e*) Her current orders are: three plain scarves, two sweaters (one plain and one patterned) and two pairs of patterned gloves. How much profit will she make on these seven items?

5 After cleaning out his shed, Henry's father gives Henry a kit for making picture frames. The only further requirements are the wood, small nails and backing hardboard. Henry has enough nails, but lengths of wood cost 92p per metre and hardboard is £4.84 per square metre.

(a) What length of wood is needed for a frame measuring 16 cm by 12 cm?

(b) What area of hardboard is required for the frame in (a)?

(c) Work out how much it will cost Henry to make this frame.

(d) If Henry charges £1.40 for the frame, how much profit will he make?

(e) He is asked to make three more frames. Two are to be 24 cm by 20 cm, and one is to be 30 cm by 24 cm. If Henry makes 80% profit on the cost of materials, how much will he charge for these three frames?

Investigation A

Choose a project or topic or idea in which you are interested, and which could develop into a small enterprise.

(a) Do a market research exercise to test the feasibility of your idea.

(b) Using the market research results, modify your idea, if necessary, and try to predict what percentage profit you might make after a week, or a month, of operating your scheme.

Presentation of information

In many magazines, periodicals and newspapers you meet some of the different ways in which mathematical information can be presented, either as a picture or chart, or in a table. Usually, the information is fairly clear and easily interpreted, requiring only a basic knowledge of bar charts, graphs, diagrams and tables.

Example 5

The table shows the number of candidates achieving grades A, B, C, D and E in 'A' level examinations in a college.

Grade	A	B	C	D	E
No. of candidates	20	32	76	44	28

We can represent this information in a number of ways.

(*a*) A line graph.

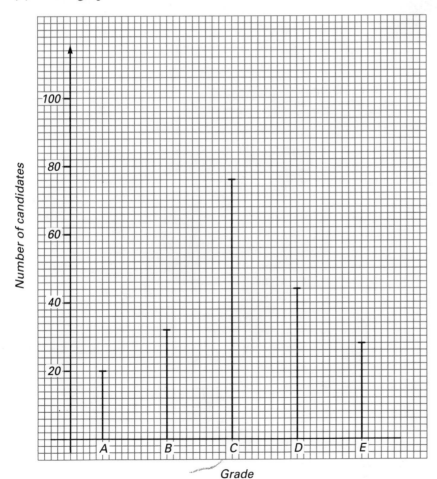

(*b*) A bar chart, either horizontal or vertical.

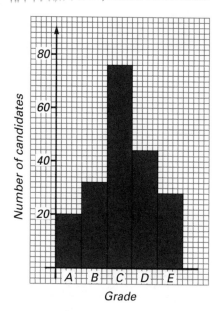

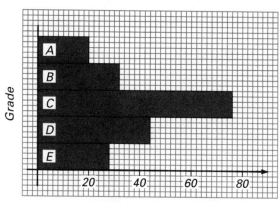

(*c*) A pie chart (here we need to work out percentages).

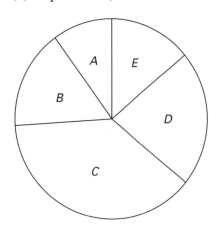

(*d*) A pictogram.

(*e*) A cumulative bar graph.

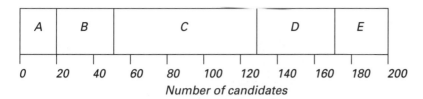

Number of candidates

(*f*) A rectangle divided up in proportion.

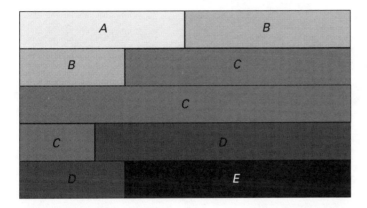

Which one of (*a*) to (*f*) do you think represents the information most clearly and honestly?

Investigation B

Look through magazines, periodicals and newspapers, and find as many ways as you can in which numerical information is represented. Classify these ways into groups (e.g. pictures only, diagrams with scales, tables of figures, etc.).

EXERCISE 4.3

1 The diagram shows the number of oarsmen who follow weight-training exercises on weekday nights.

    (*a*) How many train on Wednesdays?

    (*b*) How many train on weekday nights altogether?

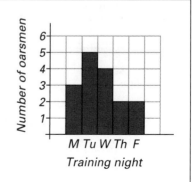

Number of oarsmen

M Tu W Th F
Training night

2 The pie chart on page 104 represents the methods by which the 24 pupils in class 3RY come to school.

    Estimate how many come by the different methods. How many come on foot?

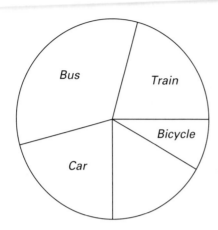

3 The share price, in pence, of a company over five years is shown.

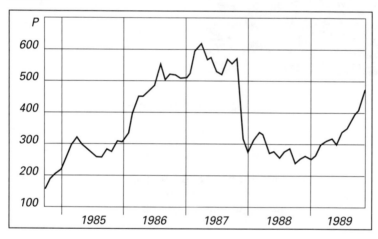

(*a*) What was the share price in June 1986?

(*b*) What was the highest share price?

(*c*) When (month and year) was this highest price?

(*d*) By how much did the share price fall in the last two months of 1987?

4 The profit analysis for a firm of stockbrokers is shown on p.105, comparing four aspects in 1988 and 1989.

(*a*) What was the figure for broking in 1989?

(*b*) Which of the four aspects showed least improvement?

(*c*) Estimate the *total* profit on Media for both years.

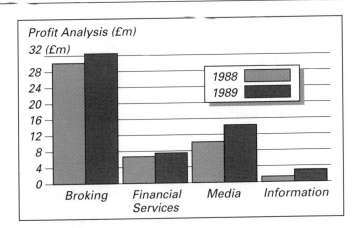

Profit Analysis (£m)

5 The figures of a Unit Trust are being compared with those of a building society and an endowment assurance over the last 15 years.

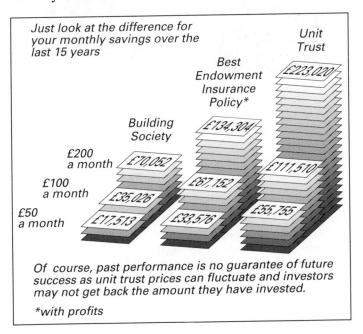

(a) How much would £50 a month in a building society have brought over the 15 years?

(b) How much would £200 a month invested in an endowment assurance have been worth after 15 years?

(c) The unit trust final figure for £100 a month is over three times the amount you would have received from a building society. Is this statement correct?

In representing information, however, there can be a tendency to mislead the reader by use of subtle (and sometimes blatant) techniques. It is worth examining some of these, in order that you can appreciate the *real* meaning of figures or diagrams.

Example 6

Which of these graphs gives a fair picture of the information?

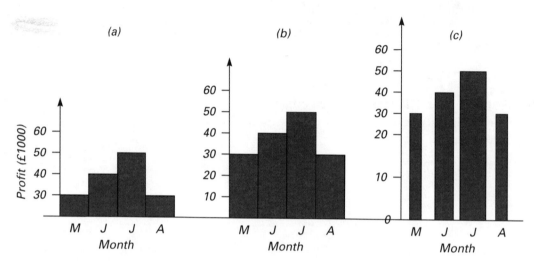

Only graph (*b*). Graph (*a*) starts at £20 000 and graph (*c*) has bars of differing widths.

A 'trick', used quite often, is to begin a bar graph from some point quite high up the scale on the vertical (*y*) axis. The differences in height are therefore exaggerated and by not beginning the graph at 'zero', the diagram conveys a false impression of the information.

EXERCISE **4.4**

In each case, state why the method of presentation deliberately
gives a false picture to the reader.

1

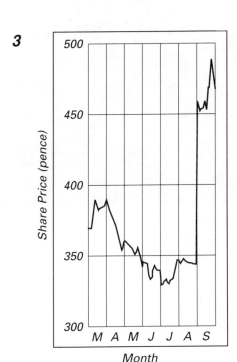

2

Here's what the new tax free benefits and monthly
maximum could have meant for you over the last 15 years...

BUILDING SOCIETY
£70,052

BEST ENDOWMENT
INSURANCE POLICY*
£134,304

£223,020
TAX FREE!

4

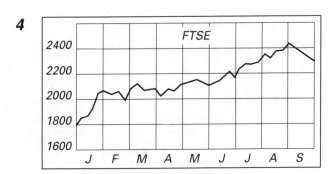

3

5 AVERAGE STAR
INVESTMENT TRUST,
COMPARED TO AVERAGE
UNIT TRUST AND AVERAGE
BUILDING SOCIETY
HIGHER RATE
ACCOUNT

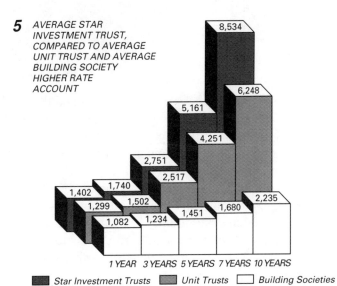

1 YEAR   3 YEARS   5 YEARS   7 YEARS   10 YEARS

▮ Star Investment Trusts   ▮ Unit Trusts   ☐ Building Societies

The figures show how an investment of £1000 in the average Star
Investment Trust (with net income re-invested) would have performed
in comparison with the same amount in the average unit trust and the
average building society higher rate account over the given periods to
1st September.

5. Foreign holidays

Due to the relative ease of air transport and the gradual reduction of
fares to foreign lands, many people choose to take their holidays
abroad. For many, the opportunities offered by a hotter climate and
guaranteed sun are the main attractions, but some people simply
prefer experiencing different cultures and places. Certainly the
number booking foreign holidays increases each year. When planning,
booking and eventually taking a holiday abroad, there are many skills
people need in order to take full advantage of the situation. A
knowledge of timetables, foreign currencies and the many types of
calculation expected in connection with such a trip will be an
advantage to the traveller.

Travelling by air

The most popular holiday resorts for British flights abroad include many on the Spanish coastline, as shown on the map on page 110.

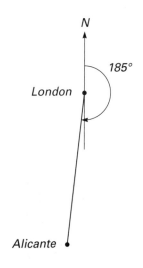

Example 1

Find (*a*) the bearing and (*b*) the distance of Alicante from London.

(*a*) Remember bearings are always measured *clockwise* from a North line.

The bearing of Alicante from London is therefore 185°.

(*b*) The distance from London to Alicante on the map is 7.8 cm.

Using the scale on the map: 0.9 cm = 100 miles,

$$\text{mileage} = \frac{7.8}{0.9} \times 100 = 866.66 \text{ miles}$$

$$= 870 \text{ miles (to the nearest ten miles).}$$

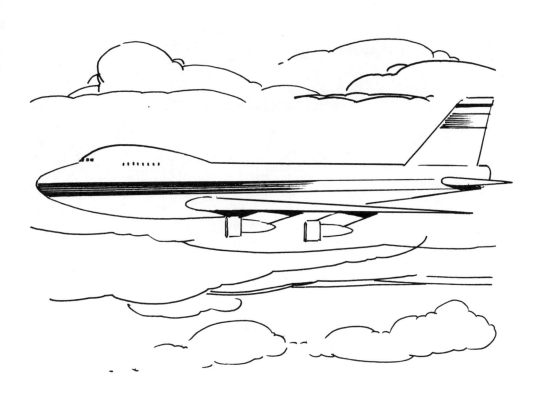

EXERCISE **5.1**

Find (*a*) the bearing and (*b*) the distance (to the nearest ten miles) of the following airports from London:

1 Reus **2** Malaga **3** Lisbon **4** Palma **5** Paris

6 (*a*) Find the bearing from Manchester to Faro on the Algarve.

    (*b*) Find the distance from Manchester to Faro.

    (*c*) Find the bearing from Faro to Manchester.

7 Find (*a*) the distance (*b*) the bearing both to and from Glasgow and Tunis airports.

8 How far is it to fly from Bristol to Paris?

9 (*a*) Find the bearing from Manchester to Ibiza.

    (*b*) Find the distance from Manchester to Ibiza.

    (*c*) Find the bearing from Ibiza to Manchester.

10 Calculate (*a*) the distance (*b*) the bearing to Minorca from the following airports: London, Manchester, Bristol and Glasgow.

11 Find the duration of each flight from London in hours and minutes:

	Destination	Flight no.	Depart (GMT)	Arrive (GMT)
(*a*)	Monastir, Tunisia	20S22	0840	1205
(*b*)	Dallas, USA	AA51	1035	2135
(*c*)	Tampa, USA	NW49	1050	0313
(*d*)	Arrecife, Lanzarote	20C52	1245	1710
(*e*)	Los Angeles	NW45	1340	0450
(*f*)	Palma, Majorca	20A00	1445	1725
(*g*)	Gibraltar	20F50	1550	1905
(*h*)	Dabolim, India	01G00	1600	0410
(*i*)	Paphos, Cyprus	20J92	1815	2255
(*j*)	Luqa, Malta	20L80	2105	0030

Investigation A

Using a world atlas examine the maps in the atlas. Many are unsuitable for finding bearings between towns. Can you explain why? Remember North lines are essential when finding bearings.

Example 2

The flight between Gatwick Airport and Funchal Airport, Madeira lasts $3\frac{3}{4}$ hours. The distance between the two airports is 1800 miles. What is the average speed of the plane?

$$\text{Average speed} = \frac{\text{distance}}{\text{time}} = \frac{1800 \text{ miles}}{3.75 \text{ hours}} = 480 \text{ m.p.h.}$$

EXERCISE 5.2

Find the average speed of the aeroplane during the following flights:

1 West Midlands Airport to Gerona, Costa Brava: distance 760 miles. Journey of duration 2 hours.

2 Manchester Airport to Ibiza: distance 1050 miles. Journey of duration $2\frac{1}{2}$ hours.

3 Stanstead Airport to Mahon, Minorca: distance 850 miles. Journey of duration $2\frac{1}{2}$ hours.

4 Gatwick Airport to Dubrovnik, Yugoslavia: distance 1080 miles. Journey of duration $2\frac{1}{2}$ hours.

5 Gatwick Airport to Varna, Bulgaria: distance 1470 miles. Journey of duration $3\frac{1}{4}$ hours.

6 Heathrow Airport to Cairo, Egypt: distance 2240 miles. Journey of duration $4\frac{3}{4}$ hours.

EXERCISE 5.3

The travel graphs opposite represent the flights made by four aircraft.

1 Can you explain why the centre portion of each graph is a straight line?

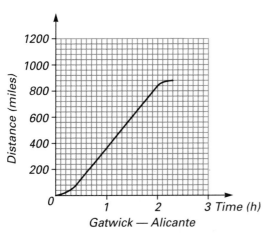

Gatwick — Alicante

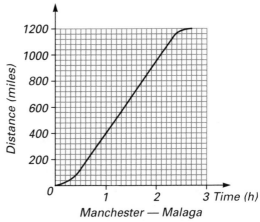

Manchester — Malaga

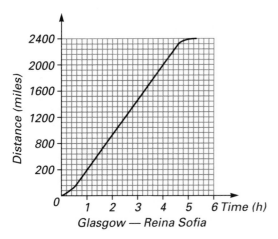

Glasgow — Reina Sofia

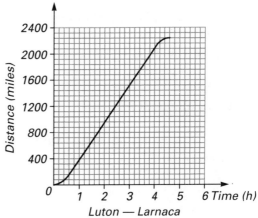

Luton — Larnaca

2 Can you explain why the ends of each graph are not straight?

3 Draw a table to compare the distances, journey times and average speeds of each of the four journeys.

4 Which plane flew the fastest?

5 How far had the plane from Glasgow travelled after 2 hours?

6 How long had the Manchester plane been in the air when it had gone 440 miles?

7 How far had the plane from Luton travelled after 3 hours?

8 After $1\frac{1}{4}$ hours, how far was the Gatwick plane from its destination of Alicante?

Sketch travel graphs for the following flights:

9 Gatwick to Palma, Majorca. A 2-hour flight of distance 800 miles.

10 Gatwick to Funchal, Madeira. An 1800-mile flight lasting $3\frac{3}{4}$ hours.

11 Gatwick to Malta. A 1300-mile flight lasting $3\frac{1}{4}$ hours.

12 What do you think happened at Amman, Jordan?

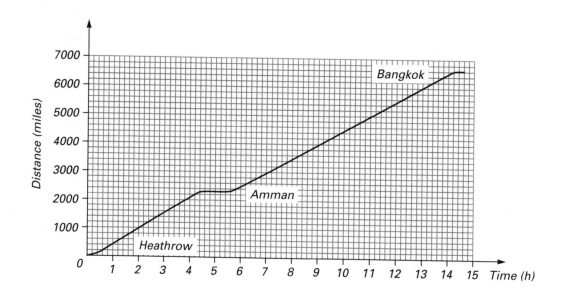

13 Find the average speed of the plane (a) between Heathrow and Amman (b) between Amman and Bangkok.

14 How far had the plane flown from Heathrow after 10 hours?

Investigation B

Sketch a number of travel graphs of aeroplane flights and ask your neighbour to describe the journeys. You might like to do the same for your neighbour's travel graphs.

Time

When travelling about the world we find we have to adjust our watches and clocks. This is because the world is divided into different time zones, as shown in the map below. We have to adjust our watches so that we always use the correct local time according to where we are in the world.

Example 3

The time in London is 4 p.m. on a Monday. What time is it in Sydney? Sydney is 10 hours in front of GMT, so the time in Sydney will be 4 p.m. + 10 hours = 2 a.m. the following day, i.e. 2 a.m. on Tuesday morning.

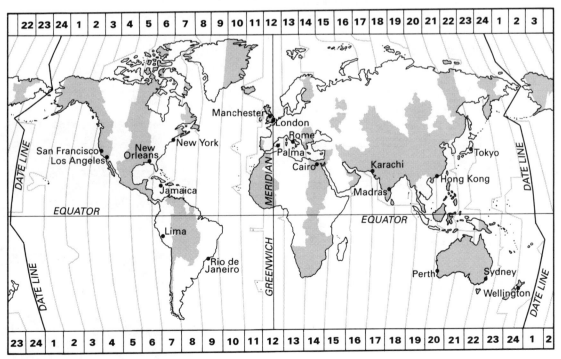

EXERCISE 5.4

1 David makes a telephone call at 3 p.m. in the afternoon to Rio in South America. What time is it there?

2 Julie 'phones her Aunt in Wellington, New Zealand. It is 8 a.m. when she calls. What is the time on her Aunt's clock?

3 Sammy makes a call to her cousin in Jamaica at 2.15 p.m. What time is it in Jamaica?

4 When it is 8 a.m. in London, what time is it in
(*a*) New Orleans (*b*) Cairo?

5 What time is it in New York when it is 5.30 p.m. in Tokyo?

6 When it is 12 noon in Perth, what time is it in (*a*) London
(*b*) Sydney (*c*) San Francisco?

7 Find the time in Rome when it is (*a*) 8 a.m. in Lima
(*b*) 9.15 p.m. in Cairo (*c*) 1.45 p.m. in Rio.

8 The business centre in Hong Kong opens at 9 a.m. in the morning. What time will it be in London?

9 Sue flies to Los Angeles on a business trip and telephones home on arrival in L.A. at 10 a.m. local time. What time will it be in Britain?

10 Omar telephones his sister in Karachi at 1.50 p.m. British time. What time is it in Pakistan?

EXERCISE 5.5

For the following, express your answers in 24-hour-clock notation.

1 A plane leaves Manchester Airport at 2000 to fly to Palma, Majorca, a flight lasting 2 h 35 min. At what local time will it arrive?

2 Mr Ghevarughese catches a 12 h 10 min flight at 1600 from Gatwick to Madras Airport in India. At what local time will he arrive in India?

3 A holiday flight leaves Heathrow on a Sunday at 0925 for Bangkok, a flight lasting $14\frac{1}{4}$ hours. At what local time will they arrive?

4 Find the local time at which an aeroplane will arrive in Cairo from Gatwick after leaving at 0830, and journeying for 5 h 50 min.

5 Find the local US time at which each of the following flights will arrive:

	Destination	Flight no.	Departure	Duration of flight
(a)	New York	BR267	1130 from Gatwick	7 h 55 min
(b)	Los Angeles	AA55	1040 from Manchester	14 h 25 min
(c)	Denver	TW701	1345 from Heathrow	13 h 45 min
(d)	New Orleans	NW49	1050 from Gatwick	16 h 50 min

6 The times on the following outbound flights to the United States are given in terms of local times (London and US time). Find the duration of each flight.

Outward	Flight no.	Depart UK time	Arrive US time
Denver	TW701	1345	2030
Chicago	TW771	1245	1500
San Francisco	TW761	1130	1747
New York	TW703	1200	1440

7 The times on the following return flights are given in terms of local times (US and London time). Find the duration of each flight.

Return	Flight no.	Depart US time	Arrive UK time
New Orleans	NW632	1035	0750
Los Angeles	NW44	1055	0745
Chicago	BA296	2035	1015
New York	BA176	2100	0840

Investigation C

The world's diameter is 7926 miles. If you board a plane leaving Heathrow Airport at noon on a Saturday and fly at an average speed of 950 miles per hour around the world, arriving back in Heathrow, what will be the approximate time, and the day? Does it make any difference if you fly to the East or to the West?

Package holidays

Package holidays are bookings made with Travel Agents who organise everything you should need for a holiday abroad: plane tickets, hotel rooms, etc. The price you pay is inclusive of all these arrangements.

Example 4

Find the cost of a holiday for 2 adults and 1 child, commencing on 15th July for 7 days to the Marina Hotel, Costa Blanca.

COSTA BLANCA from £139   FLIGHTS TO ALICANTE   SEE PAGES 22-23 OF BROCHURE

HOTEL	MARINA ④		CHILD REDUCTION	PRESIDENTE ④		CHILD REDUCTION
Prices include	Twin B wc bal/FB			Twin B wc bal/FB		
Holiday Number	EJ2250			EJ2257		
Nights in hotel	7	14		7	14	
DEPARTURES ON OR BETWEEN — 23 Apr-5 May	157	221	50%	141	220	70%
6-23 May	168	229	50%	160	226	70%
24-30 May	196	269	20%	186	271	35%
31 May-16 Jun	179	264	35%	181	272	50%
17-23 Jun	187	272	30%	191	288	45%
24 Jun-7 Jul	211	301	30%	196	309	45%
8-14 Jul	221	319	25%	206	322	40%
15-21 Jul	239	348	25%	234	359	40%
22 Jul-21 Aug	251	355	20%	242	369	35%
22-28 Aug	235	328	20%	229	320	35%
29 Aug-4 Sep	221	304	25%	223	317	40%
5-18 Sep	212	301	25%	216	309	40%
19-25 Sep	206	287	30%	210	301	45%
26 Sep-16 Oct	193	261	30%	197	269	45%
17-25 Oct	194	–	25%	199	–	40%

From the above table: one child gets a 25% reduction:

$$£239 \times \frac{25}{100} = £59.75, \text{ so child's cost is } £239 - £59.75 = £179.25$$

$$\text{cost of 2 adults is } £239 \times 2 = £478.00$$

$$\text{Total cost} = £657.25$$

EXERCISE **5.6**

1 What is the (*a*) earliest (*b*) latest date on which you can leave for a holiday on the Costa Blanca?

2 What can you say about the way the prices change during the advertised period? Can you explain why they vary in this way?

3 (*a*) What is the price of the cheapest holiday advertised?

(*b*) Can you comment on the table heading?

4 Why do the columns headed '14' have a dash for the last entry?

5 A 14-day holiday is booked beginning on 22nd August. On what date does the holiday finish?

Find the cost of the following holidays:

6 2 adults staying at the Presidente, beginning 22nd July for 14 days.

7 3 adults for 7 days beginning 24th May at the Marina.

8 2 adults and 1 child leaving on 5th September for 14 days in the Marina.

9 2 adults and 3 children at the Presidente for 7 days, beginning on 29th August.

10 4 adults and 2 children at the Marina for 14 days from 12th September.

EXERCISE 5.7

YUGOSLAVIA (ISTRIAN RIVIERA) from £143 FLIGHTS TO PULA   SEE PAGES 112-113 OF BROCHURE

HOTEL	LUCIJA COMPLEX		CHILD REDUCTION	APOLLO		CHILD REDUCTION	MUTILA		CHILD REDUCTION	MONTAURO		CHILD REDUCTION
Prices include	Twin sh wc/BB			Twin sh wc/BB			Twin sh wc/HB			Twin sh wc bal/HB		
Holiday Number	EJ7655			EJ7650			EJ7651			EJ7656		
Nights in hotel	7	14		7	14		7	14		7	14	
1-5 May	143	179	35%	154	199	35%	145	190	35%	169	234	35%
6-23 May	151	199	35%	163	209	35%	148	218	35%	177	249	35%
24-30 May	176	229	15%	187	251	15%	163	238	15%	209	305	15%
31 May-16 Jun	169	225	30%	183	247	30%	178	242	30%	203	299	30%
17-23 Jun	174	249	25%	189	273	25%	184	246	25%	211	325	25%
24 Jun-7 Jul	199	279	25%	215	309	25%	212	252	25%	241	355	25%
8-14 Jul	209	293	20%	226	319	20%	217	275	20%	253	360	20%
15-21 Jul	219	304	20%	233	329	20%	229	306	20%	258	372	20%
22 Jul-21 Aug	229	315	10%	243	344	10%	232	315	10%	269	396	10%
22-28 Aug	219	299	10%	232	325	10%	228	294	10%	257	379	10%
29 Aug-4 Sep	206	269	20%	215	287	20%	214	285	20%	239	339	20%
5-18 Sep	193	255	20%	199	274	20%	202	262	20%	227	319	20%
19-25 Sep	182	237	25%	189	256	25%	192	257	25%	218	299	25%
26-30 Sep	170	—	25%	179	—	25%	177	—	25%	197	—	25%

(DEPARTURES ON OR BETWEEN)

Look at the table and answer the following questions:

1 Which is the cheapest holiday?

2 Write down the departure dates for which the Lucija Complex is dearer than the Mutila on a 14-day holiday.

3 On what date would you arrive back from a 14-day holiday which started on 28th July?

4 Holidays booked on 24th May receive a child reduction of only 15%. How do you explain this sudden change in reduction for the end of May?

5 Which hotel has the greatest range in prices for a 7-day holiday?

Find the cost of the following holidays:

6 2 adults booked into the Mutila for 14 days beginning 15th July.

7 A 7-day holiday beginning on 22nd August for 2 adults and 1 child in the Montauro.

8 4 adults at the Apollo for 14 days beginning 6th May.

9 2 adults and 2 children at the Lucija Complex for 14 days beginning 7th August.

10 4 adults and 4 children starting a holiday on 19th September for 7 days at the Apollo.

Investigation D

Obtain your own package holiday brochures from a travel agent. In groups, act out the process of booking a holiday, keeping notes of what you are booking, and the costings.

Foreign currencies

When going abroad it is usually necessary to change currencies. Rates of exchange are advertised at banks, and in newspapers. These rates change from day to day, and even by the hour. When we actually change our £ sterling into a foreign currency we receive the current rate of exchange. Banks in major towns, at airports and even on boats will exchange money, but all have different charges for doing so.

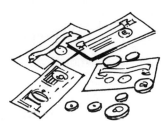

Foreign currency for one pound sterling (£)			
Austria	22.10 schillings	Malta	£M0.572
Belgium	66.80 francs	Norway	11.60 krone
Canada	C$2.04	Portugal	255 escudos
Denmark	12.17 krone	S. Africa	4.25 rand
Eire	1.175 I-punt	Spain	205 pesetas
France	10.67 francs	Sweden	10.85 kronor
W. Germany	3.15 D-marks	Switzerland	2.65 francs
Greece	3.15 drachmae	Turkey	2325 lira
Holland	3.56 guilders	USA	$1.6775
Italy	2340 lira	Yugoslavia	4450 dinars
Japan	225 yen		

Example 5

Change £2.50 into Italian lira using the above exchange rates.

£2.50 × 2340 = 5850 lira

Example 6

What would be the cost of a radio priced at 4200 pesetas in terms of £ and pence?

4200 ÷ 205 = 20.4878 = £20.49 to the nearest penny.

Frequently when exchanging amounts of money we need to round off to the nearest whole number in the amount of currency. If the exchange rate in the above table is given as a decimal, we need to round off to two decimal places.

EXERCISE 5.8

Change the following amounts of money for a holiday in the country indicated, clearly stating the currency in each of your answers.

1 £100 – France

2 £200 – Greece

3 £150 – Spain

4 £80 – Eire

5 £175 – Malta

6 £250 – Yugoslavia

7 £300 – United States

8 £120 – Japan

9 £140 – Denmark

10 £220 – Austria

Change the following amounts of foreign currency into £ and pence, rounding off to the nearest penny.

11 2050 pesetas (Spain)   **12** 400 D-marks (Germany)   **13** C$200 (Canada)

14 180.25 krone (Norway)   **15** 15.30 I-punts (Eire)   **16** 50 000 lira (Italy)

17 50 000 lira (Turkey)   **18** 50.10 guilders (Holland)

19 1080.50 francs (Belgium) **20** 208 francs (Switzerland)

21 How many Portuguese escudos would be given for £200?

22 What would be the price of a 50 kronor shirt on a Swedish market, in £ and pence?

23 How much would a Turkish vase cost in £ sterling if priced at 42 000 lira?

24 Gary goes to the bank to draw out $500 for a trip to America. How much money, in £ sterling, does he exchange?

25 Maralyn has exchanged £50 for francs for a one-day visit to Paris, but finds she does not need the money. The following day when she returns to the bank the exchange rate has increased by 0.15 francs. Calculate (*a*) the amount of francs obtained for the visit (*b*) the profit or loss, in £ sterling, after the money has been exchanged back into £ from francs.

EXERCISE 5.9

1 Change the following amounts in Japanese yen into £ and pence using the conversion graph: (*a*) 400 (*b*) 850 (*c*) 1000 (*d*) 470 (*e*) 930.

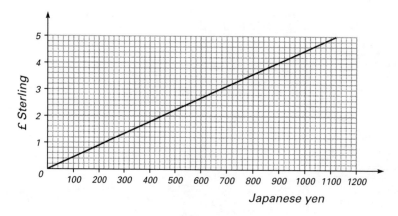

2 Change the following amounts of sterling into yen using the conversion graph: (*a*) £2 (*b*) £3 (*c*) £4.50 (*d*) £1.40 (*e*) £3.05.

3 Change the following amounts in Greek drachmae into £ and pence using the conversion graph: (*a*) 5 d (*b*) 9 d (*c*) 16.50 d (*d*) 6.75 d (*e*) 11.25 d.

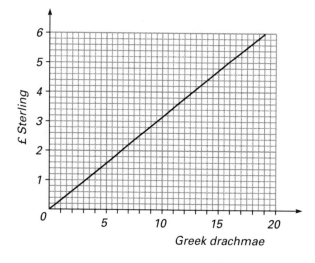

4 Change the following amounts of sterling into Greek drachmae using the conversion graph: (*a*) £4 (*b*) £2 (*c*) £3.70 (*d*) £5.30 (*e*) £1.50.

Investigation E

Over a period of a few weeks keep a note of the exchange rates
between the £ and a number of foreign currencies. Notice how they
change. You could use a graph to show the results of your
investigation

Weather at destination

EXERCISE 5.10

1 What is the average daily maximum temperature in
September on the Costa Brava?

2 Which are the hottest months on the Costa Brava?

3 Write the hours of sunshine on the Costa Brava as a fraction
(in its lowest terms) of the hours in a day for (*a*) August
(*b*) October.

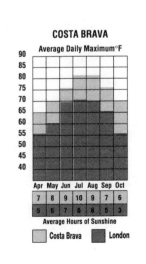

COSTA BRAVA

Average Daily Maximum°F

	Apr	May	Jun	Jul	Aug	Sep	Oct
	7	8	9	10	9	7	6
	5	6	7	6	6	5	3

Average Hours of Sunshine

Costa Brava   London

4 What is the greatest difference in temperature between the Costa Brava and London?

5 Of the two resorts in N. Africa, Egypt and Tunisia, which is the hotter?

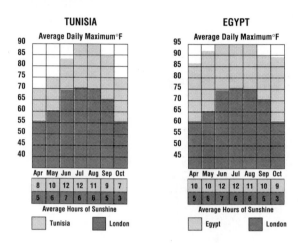

6 Which resort has more hours of sunshine over the period April–October?

7 In which month is the temperature the same for the two resorts?

8 In which month is there the least difference in temperature between Egypt and London?

9 What is the average daily temperature in July in (a) Egypt (b) Tunisia (c) London?

10 What is the difference between the average daily maxiximum temperature in May for Tenerife compared to the other resorts above?

11 What is (a) the highest (b) the least, average daily maximum temperature in Tenerife?

12 What is (a) the greatest (b) the least, difference in temperature between Tenerife and London?

13 What is the range in average daily maximum temperatures for Tenerife for the 7-month period?

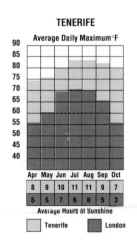

14 Draw similar bar charts for the following resorts:

| | °F Average daily maximum temperatures | | | | | | | Hours of sunshine per day | | | | | | |
	APR.	MAY	JUN.	JUL.	AUG.	SEPT.	OCT.	APR.	MAY	JUN.	JUL.	AUG.	SEPT.	OCT.
Ibiza	68	73	79	84	85	81	74	8	10	11	11	11	8	6
Costa Blanca	65	74	80	86	86	83	76	8	10	10	12	10	8	7
Lisbon Coast	64	70	76	80	80	76	70	9	10	11	12	12	9	7
Algarve	65	74	77	84	85	80	73	9	10	12	12	11	9	7

15 Can you draw *one* bar chart to combine the information for both the Lisbon Coast and the Algarve?

6. Travel

Timetables

When first seen, bus, train and aeroplane timetables often look quite complicated. However, once you begin to use timetables, you can usually find the information needed without much trouble. Careful reading and double checking helps to avoid mistakes, especially as most timetables are written using the 24-hour clock.

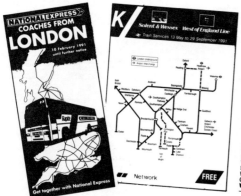

SOLENT AND WESSEX
Southampton—Basingstoke—Woking, Waterloo

Sundays—contd

	80 ◇	⚥	91 ◇	63		80 ◇	⚥	91 ◇	63
Southampton									
St. Denys	1534	1600	1613	....		1634	1645	1713	....
Swaything	1538					1638			
Southampton Parkway	1541					1641			
Eastleigh	1544	1609	1621			1644	1655	1721	
Shawford	1552c					1652c			
Winchester	1556					1656			
Micheldever	1602	1620	1632			1702	1706	1732	
Basingstoke	1611					1711			
Hook	1623	1637	1652	1659	1718	1723	1725	1752	1759
Winchfield				1705					1805
Fleet				1709					1809
Farnborough (Main)				1714					1814
Brookwood				1719					1819
Woking				1725					1825
Surbiton 55	1645			1730	1738	1745			1830
Wimbledon 55,51	⊕ ar 1724			1754		1824			1854
Clapham Junction 55,51	⊕ ar 1731			1801		1831			1901
Waterloo 55	⊕ ar 1712			1806		1812			1906
	1720		1748	1814	1816	1820		1848	1914

Example 1

The timetable shows the train times from King's Cross, London to Newcastle upon Tyne on Mondays to Fridays, until 1300.

(a) At what time does the 0930 arrive in Newcastle?

(b) I wish to arrive in Newcastle at 1402. What time train should I catch from King's Cross?

(c) Which trains take less than 3 hours for the journey?

King's Cross depart	Newcastle arrive
0600	0936
0730	1043
0800	1111
0900	1202
0930	1250
1000	1302
1030	1319
1100	1402
1130	1445
1200	1452
1230	1548
1300	1559

(*a*) The 0930 arrives at 1250.

(*b*) I need to catch the 1100 from King's Cross.

(*c*) The 1030, 1200 and 1300 trains take under three hours.

Example 2

There are five buses passing each weekday through the villages of
Oakton, Horting and Newton to the town of Tadham.

Oakton	0730	0945	1245	1500	1730
Horting	0755	1010	1310	1525	1755
Newton	0831	1046	1346	1601	1831
Tadham	0848	1103	1403	1618	1848

(*a*) At what time does the 1245 from Oakton arrive at Tadham?

(*b*) Mr Taylor catches the 1010 bus from Horting. At what time will
he reach Tadham?

(*c*) How long does the bus take to travel from Oakton to Newton?

(*d*) Julian is meeting Sandra in Tadham at 6.50 p.m. At what time
should he aim to be at the bus stop in Horting?

(*a*) The 1245 arrives at 1403.

(*b*) It will reach Tadham at 1103.

(*c*) The bus takes 61 minutes.

(*d*) He should be at the bus stop before 1755.

EXERCISE **6.1**

Use the coach timetable below to answer these questions.

Brownside	0745	1045	1315	1515	1800
Bilstone	0805	1105	1335	1535	1820
Camford Bridge	0828	1128	1358	1558	1843
Worling	0856	1156	1426	1626	1911
Stangley	0922	1222	1452	1652	1937

1 At what time does the 1515 from Brownside arrive in Worling?

2 At what time does the 1358 from Camford Bridge arrive in Stangley?

3 How long does the coach take to travel from Bilstone to Worling?

4 How long does the coach take to travel from Brownside to Camford Bridge?

5 'It's about 100 minutes from Brownside to Stangley on the coach,' says Anne. Is she correct?

6 Jane lives in Bilstone, and has arranged to meet her friend at Worling at noon. What is the latest time at which she must be at the coach stop at Bilstone?

7 Jane catches the coach back from Worling at 6.30 p.m. At what time will she arrive back in Bilstone?

8 During the summer months an extra evening coach is put on, starting from Brownside at 2030. Make a list of the times at which this coach will arrive at the other four stops.

9 Aziz has to be in Stangley by 5.00 p.m. Will he be in time if he gets to the coach stop at Camford Bridge by 3.45 p.m.?

10 There is a coach from Stangley which will get Aziz back home in Camford Bridge at 10.48 p.m. At what time will it leave Stangley?

Fares

Most bus and coach companies, and many local train services, have a fares table. From these you can work out the fares for your journey. If you live near a railway station, and you are also near to a bus route, you can use these tables to compare travel costs.

Example 3

The table shows the cost, in pence, of travelling between Oakham and Tadham, as in Example 2.

	Horting	Newton	Tadham
Oakham	50	100	120
Horting	–	72	90
Newton	–	–	34

(*a*) How much is the fare from Oakham to Newton?

(*b*) Four people travel from Horting to Tadham. How much is the total fare?

(*c*) Children under 14 years of age pay half fare. How much will it cost for Mr Sanderson and his three children, all under 14, to travel from Oakham to Tadham?

(*a*) The fare from Oakham to Newton is 100p or £1.00.

(*b*) The total fare is $4 \times 90p = £3.60$.

(*c*) The total fare will be $£1.20 + (3 \times 60p) = £1.20 + £1.80 = £3.00$.

Example 4

A cruise ship on the river Clyde goes from Helensburgh to Tighnabruaich on Fridays. The ship stops at various places on the way. The fares are given in the table. (A = adult fare, F = family fare)

Fares	Helensburgh		Kilcreggan		Dunoon		Rothesay		Tighnabruaich	
(£)	A	F	A	F	A	F	A	F	A	F
Helensburgh	*	*	*	*	5.00	11.50	6.50	14.70	7.50	16.90
Kilcreggan	*	*	*	*	4.00	9.00	5.00	11.30	6.50	14.70
Dunoon	5.00	11.50	4.00	9.00	*	*	5.00	11.30	6.50	14.70
Rothesay	6.50	14.70	5.00	11.30	5.00	11.30	*	*	5.00	11.30
Tighnab'ch	7.50	16.90	6.50	14.70	6.50	14.70	5.00	11.30	*	*

(a) How much is the adult fare from Helensburgh to Dunoon?

(b) Andrew offers to go with Sarah from Rothesay to Helensburgh. How much will it cost him for both of them?

(c) A family decides to take the cruise from Kilcreggan to Tighnabruaich, returning later in the day. How much will the return fare cost the family?

(a) The adult fare from Helensburgh to Dunoon is £5.00.

(b) The fare from Rothesay to Helensburgh is £6.50. It will cost Andrew £13.00 for the fare for both himself and Sarah.

(c) The family fare from Kilcreggan to Tighnabruaich is £14.70; the return fare will be double, i.e. £29.40.

EXERCISE 6.2

1   What is the meaning of the asterisks (*) in the fares table above?

2   Three people join the ship at Rothesay, for a trip to Helensburgh. How much will the fares be altogether?

3   The adult fare for a ferry on Lake Windermere is £5.20: for children under 12 years of age the fare is half the adult fare. How much will it cost Mr and Mrs Sowerby and their three children, all under 12, to take the ferry?

4 The passenger fares for the ferry from Lymington to Yarmouth on the Isle of Wight are shown in the table.

(a) Mrs Gray takes her son Philip across to the Isle of Wight from Lymington. How much will the single fares cost her?

(b) The next day Mr Gray goes across from Lymington to Yarmouth. He buys a cheap-day return for himself, and pays for Mrs Gray and their son to return to Lymington. How much do these fares cost Mr Gray?

	Single	Return	Cheap-day return
Adult	£2.60	£5.20	£3.70
Child	£1.30	£2.60	£1.85
Dog	£1.30	£2.60	£1.85

(c) For a birthday treat, Michelle and her friends cross on the ferry from Lymington to Yarmouth for the day. Altogether there are seven children, three adults and Michelle's two dogs in the party. How much will these fares be, at the cheap-day return rate?

5 The fares charged by an airline company for flights to or from London are shown in the table.

Destination	Fare type (£)		
	Economy	Supersaver	Latesaver
Aberdeen	88.00	65.00	49.00
Belfast	75.00	43.00	n.a.
Inverness	90.00	69.00	49.00
Jersey	55.00	n.a.	n.a.
Manchester	60.00	45.00	33.00

A return fare is twice the single fare. (n.a. = not available)

(a) Mr Forbes lives in Jersey and has a meeting in London. How much will a return flight cost?

(b) Five members of a company fly from London to Belfast. They can have a supersaver flight on the outward journey, but can only have an economy flight on their return. How much will these fares be in total?

(c) An examination board arranges a committee meeting in London. Two members of the committee live in Aberdeen, one in Inverness, three in Manchester and two in Belfast. What is the cheapest cost of flying all eight people to London?

Travel graphs

In Chapter 5 you met some travel graphs of journeys by aircraft. We now look at some travel graphs of journeys that could be made on roads or by rail.

Example 5

The diagram represents the bicycle ride made by Lorna, a keen cyclist, from her home in Parkmill to her Uncle Barry's house in New Green. She passed through the villages of Langaith and Morelandby on the way.

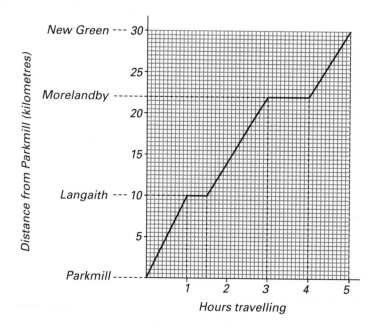

(*a*) What distance is represented by each small square on the vertical (distance) axis?

(*b*) How far is Langaith from Parkmill?

(*c*) How long did Lorna take to cycle to Langaith?

(*d*) What was her average speed on this part of the journey?

(*e*) For how long did she rest at Langaith?

(*f*) How far was the next stage, from Langaith to Morelandby?

(*g*) How long did she take to cycle to Morelandby?

(*h*) Work out her average speed for the whole journey to her Uncle's house (i) when she was actually cycling (ii) including the resting times at Langaith and Morelandby.

(*a*) Each small square stands for *half* a kilometre.

(*b*) Langaith is 10 km from Parkmill.

(*c*) She took one hour.

(*d*) Her average speed was therefore 10 km per hour.

(*e*) She rested for half an hour at Langaith.

(*f*) From Langaith to Morelandby is 22 – 10 = 12 km.

(*g*) She took three hours.

(*h*) The whole journey was 30 km.
   (i) She was actually cycling for $1 + 1\frac{1}{2} + 1 = 3\frac{1}{2}$ hours.

   Her average speed was therefore $\frac{30}{3.5} = 8.571428...$km/h, or,

   more sensibly, about 8.6 km/h.

   (ii) If the resting times are included, she took 5 hours.

   Her average speed, including stops, was $\frac{30}{5} = 6$ km/h.

EXERCISE **6.3**

1 One Saturday Lynn, a keen hiker, decides to walk to her friend's house. Her friend lives 14 km away. Lynn starts at noon, and the diagram overleaf represents her walk.

(*a*) At what time did she first stop for a rest?

(*b*) How far had she walked by this time?

(c) What was her average walking pace?

(d) At what time did she start walking again?

(e) How long was her second rest?

(f) At what time did she start to walk again, after her second rest?

(g) How long did it take her altogether to reach her friend's house?

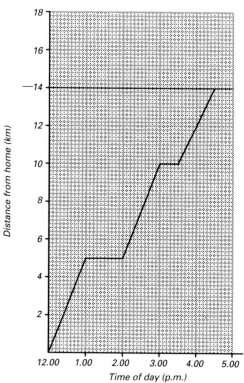

2

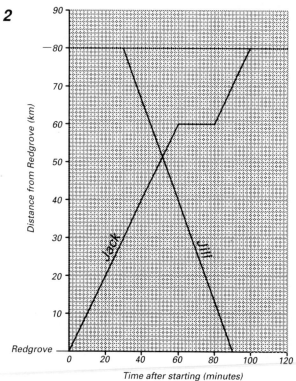

Jack lives in Redgrove, and drives to Jill's house, 80
kilometres away, stopping for a cup of tea on the way.

Due to a misunderstanding, Jill drives to Jack's house,
leaving half an hour after Jack has left for her house.
The diagram on page 136 represents their journeys.

(*a*) After how long on the road did Jack stop?

(*b*) What was his average speed for this part of the journey?

(*c*) For how long did he stop for a cup of tea?

(*d*) How long did it take him to reach Jill's house?

(*e*) What was Jill's average speed?

(*f*) At what time did they pass each other?

(*g*) How far away from Jack's house were they then?

3 David has a racing bike, and goes for a ride, starting at
9.00 a.m. one morning. The diagram represents his journey
to a café, 30 km away, and back home again.

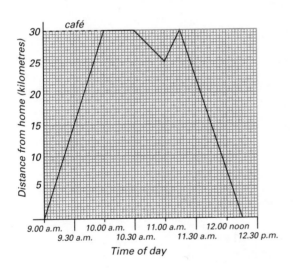

(*a*) How far has he travelled by 9.30 a.m.?

(*b*) For how long does he rest at the café?

(*c*) At what time does he start to ride back home?

(*d*) He left his watch at the café. How far on the homeward
journey had he travelled before he turned round to go
back to the café for his watch?

(*e*) What was his average speed on the last part of the
journey home?

4 A family left their London home at 6.00 p.m. on a Friday evening to drive north on holiday. Their car journey is represented in the diagram.

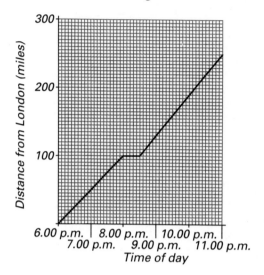

(*a*) When did they stop for a break in their journey?

(*b*) How far had they travelled by this time?

(*c*) What was their average speed over this part of the journey?

(*d*) How long was the break in the journey?

(*e*) At what time did they restart?

(*f*) When did they reach their destination?

(*g*) How far away was this from their home in London?

5 A private aeroplane flies from Heathrow Airport at 10.00 a.m. one morning. The diagram opposite represents its journey.

(*a*) The plane landed at airport A, 300 miles away. What was the plane's average speed during this flight?

(*b*) How long was the plane on the ground before taking off again?

(*c*) How long was the next flight, from A to B?

(*d*) Another aeroplane left Heathrow at 11.45 a.m. and flew
directly to B, where it landed at the same time as the
first plane. What was the second plane's average speed?

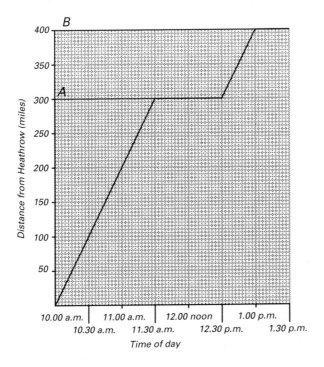

Investigation A

(*a*) Imagine a simple journey that you might make, either by car or on
a bicycle. Include at least one stop on the journey.

(*b*) Draw the travel graph of your journey, and make up a story to
match your graph.

(*c*) Now show your graph to someone else, and see if that person can
interpret it and tell the story from the graph.

Travel leaflets

In travel leaflets, whether for regular services or for special trips, the
information can be presented in a number of different ways. You will
need to look quite carefully at any leaflet in order to ensure that you
understand fully the times, costs and conditions.

Example 6

The 'Speedy' coach runs to Birmingham from Ralph's home town, Greenstone. Both outward and return timetables and the fares are shown below.

Greenstone (depart)	0700	0830	1000	1300	1730
Birmingham (arrive)	1215	1350	1515	1820	2245
Birmingham (depart)	0945	1415	1545	1745	1945
Greenstone (arrive)	1500	1930	2100	2300	0100

Speedy fares	Adult	Child
Single	£17	£12
Day return	£20	£14
Ordinary return	£25	£18

(a) How long does the 0830 coach take to travel to Birmingham?

(b) 'Meet me at 1820 at Birmingham, Henry' says Ralph over the telephone. Which coach will Ralph need to catch from Greenstone?

(c) If Ralph (who pays the child's fare) and his parents, catch this coach, how much will the total fares be, if they buy single tickets?

(d) Ralph's sister intends to go to Birmingham for the day, but she needs to be back in Greenstone before midnight. What is the longest time that she can spend in Birmingham?

(e) How much will she have to pay (she is an adult)?

(a) From 0830 to 1350 is 5 hours and 20 minutes.

(b) He will need to catch the 1300 coach.

(c) Their total fares will be £17 + £17 + £12 = £46.

(d) From 1215 until 1745 is $5\frac{1}{2}$ hours.

(e) The adult day return fare is £20.

EXERCISE 6.4

1 An airline has flights on the route between Liverpool and
Heathrow. The table shows the flight times, frequency, and
facilities available.

LIVERPOOL – Heathrow				HEATHROW – Liverpool			
Frequency	Depart	Arrive	Meal	Frequency	Depart	Arrive	Meal
Daily	0700	0745	B'kfast	Daily	0810	0900	B'kfast
Daily ex. Sa. Su.	1010	1100	Snack	Daily ex. Sa. Su.	1145	1235	Snack
Daily	1305	1355	Lunch	Daily	1515	1605	Tea
Daily	1635	1725	Tea	Daily	1755	1845	Dinner
Daily ex. Sa.	1925	2015	Dinner	Daily ex. Sa.	2045	2135	Dinner

(a) What does 'ex. Sa. Su.' mean?

(b) One flight takes five minutes less than the others. Which
one?

(c) Which is the latest flight from Heathrow that will get
me to Liverpool by 7.00 p.m.?

(d) Ian, who is based in Liverpool, has a meeting in London
at 3.30 p.m. It takes an hour to travel from Heathrow to
the office where the meeting is to take place. What
flight should he book from Liverpool?

2 A ferry sails from Mallaig on the west coast of Scotland on
a round trip of four islands, Eigg, Muck, Rhum and Canna.
The table shows the times of departure of the ferry from the
islands, and the arrival times back at Mallaig.

	Mondays	Wednesdays	Saturdays
Mallaig	1100	1100	1230
Eigg	1230	1230	1400
Muck	–	1315	1445
Rhum	1400	1430	1600
Canna	1500	1530	1700
Mallaig	1745	1800	1930

(*a*) How long does it take to sail from Muck to Rhum?

(*b*) On which days can you travel to Muck?

(*c*) For how long is the ferry at sea on a Saturday?

3 On a Friday and Saturday the ferry travels round the islands in the reverse order.

	Fridays	Saturdays
Mallaig	0500	0500
Canna	0730	0730
Rhum	0830	0830
Muck	–	0945
Eigg	0945	1030
Mallaig	1115	1200

(*a*) How long does the whole round trip take on a Friday?

(*b*) On Friday, Andy catches the 7.30 a.m. ferry at Canna. At what time will he land on Eigg?

(*c*) On Saturday, Robert makes the same trip. How much longer than Andy does it take him?

4 The timetable of a coach company is partially torn, so that not all of the times are legible.

Swanton	0730	1245	1815
Mosey	0850	1405	
Arlott	1000		
Frindle	1140		

(*a*) How long is the coach ride from Mosey to Frindle?

(*b*) Assuming the same travelling times, at what time will the 1245 arrive in Frindle?

(*c*) Complete the rest of the missing times.

(*d*) Will the 1815 from Swanton get me to Arlott by 8.30 p.m.?

5 The fares for the coach company in question 4 are shown in the table. Children under 16 pay half the adult fare.

	Mosey	Arlott	Frindle
Swanton	£3.54	£5.58	£7.06
Mosey	–	£3.29	£5.88
Arlott	–	–	£4.12

(*a*) How much is the fare from Mosey to Frindle?

(*b*) A lady and her 8-year-old son travel from Swanton to Arlott. How much will the fares cost her?

(*c*) The seven members of the Mosey under-12 table-tennis team travel from Mosey to Frindle on the coach. How much are their fares?

(*d*) Next week all fares are going up by 8%. Draw up a table showing the new prices, rounded to the nearest penny.

Investigation B

Imagine that you have won two tickets for a sporting event in London next Saturday afternoon. You will be collected at any London main line station that you nominate, and be taken to the event.

Work out how much it would cost for you and a friend to travel from your home to London, and back, as cheaply as possible, using public transport (taxi, bus, coach, train, etc.). (You will need to contact local bus, train or coach companies.)

Maps and bearings

Early in Chapter 5 there are questions on bearings from London to European places. Look back at Example 1 in Chapter 5, then try these questions about bearings in the UK. Remember to draw in a North line through the place *from which* you are measuring the bearing.

EXERCISE 6.5

1 The bearing of Lincoln from Nottingham is 056°, and the bearing of Gainsborough from Lincoln is 320°. It is 34 miles from Lincoln to Nottingham, and 16 miles from Lincoln to Gainsborough. Taking measurements from the diagram, estimate the distance and bearing of Gainsborough from Nottingham.

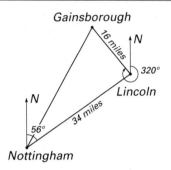

2 From the top of Helvellyn, Penrith is on a bearing of 050°, and Shap is on a bearing of 086.° If both places are six miles from Helvellyn, use the diagram to find the distance and bearing of Shap from Penrith.

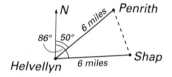

3 The diagram shows the distances and bearings of Manchester and Exeter airports from Heathrow.

(*a*) Make a scale drawing.

(*b*) Estimate the distance and bearing from Manchester to Exeter.

(*c*) What is the bearing from Exeter to Manchester?

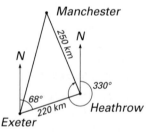

4 An aeroplane flies from an airport on a bearing of 064° for a distance of 120 km, then turns on to a bearing of 168° for 136 km.

(*a*) Make a scale drawing of the flight so far.

(*b*) How far is the aeroplane from the airport?

(*c*) On what bearing should the aeroplane fly in order to land back at the airport?

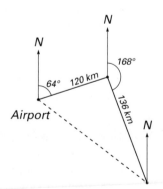

5 The bearing of B from A is $x°$. By using the diagrams, or otherwise, find a rule which will enable you to find the bearing of A from B, if you know the value of x.

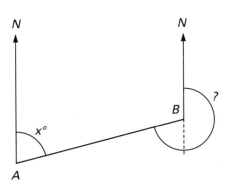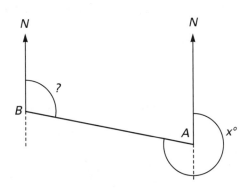

Investigation C

(a) Using a road atlas, or map (you may need to visit a library), estimate the distance round the M25 London Orbital road.

(b) It has been suggested that a fourth lane is required all the way along the M25, in both directions. Make a list of the advantages and disadvantages of such a proposal. Compare your list with those of other pupils in your class, and try to agree on the four most important advantages, and disadvantages.

Investigation D

(a) Mrs Stanton, a Science Moderator, is coming to your school by car, and has asked for a map and directions. Make a sketch map of the roads around your school, and write down instructions so that she can find her way to your school.

Compare your map and instructions with someone else's and see if you can make any improvements.

(b) On the day of the visit, Mrs Stanton telephones to say that her car will not start, and that she is coming on the train.

Describe to her the best way to get to your school from the nearest railway station.

Write down the instructions that you would give her.

Try out your set of instructions on someone who does not know your school very well, to see how good (or bad!) they are.

Town plans

A British road atlas often includes street plans of the larger towns and cities. If you are travelling by car, these plans can be very useful, so long as you know how to read them, and where you are when you start!

Example 7

Here is a town plan of Brighton.

(*a*) On some roads there are arrows. What do you think they mean?

(*b*) How would I get from the museum on Preston Road to the station in Buckingham Place?

(*c*) Describe how to get to the West Pier if you are travelling south along Lewes Road.

(*d*) Approximately how long would it take, walking at three miles per hour, to reach the Palace Pier from the museum?

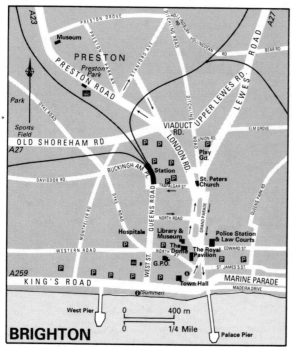

(*a*) The arrows signify one-way streets.

(*b*) Go southwards along Preston Road (A23). After about half a mile, follow the one-way system left along Stanford Avenue and then turn right going over the railway. Continue on along London Road. When you see St. Peters Church on the left, turn right along Trafalgar Street. After about ¼ mile, the station is on the right.

(*c*) Keep going along Lewes Road, past St. Peters Church on the right, along Grand Parade, past the Royal Pavilion on the right. At the sea front, turn right along King's Road. The West Pier is a little over half a mile along King's Road.

(*d*) It is a little over two miles, approximately, from the museum to the Palace Pier. It will take between 40 and 45 minutes.

_ EXERCISE **6.6** _

1 (*a*) In the Canterbury town plan, in which direction is the hospital in South Canterbury Road from the swimming pool in Kingsmead Road?

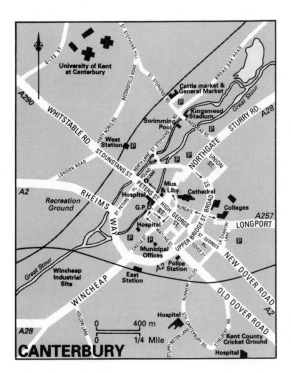

(*b*) About how long will it take to walk from East Station along Castle Street to the Cathedral, at a walking pace of three miles per hour?

(*c*) Describe how to get from the Kent County Cricket Ground in Old Dover Road to the Recreation Ground on Rheims Way

2 (a) If you are on a train coming into Central Station, having just crossed over Derby Road, in which direction are you travelling?

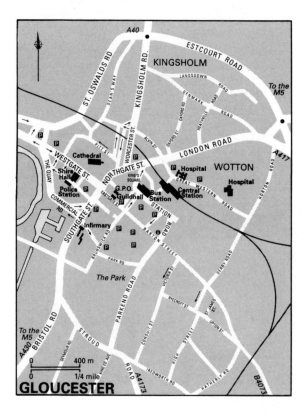

(b) A pedestrian is injured at the junction of Stroud Road and Parkend Road, and is taken to the Infirmary on Southgate Street. How far, approximately, is this journey?

(c) As you leave Central Station in a train, going north-west, which road goes under the railway line?

3 (*a*) Approximately how far is it from the library in Queens Road to the station in Station Road?

(*b*) Name the roads which you would travel along, if you went from Fen Causeway on the A603 to the roundabout at the east end of Chesterton Road.

(*c*) If you are on the river Cam, with 'The Backs' on your right, in which direction are you moving?

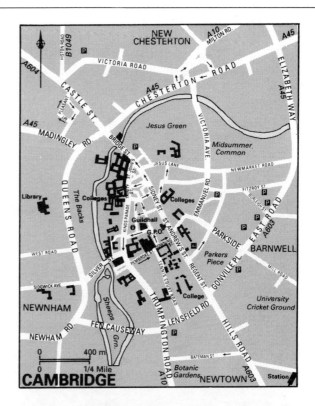

4 (*a*) What are the names of the two rivers which flow through Aberdeen?

(*b*) About how long is Anderson Drive?

(*c*) Name three of the roads that cross over the railway line going north from the station.

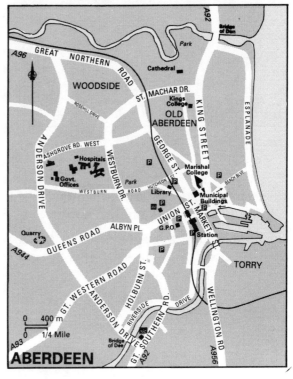

5 (*a*) How far is it from The Circus to the Police Station?

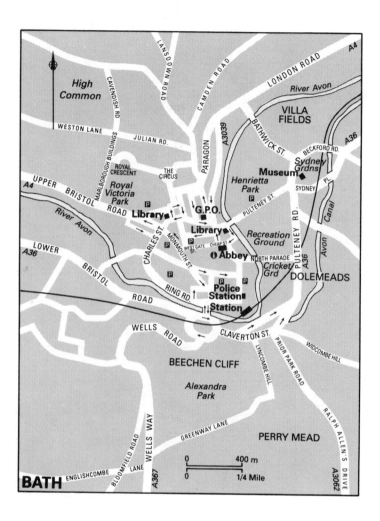

(*b*) I am travelling east along Englishcombe Lane. Describe how to get to Beckford Road.

(*c*) In which direction am I travelling if I am coming into Bath along the A4, London Road?

Conversion graphs and charts

In Investigations D and E in Chapter 2 you may have drawn a **conversion graph,** or used a **conversion chart** to change feet and inches into centimetres. First let us look at conversion graphs.

It is common to have travelling distances measured either in miles or in kilometres. There are three simple conversions that are usually sufficiently accurate, these are : 8 km = 5 miles, or 1 km = $\frac{5}{8}$ mile (= 0.625 mile), or 1 mile = 1.6 km.

To make a conversion graph, you must have at least two points which you know are correct. It is always worth marking three points, if you can. On this graph, we know that 8 km = 5 miles, and therefore 16 km = 10 miles. Also 0 km = 0 miles, so the graph passes through the origin.

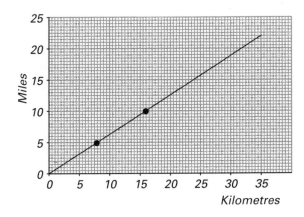

EXERCISE 6.7

1 Make your own conversion graph for changing miles into kilometres, for use when travelling by car. (You will need to make the 'miles' axis go up to 100 miles or more.)

2 An inch is about 2.5 centimetres. Make up a conversion graph, up to 10 inches, to convert inches into centimetres. Use your graph to change (*a*) 7 inches into centimetres (*b*) 3.8 inches into centimetres (*c*) 16 cm into inches.

3 Make a conversion graph for gallons and litres, up to about 8 gallons. Use the fact that 4.5 litres is about 1 gallon.

Use your graph to change (*a*) 4 gallons into litres (*b*) 6.4 gallons into litres (*c*) 15 litres into gallons (*d*) 24.8 litres into gallons.

4 On a street map of a town, 6 cm represents 1 mile. Draw a conversion graph, and use it to estimate what distance (*a*) 18 cm represents (*b*) 34 cm represents (*c*) 4.5 miles is on the map (*d*) 7.2 miles is on the map.

5 For attending a meeting, car expenses of 27p per mile are allowed. Draw a conversion graph to work out expenses for journeys up to 50 miles. From your graph, estimate (*a*) the expenses allowed for a journey of (i) 8 miles (ii) 34.6 miles (*b*) the distance travelled for expenses of (i) £5.40 (ii) £4.00.

Example 8

Use these conversion tables to change

(*a*) 3 litres into gallons

(*b*) 12 litres into gallons

(*c*) 7½ litres into gallons

(*d*) 4 miles into kilometres

(*e*) 6.5 miles into kilometres

(*f*) 29 miles into kilometres.

Litres	Gallons	Miles	Km
1	0.22	1	1.61
2	0.44	2	3.22
3	0.66	3	4.83
4	0.88	4	6.44
5	1.10	5	8.05
6	1.32	6	9.66
7	1.54	7	11.27
8	1.76	8	12.87

(*a*) 3 litres = 0.66 gallons.

(*b*) As 12 litres is not in the table, we have to devise other methods. Here are three possible ways:
   (i)   Double the 6-litre equivalent: $2 \times 1.32 = 2.64$ gallons.
   (ii) Multiply answer (*a*) by 4: $4 \times 0.66 = 2.64$ gallons.
   (iii) Add together the 8-litre and 4-litre equivalent: $1.76 + 0.88 = 2.64$ gallons.

(*c*) As 1 litre = 0.22 gallons, then $\frac{1}{2}$ litre = 0.11 gallons. So $7\frac{1}{2}$ litres = 1.54 + 0.11 = 1.65 gallons.

(*d*) 4 miles = 6.44 km.

(*e*) As 1 mile = 1.6 km, then $\frac{1}{2}$ mile = $\frac{1.61}{2}$ = 0.805 km.

So 6.5 miles = 9.66 + 0.805 = 10.465, or 10.47 km, rounded to two decimal places, like the distances in the table.

(*f*) There are many ways of working out 29 miles : $(6 \times 5) - 1$, or $(4 \times 7) + 1$ are two ways.

The first will give $(6 \times 8.05) - 1.61 = 48.30 - 1.61 = 46.69$ km.

The second will give $(4 \times 11.27) + 1.61 = 45.08 + 1.61 = 46.69$ km.

Example 9

This type of conversion table enables you to change from either unit to the other. Use it to change:

(*a*) 3 kg into lb

(*b*) 4.2 kg into lb

(*c*) 20 kg into lb

(*d*) 4 lb into kg

(*e*) 3.6 lb into kg

(*f*) 14 lb into kg.

kg		lb
0.05	0.1	0.22
0.23	0.5	1.10
0.45	1	2.20
0.91	2	4.41
1.36	3	6.61
1.81	4	8.82
2.27	5	11.02

The middle column stands for the unit we are changing *from*. To change *from kg to lb*, we use the middle and 'lb' columns, and to change *from lb to kg*, we use the middle and 'kg' columns.

(*a*) From 3 kg into lb, we use the middle and 'lb' columns to give 3 kg = 6.61 lb.

(*b*) 0.1 kg = 0.22 lb, so 0.2 kg = 0.44 lb.
Hence 4.2 kg = 8.82 + 0.44 = 9.26 lb.

(*c*) As 5 kg = 11.02 lb, then 20 kg = $4 \times 11.02 = 44.08$ lb.

(*d*) From 4 lb into kg will give 4 lb = 1.81 kg.

(*e*) As 3.6 = 3 + 0.5 + 0.1, we can add 1.36 + 0.23 + 0.05 = 1.64 kg.

(*f*) We can use $14 = (3 \times 5) - 1$, or $(2 \times 5) + 4$.

So $14 \text{ lb} = (3 \times 2.27) - 0.45 = 6.81 - 0.45 \quad = 6.36 \text{ kg}$.

or $\qquad (2 \times 2.27) + 1.81 = 4.54 + 1.81 \quad = 6.35 \text{ kg}$.

Why are these two answers slightly different?

EXERCISE 6.8

Use the appropriate chart to convert:

1 4 kg into lb

2 4 lb into kilograms

3 6 litres into gallons

4 10 miles into kilometres

5 $3\frac{1}{2}$ litres into gallons

6 0.55 gallon into litres

7 4.5 miles into kilometres

8 3.1 lb into kilograms

9 60 miles into kilometres

10 9 kg into lb

11 9 lb into kilograms

12 17 litres into gallons

13 26 miles into kilometres

14 45 lb into kilograms

15 18.7 kg into lb

16 24.4 lb into kilograms

17 From the mileage counter on my car, I have travelled a total distance of 37.4 miles today. Use the chart to estimate this distance in kilometres.

18 At a garage the pump registers that I have put 30 litres of petrol into the petrol tank of my car. How many gallons is this, to the nearest half gallon?

19 A bag of potatoes weighs 56 lb. What is this weight in kilograms? Give your answer to the nearest kilogram.

20 At the clinic, baby Kerry weighs 4.31 kg. What is her weight in pounds (lb), to the nearest half pound?

7. Motoring

Many people, at some time in their lives, own a motor car. Indeed, most people usually buy and sell cars at regular intervals, and spend considerable amounts of time driving, cleaning and tending to their cars.

Example 1

Martin needs a Ford Escort van, advertised at £4000, for his business.

(a) Calculate the cash price plus 15% VAT on its commercial value.

(b) Find the additional amount he will have to pay if he buys the car on HP with a 10% deposit and monthly payments of £151.12 over 3 years.

(a) $£4000 \times \dfrac{15}{100} = £600$ Cash price = £4000 + £600 = £4600.

(b) Deposit: 10% of £4600 = $4600 \times \dfrac{10}{100} = £460$.

Payments: £151.12 × 12 × 3 = £5440.32.

Total amount paid out is £5440.32 + £460 = £5900.32.

Additional cost is £5900.32 − £4600 = £1300.32.

EXERCISE 7.1

1 What is the price of (a) the cheapest (b) the dearest car?

2 How many cars cost more than £5000?

3 What fraction of all the cars cost between £4000 and £4999?

4 What is the most common price of car?

5 What would it cost to buy the most expensive Vauxhall car?

6 Gail wants a cheap 1.3L engined car. What would you recommend as the cheapest buy?

ESCORT 1.3 L 5-door, in blue.	
VAUXHALL Nova, excellent value	£4995
FORD Granada 2.8 GL, all possible extras	£4295
VW Golf, nice clean car	£4595
FORD Fiesta 1.1 Pop Plus	£4295
AUSTIN Maestro 1.6 HL, 5-sp, in gold met	£3795
VOLVO 240 GL, in white, immaculate condition	£3695
GRANADA 2 litre IGL, blue metallic	£5595
VOLVO 240 GL, 5-speed, PS sunroof	£5995
TALBOT Salara Minx, in red, excellent value	£5595
FORD Granada 2- Litre I GL, 5-sp, beautiful con	£3695
NISSAN Micra SGL, low mileage, blue metallic	£5995
AUSTIN Maestro 1.3, in red, a must at	£3795
FIAT Panda, 11,000 miles only, a must at	£3195
SIERRA 1.8 L, excellent value	£2795
VAUXHALL Carlton GL 1.8, 5-spd, in green met	£4995
FORD Fiesta, in red, very clean car	£5295
VAUXHALL Astra 1.3 Estate, in white	£3195
ASTRA 3-door 1.3L, 41,000 miles	£2995
RENAULT 11 GTL, two tone, excellent value	£3895
PEUGEOT 205 in blue, one owner	£3395
FORD Fiesta 1.1 Pop Plus, blue	£3595
FORD Orion GL 1.6, 5-spd, in blue met	£3195
FORD Escort 1.3 5-dr, in red	£3495
FORD Orion 1.6 GL, 29,000 miles only	£3595
VAUXHALL Nova Swing, 1 litre hatch	£4395
FORD Escort 1.1 L 3-door	£3195
FORD XR3i, beautiful condition	£2895
	£4295

7 Martin wants a car with a 1.6L engine. What is (*a*) the cheapest (*b*) the dearest car available?

8 How much more would it cost to buy the Peugeot 205 on HP terms of 20% deposit and monthly repayments of £170.52 over 2 years?

9 Haroon has a car valued at £600 to trade-in against the red Ford Fiesta. Using the trade-in as a deposit and monthly repayments of £98.23 over 3 years, how much will the car have cost him in deposit and repayments?

10 What would be the additional cost of buying the Volvo 240 using an HP agreement, with a £595 deposit and monthly repayments of £154.20 over 4 years?

COMMERCIALS

FORD Cargo 0811 Box Van, B reg, 46,500 miles (74,850 Kms)	£7495
AUSTIN Maestro 500L Panel Van, 27,480 miles	£3895
AUSTIN Maestro 500L Panel Van, 30,550 miles	£3550
ESCORT 1.3 Panel Van, 24,655 miles, as new	£4195
ESCORT 1.3 Panel Van, 26,168 miles, drives and looks like a car	£3995
ESCORT 1.3 Panel Van, 29,190 miles, superb	£3895
ESCORT 1.3 Panel Van, 56,524 miles, showroom condition	£3595
TRANSIT 100 Panel Van, side/rear loading, 20,189 miles	£5395
TRANSIT 100 Panel Van, side/rear loading, 26,350 miles	£4895
TRANSIT 100 Panel Van, side/rear loading, 40,279 miles	£4495
TRANSIT High Roof Panel Van, 43,125 miles	£4995
FIAT Ducato Diesel Van, side/rear loading, 2495cc, 5-speed gears, 42,662 miles	£4495
VOLKSWAGEN LT31, large volume, high roof van, magnificent strong construction	£5400
VOLKSWAGEN LT31, large volume, high roof van, recon engine, ready for work	£4995
VOLKSWAGEN LT31 Luton Van	£4350
FREIGHT ROVER Sherpa, light tipper truck, 27,850 miles, hardly run-in	£3895

All commercial vehicles carry written warranty. All commercial vehicles plus 15% VAT. Finance and part exchange available. Every commercial listed above is one previous owner and in superior condition.

11 Calculate the cash price of these vehicles, inclusive of VAT:

(*a*) Austin Maestro Van, 30 550 miles

(*b*) Volkswagen Luton Van

(*c*) Escort 1.3L Van, 29 190 miles.

12 What is the price, inclusive of VAT, of the (*a*) cheapest (*b*) dearest van?

13 Samantha would like a diesel van. What would she pay for one?

14 Find the additional cost of buying the Freight Rover Sherpa on HP with a 20% deposit and monthly repayments of £138.36 over a 3 year period.

15 How much more than the cash price would it cost to buy the High Roof Transit with an £800 trade-in as deposit, and monthly repayments of £181.35 over 3 years?

16 What is the cash price of the Ford Largo Box Van?

Paying for cars and the hidden extras

When buying new cars we find there may be many hidden extras for which we are charged above the basic price of the car. The dealer himself pays for some of these extras, which he then adds to the price of the car.

Example 2

Car Tax is 'ten per cent of five-sixths of the cost', to the nearest £.

(*a*) What is the car tax on a new car costing £5000, to the nearest £?

(*b*) What will be the advertised price of the car, inclusive of VAT (at 15%)?

(*a*) $£5000 \times \dfrac{5}{6} \times \dfrac{10}{100} = \dfrac{250\,000}{600} = £416.67 = £417,$

to the nearest £.

(*b*) Basic price + car tax = £5000 + £417 = £5417.

VAT: $£5417 \times \dfrac{15}{100} = £812.55 = £813$, to the nearest £.

The advertised price of the car will be £5417 + £813 = £6230.

Example 3

Find the percentage increase in the price of a £8800 car after the addition of £230 extras.

$\dfrac{£230}{£8800} \times \dfrac{100}{1} = 2.6\%$, correct to one decimal place.

EXERCISE 7.2

Calculate to the nearest £ for each car (*a*) the car tax due (*b*) the advertised price after addition of both car tax and VAT (at 15%):

1 A Rover for £8100

2 A Lada Riva for £5200

3 A Renault 5 for £4300

4 A Peugeot costing £6600

5 A Citroen for £5400

6 A Nissan Bluebird for £7000

7 A BMW 520 for £13000

8 A Mercedes for £35 000

Find the total cost of buying each new car (the price shown for each car includes tax and VAT at 15%):

9
Car	£8510.00
Delivery	£165.00
Number plates	£16.50 + VAT

10
Car	£9617.00
Delivery	£124.52 + VAT
Number plates	£30.48 + VAT

11
Car	£7259.00
Delivery	£260.87 + VAT
Road tax	£60.00
Number plates	£42.70
Petrol	£15.00

12
Car	£4455.00
Delivery	£135.00 + VAT
Number plates	£10.00 + VAT
Petrol	£5.00

Find the percentage increase in the price of each new car by the addition of the 'hidden extras':

13 Car £6750, delivery and number plates £276 + VAT, road fund licence £100, petrol £18.

14 Car £32 140, extra car features £250, road fund licence £100.

15 Car £10 450, delivery £150, number plates £28.

16 Car £6624, delivery £150, number plates £23, inspection £52.

17 Car £7999, delivery and number plates £200, inspection £65, road fund licence £100.

18 Car £8415, delivery £140 + VAT, number plates £24.50 + VAT, road fund licence £100, pre-delivery inspection £63, petrol £15.

EXERCISE 7.3

The table below shows the monthly repayments necessary on a car loan of varying time and interest rate.

FLAT RATE	10%			12%		
PERIOD	2 yrs	3 yrs	4 yrs	2 yrs	3 yrs	4 yrs
£50.............	£2.50	£1.81	£1.46	£2.59	£1.89	£1.55
£100............	£5.00	£3.62	£2.92	£5.17	£3.78	£3.09
£200............	£10.00	£7.23	£5.84	£10.34	£7.56	£6.17
£500............	£25.00	£18.06	£14.59	£25.84	£18.89	£15.42
£600............	£30.00	£21.67	£17.50	£31.00	£22.67	£18.50
£800............	£40.00	£28.89	£23.34	£41.34	£30.23	£24.67
£1000...........	£50.00	£36.12	£29.17	£51.67	£37.78	£30.84
£2000...........	£100.00	£72.24	£58.34	£103.34	£75.56	£61.68
£3000...........	£150.00	£108.36	£87.51	£155.01	£113.34	£92.52
£4000...........	£200.00	£144.48	£116.68	£206.68	£151.12	£123.36
£5000...........	£250.00	£180.60	£145.85	£258.35	£188.90	£154.20

SUM BORROWED

Use the table to calculate (*a*) the monthly repayments (*b*) the total cost of buying cars at the following prices:

1 £4000 at 10% over 4 years.

2 £3800 at 12% over 2 years.

3 £6700 at 12% over 4 years.

4 £8900 at 10% over 3 years.

5 £12 350 at 10% over 4 years.

6 £5900 at 12% over 3 years.

7 £4750 at 10% over 2 years.

8 £6450 at 12% over 4 years.

9 £9350 at 12% over 3 years.

10 £7950 at 10% over 3 years.

11 Estimate the monthly repayments for a £6000 car at 11% over 3 years.

12 Estimate the monthly repayments for a £10 000 car at $11\frac{1}{2}$% over 3 years.

13 Mark can afford no more than £100 per month repayments over a 3-year period. What is the maximum price of car he could afford at interest rates of (*a*) 10% (*b*) 12%?

14 Sheila can only afford a loan with repayments of up to £80 per month over a 4-year period. What is the maximum price of car she could afford at interest rates of (*a*) 10% (*b*) 12%?

15 You want to pay no more than £130 per month in repayments on a loan. Find the six maximum amounts you could borrow for the different periods of time and percentage rates in the table.

Depreciation

Cars depreciate in value, that is, a car's value decreases with time as the car gets older.

Example 4
A car costing £8000 loses 20% of its value in the first year, and 10% in the second year. What is its value at the end of the second year?

$$£8000 \times \frac{20}{100} = £1600$$

so depreciated value is £8000 − £1600 = £6400 at the end of the first year.

$$£6400 \times \frac{10}{100} = £640$$

so depreciated value is £5760 at the end of the second year.

Example 5
A car bought for £6650 is valued at £5875 one year later. What is its percentage depreciation over the year?

Depreciation over the year is £6650 − £5875 = £775.

Percentage depreciation is $\frac{£775}{£6650} \times \frac{100}{1} = 11.7\%$, to one decimal place.

EXERCISE 7.4

1 A car costing £5400 has depreciated in value by 30%. What is its present value?

2 A car is valued at £3050, but depreciates in value by a further 10% the next year. What will be its value at this time?

3 Ali buys a new car costing £9400, but is told its value would depreciate by $22\frac{1}{2}$ % in its first year. What will be its value after one year?

4 A new car valued at £7790 will depreciate by 20% in the first year, and then by 10% in its second year. What will be its value after the two-year period?

5 Calculate the present value of a car which cost £8300 when new, if its depreciation was $22\frac{1}{2}$ % and $12\frac{1}{2}$ % over the first and second years respectively.

6 Find the present value of a car which cost £6250 to buy two years ago, but which has depreciated at a rate of 15% in the first year, and 10% in the second year.

7 Find the percentage depreciation on a £11 300 car which is now valued at £9150.

8 Calculate the percentage depreciation on a £5200 car which is now valued at £4050.

9 What is the percentage depreciation in value of a car which was priced at £4500, but had a value of only £3800 one year later?

10 Find the percentage depreciation on a £10 600 car which is now valued at £8550.

Calculate the percentage depreciation for each of the following cars (*a*) in the first year (*b*) in the second year, rounding your answers correct to one decimal place.

	Value two years ago	Value one year ago	Present value
11	£5750	£5150	£4250
12	£21 350	£18 900	£15 900
13	£7600	£6800	£5650
14	£4975	£4200	£3475
15	£3725	£3050	£2525

EXERCISE **7.5**

In questions 1–4 the graphs show the depreciating value of cars over time.

1 *Value (£)*

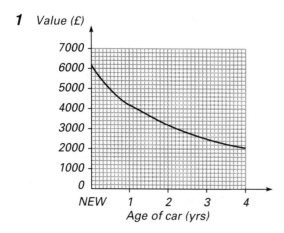

Age of car (yrs)

(*a*) Explain why you think the graph is this shape.

(*b*) What is the value of the car after 18 months?

(*c*) By how much has the value depreciated after (i) 2 years (ii) 4 years?

2 *Value (£)*

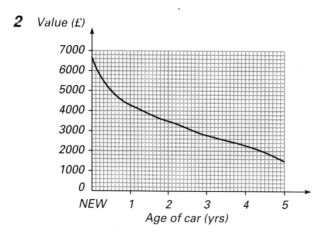

Age of car (yrs)

(*a*) What is the value of the car after (i) 1 year (ii) $2\frac{1}{2}$ years (iii) 3 years?

(*b*) By how much has the value depreciated after (i) 1 year (ii) 4 years?

(*c*) By how much has the value depreciated in the (i) 2nd year (ii) 4th year?

3

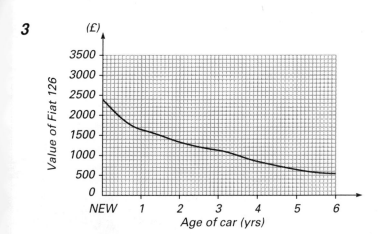

(*a*) What is the value of the car (i) new (ii) after 3 years
(iii) after 6 years?

(*b*) By how much has the value depreciated after (i) 1 year
(ii) 2 years (iii) 5 years?

(*c*) What is the percentage depreciation in the (i) 1st year
(ii) 2nd year (iii) 3rd year?

4

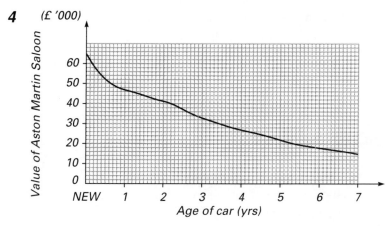

(*a*) Describe what you think will happen to the value of the
car as it continues to grow older than 7 years.

(*b*) What is the value of the car (i) new (ii) after 3 years
(iii) after 5 years?

(*c*) What is the value of the car after (i) 15 months
(ii) 2½ years (iii) 6 years 3 months?

(*d*) What is the percentage depreciation in the (i) 1st year
(ii) 3rd year (iii) 5th year?

Draw graphs to show the depreciation of these cars:

	Model	New	After 1 yr	After 2 yrs	After 3 yrs	After 4 yrs	After 5 yrs
5	Austin metro 1.0L	5599	3950	3275	2700	2310	1750
6	Fiat strada 85	6990	4400	3575	2900	2400	1825
7	Ford sierra 1.6	7500	5000	4000	3250	2575	2125
8	Mazda 929 Estate	8849	5700	4650	3775	3200	2450
9	Porsche carrera	33 768	26 250	22 400	19 000	16 200	13 900

Investigation A

Using one of the popular motoring magazines find the cost of a particular car which is new, then refer to the section on Used Car prices over a number of years. Draw a graph to show how the value of the car depreciates. Can you describe which types of car depreciate in value (*a*) the most (*b*) the least?

Car insurance

In Great Britain it is illegal to drive without some form of car insurance. The cost of insurance depends on the car, the driver, and the district in which the car is normally kept. To encourage safe driving most insurance companies give a reduction known as a **No Claims Discount (NCD),** depending on the number of years for which you have not made a claim on your insurance:

Years without claiming	1	2	3	4 or more
No Claims Discount (NCD)	30%	40%	50%	60%

The tables below show the cost of insurance for two different types of car insurance: *Third Party, Fire and Theft,* and *Comprehensive* (your own vehicle is insured if an accident is your fault).

Insurance group: this is determined by the make and model of your car.

Region: this depends on where in the country the car is kept.

Third Party, Fire & Theft							Comprehensive						
	Insurance group							Insurance group					
Region	1	2	3	4	5	6	Region	1	2	3	4	5	6
1	132	151	179	207	240	271	1	265	307	373	442	523	602
2	144	164	195	227	261	295	2	290	337	408	482	570	659
3	155	176	209	242	281	317	3	312	411	438	518	613	706
4	168	191	227	263	304	343	4	336	391	473	559	662	764
5	182	207	247	285	331	373	5	367	425	515	609	720	830
6	199	227	269	311	361	407	6	399	464	561	664	787	906

Example 6

Calculate the comprehensive insurance for a car in group 3, region 3, after deduction of a discount through no claim having been made for 3 years.

Group 3, region 3, comprehensive insurance: £438.

3 years NCD is 50%: $£438 \times \dfrac{50}{100} = £219.$

Insurance premium is £438 − £219 = £219.

EXERCISE 7.6

Calculate the insurance premium due for each of the following cars:

1 Comprehensive insurance for a car in group 2, region 3 with a discount after 2 years' safe driving.

2 Third party, fire and theft insurance for a car in group 5, region 4 with a discount after 6 years' safe driving.

3 Third party, fire and theft insurance for a car in group 1, region 1 with a discount after 1 year's safe driving.

4 Comprehensive insurance for a car in group 2, region 3 with a discount after 3 years' safe driving.

5 Third party, fire and theft insurance for a car in group 2, region 6 with a discount after 10 years' safe driving.

6 Comprehensive insurance for a car in group 6, region 4 with a discount after 4 years' safe driving.

7 Comprehensive insurance for a car in group 4, region 2 with a discount after 2 years' safe driving.

8 Comprehensive insurance for a car in group 3, region 5 with a discount after 5 years' safe driving.

9 Explain why a Mini (insurance group 1) might cost less to insure than an MG Montego (insurance group 6).

10 Brian lives in region 3, and has an Escort 1.6 which is in insurance group 4. He has a 60% NCD and wants to change from third party, fire and theft to comprehensive insurance. How much more will it cost him?

11 Shirley has a Mini which is in group 1, and which is kept in region 4. She has third party, fire and theft insurance, and presently holds a NCD of 40%. How much will her premium be next year?

12 Cecil lives in region 5, and owns an MG Montego, a car in insurance group 6. He held a NCD of 60% on a comprehensive insurance policy, but was involved in an accident and his NCD fell to 30%. How much will he lose over the 3 years until his NCD rises to 60% again?

13 Vivek owns a Hyundai Pony, which is classified in group 3. He lives in region 2, has third party, fire and theft insurance, and has not made a claim for 3 years. If he does not make a claim in the next 12 months and changes his policy to comprehensive on renewal, what difference will this make to his premium?

14 Bernice is expecting to receive a comprehensive insurance renewal notice for her Lancia (group 6). She lives in region 5 and will have a NCD after having a clear record for 3 years. Following deduction of NCD she also receives a 10% 'only driver' deduction. What should she expect to pay?

Investigation B

Explain why it should cost more to insure a car kept in an inner city than a car kept in a quiet rural area. What details would an insurance company want if you asked them for a quotation for car insurance?

Averages

The average speed of a car is a useful statistic since it helps us understand how slow or how fast an entire car journey has been taken. Another important average these days with petrol prices continuing to rise is the mileage per gallon (m.p.g.) of the car. This tells us how many miles, on average, the car will travel for each gallon of petrol. The higher the m.p.g., the cheaper it will be to run the car.

Example 7

A car takes $2\frac{1}{2}$ hours to complete a journey of 85 miles. What is its average speed?

$$\text{Average speed} = \frac{\text{total distance}}{\text{total time}} = \frac{85}{2.5} = 34 \text{ m.p.h.}$$

Example 8

A car has a rating of 40 m.p.g. How far is it expected to travel on $5\frac{1}{2}$ gallons of petrol?

$$\text{Mileage per gallon (m.p.g.)} = \frac{\text{total distance (miles)}}{\text{number of gallons}}$$

So total distance (miles) $= \text{m.p.g.} \times \text{number of gallons}$

$$= 40 \times 5\frac{1}{2} = 220 \text{ miles.}$$

The metric equivalent to m.p.g. is km/litre. Write down a similar formula to find the km/litre of a car.

Investigation C

1 gallon is 0.22 litres, and 1 km is approximately $\frac{5}{8}$ of a mile.

Can you find how many km/litre there are in each mile/gallon?

EXERCISE 7.7

1 A car takes $2\frac{1}{2}$ hours to complete a journey of 100 miles. What is its average speed?

2 The same car as in question 1 uses $3\frac{1}{2}$ gallons of petrol to complete the journey. What is its m.p.g.?

3 Derek is about to go on a long journey of 720 km in a car he knows uses 16 km/litre.

   (a) How many litres of petrol will he need?

   (b) What will be the cost of the petrol at a price of 42p per litre?

4 Susan averages a speed of 60 m.p.h. on the motorway. How long will it take her to cover a distance of 270 miles?

5 Ali keeps a notebook in his car in which he can check the fuel consumption of his car each time he fills up at a petrol station:

	Mileage (miles)	Petrol (gallons)	m.p.g.
	23 142	–	–
(a)	23 366	7	
(b)	23 558	$6\frac{1}{2}$	
(c)	23 828	8	
(d)	23 995	$5\frac{1}{4}$	
(e)	24 236	$7\frac{1}{2}$	

Calculate the m.p.g. on each occasion.

6 Frederick makes a journey consisting of 130 miles on a motorway lasting $2\frac{1}{2}$ hours, and 35 miles across country roads lasting 1 hour. What was the average speed of the entire journey?

7 A car's fuel consumption is described as follows:
Urban cycle: 34.4 m.p.g.   Steady 55 m.p.h.: 46.3 m.p.g.
Steady 75 m.p.h.: 35.3 m.p.g.

(*a*) Calculate the number of gallons needed if the car is about to cover 10 miles on the motorway at a steady 75 m.p.h., and 10 miles through a city.

(*b*) Why do you think the lowest figure is for the urban cycle?

(*c*) Give a reason why the higher speed of 75 m.p.h. is less economical than 55 m.p.h.

8 Calculate the cost of a journey of 550 km in a car averaging 16 km/litre, if petrol is 41.2p per litre.

9 Find the fuel consumption, in km/litre, if a car averages (*a*) 36 km on 3 litres (*b*) 125 km on 12.5 litres (*c*) 258 km on 22 litres.

10 Mark takes $3\frac{1}{2}$ hours to drive the 240 miles from his house to London, and $3\frac{3}{4}$ hours on the return trip. What is his average speed (*a*) on his way to London (*b*) on his return journey home (*c*) for the entire journey?

11 A Ford Fiesta uses $3\frac{1}{2}$ gallons over 112 miles, while a Ferrari Cabriolet uses $2\frac{3}{4}$ gallons over 77 miles. Find out which is the more economical car to run, giving an explanation for your answer.

12 A foreign car will average 12.5 km/litre on the roads. How much petrol will you need to buy for a journey lasting (*a*) 240 km (*b*) 95 km (*c*) 300 km?

13 Susie finds she can drive at an average speed of 40 m.p.h. on the better roads. How long will it take her to make a journey of 70 miles on such roads?

14 Wai makes a journey in three stages: (*a*) 45 miles taking $1\frac{1}{4}$ hours (*b*) 66.6 miles taking 1 h 48 min (*c*) 80 miles taking 1 h 12 min. Calculate the average speed for each stage, and (*d*) the average speed for the entire journey.

The garage forecourt

At a petrol station many services are provided. We can fill up with oil, put air in the tyres, and check the water level in the radiator. Motoring has become more complicated since we need to know about both imperial and metric measures.

Example 9

Using the chart change (*a*) 7 litres into gallons (*b*) 5 gallons into litres.

Using the centre column of the chart (*a*) 7 litres becomes 1.54 gallons (*b*) 5 gallons becomes 22.73 litres.

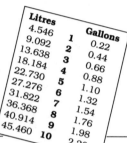

Litres		Gallons
4.546	1	0.22
9.092	2	0.44
13.638	3	0.66
18.184	4	0.88
22.730	5	1.10
27.276	6	1.32
31.822	7	1.54
36.368	8	1.76
40.914	9	1.98
45.460	10	2.20

EXERCISE 7.8

1 Using the chart in Example 9, change into gallons
(*a*) 2 litres (*b*) 10 litres (*c*) 6 litres.

2 Using the chart in Example 9, change into litres
(*a*) 4 gallons (*b*) 9 gallons (*c*) 7 gallons.

3 Calculate the cost of buying petrol:

(*a*) 36 litres at 39.6p per litre   (*b*) 27.2 litres at 41.8p per litre

(*c*) 45.4 litres at 42.3p per litre   (*d*) 32.9 litres at 38.9p per litre

(*e*) 50.7 litres at 40.1p per litre   (*f*) 40.71 litres at 40.7p per litre

4 A petrol tank is $\frac{1}{4}$ full, and has a capacity of 8 gallons.

How much petrol will be needed to fill it?

5 A petrol tank is $\frac{3}{8}$ full, and has a capacity of 12 gallons.

How much petrol will be needed to fill it?

6 A petrol tank is $\frac{3}{4}$ full, and requires 3 gallons to fill it.

What is the capacity of the tank?

7 A petrol tank is $\frac{3}{8}$ full, and requires 10 gallons to fill it.

What is the capacity of the tank?

8 A petrol tank is $\frac{5}{8}$ full, and requires 9 gallons to fill it.

What is the capacity of the tank?

9 Draw a conversion graph for this table:

(a) Use your conversion graph to change these amounts of money written in pence per gallon into pence per litre:
(i) 190p (ii) 230p (iii) 185p (iv) 205p (v) 275p.

(b) Use your conversion graph to change these amounts of money written in pence per litre into pence per gallon:
(i) 44p (ii) 39p (iii) 54p (iv) 62.1p (v) 39.5p.

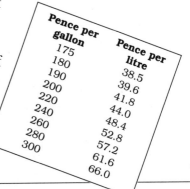

Pence per gallon	Pence per litre
175	
180	38.5
190	39.6
200	41.8
220	44.0
240	48.4
260	52.8
280	57.2
300	61.6
	66.0

10 How much will it cost to fill a petrol tank needing 10 gallons, if petrol is priced at 39.6p per litre?

Example 10

As a result of metrication, the EEC has adopted the **bar** as the standard measure for tyre pressure. Use the table to change these pressures in p.s.i. (pounds per square inch) into bars: (a) 16 p.s.i. (b) 22 p.s.i.

psi	0	1	2	3	4	5	6	7	8	9
0–9	—	.07	.14	.21	.28	.35	.41	.48	.55	.62
10–19	.69	.76	.83	.90	.97	1.03	1.10	1.17	1.24	1.31
20–29	1.39	1.45	1.52	1.59	1.66	1.72	1.79	1.86	1.93	2.00
30–39	2.07	2.14	2.21	2.28	2.34	2.41	2.48	2.55	2.62	2.69

From the table, (a) 16 p.s.i. is in the range 10–19, and is 10 + 6 or 1.10 bars. (b) 22 p.s.i. is in the range 20–29, and is 20 + 2 or 1.52 bars.

EXERCISE **7.9**

Using the table in Example 10 convert these pressure measurements to bars:

1 2 p.s.i.   **2** 9 p.s.i.   **3** 15 p.s.i.   **4** 19 p.s.i.   **5** 24 p.s.i.

6 37 p.s.i.   **7** 31 p.s.i.   **8** 39 p.s.i.   **9** 14 p.s.i.   **10** 20 p.s.i.

EXERCISE 7.9 *(continued)*

Write down the speed in (*a*) m.p.h. (*b*) km/h:

11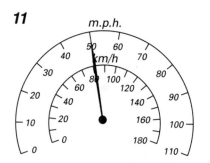

12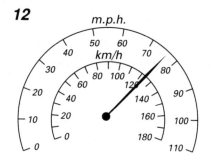

13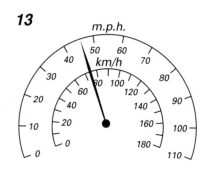

14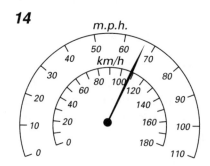

15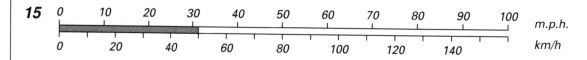

16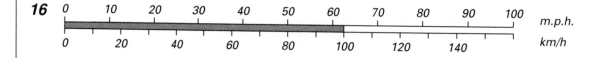

17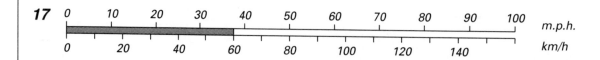

18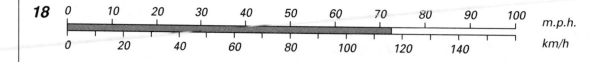

Estimate the radio frequency indicated by the needle (*a*) at MW (*b*) at LW.

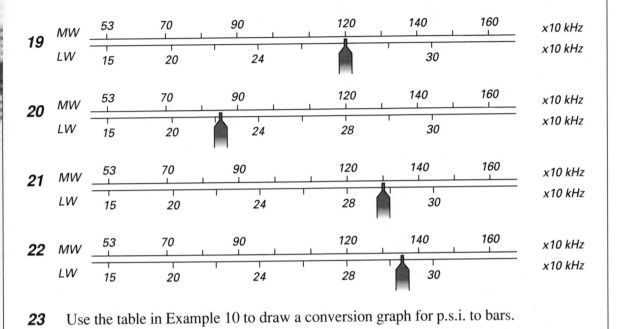

19

MW | 53 | 70 | 90 | 120 | 140 | 160 | x10 kHz

LW | 15 | 20 | 24 | | 30 | | x10 kHz

20

MW | 53 | 70 | 90 | 120 | 140 | 160 | x10 kHz

LW | 15 | 20 | 24 | 28 | 30 | | x10 kHz

21

MW | 53 | 70 | 90 | 120 | 140 | 160 | x10 kHz

LW | 15 | 20 | 24 | 28 | 30 | | x10 kHz

22

MW | 53 | 70 | 90 | 120 | 140 | 160 | x10 kHz

LW | 15 | 20 | 24 | 28 | 30 | | x10 kHz

23   Use the table in Example 10 to draw a conversion graph for p.s.i. to bars.

Networks

Networks are used as diagrams to aid us in planning routes,
particularly when it comes to finding the most economical journeys.

Example 11

A company based in Liverpool sends out mail using a courier
despatch to its nearest regional centres, which then pass on the mail to
the centres nearest to them. Find the despatch plan to give the
minimum mileage.

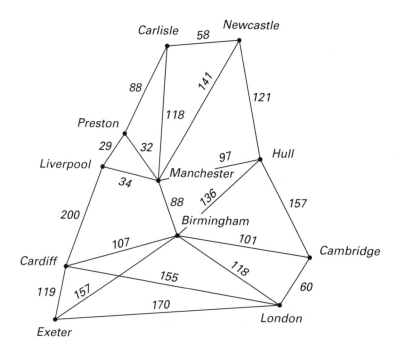

The best way, starting from Liverpool, is to use the shortest distances
from the towns who have received their despatch. Starting from
Liverpool the nearest town is Preston (29 miles):

Liverpool •
29 /
• Preston

The next nearest town is Manchester (from Preston 32 miles):

The next nearest towns are Carlisle (from Preston 88 miles) and Birmingham (from Manchester 88 miles):

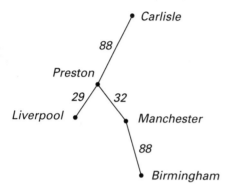

The first nearest, however, is not always the best. You need to consider later stages: it may be necessary to try different routes before finding the one with the minimum mileage.

EXERCISE 7.10

1 Complete Example 11 above. The minimum mileage using the best routes comes to 779 miles.

2 Using the same network as in Example 11, find the minimum mileage if the company had been based in (a) Newcastle (b) Birmingham (c) London. What can you deduce from your answers?

3 Calculate the minimum mileage for a company based in (a) Aberdeen (b) Glasgow (c) Newcastle.

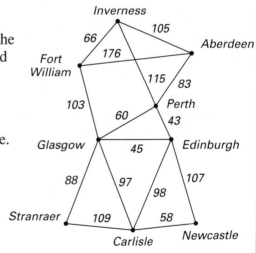

4 Find the minimum mileage for a company based in
(*a*) Manchester (*b*) Cardiff (*c*) Shrewsbury.

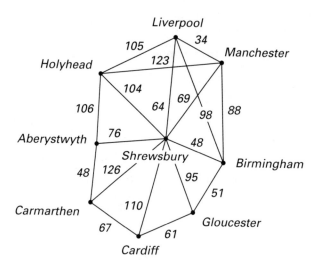

5 Calculate the minimum mileage for a company based in
(*a*) London (*b*) Maidstone (*c*) Guildford.

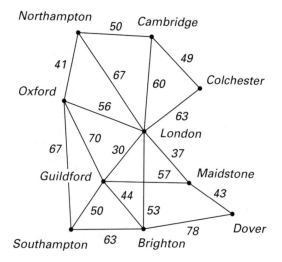

Shortest complete routes

An alternative to sending out several despatch couriers is to have one
courier who visits each centre in turn, then returns to headquarters.
To reduce costs, it is important to plan the shortest route possible.

Example 12

Find the shortest route from the headquarters in Liverpool.

There are only three different routes possible:

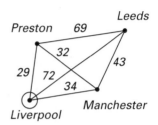

Liverpool → Preston → Leeds → Manchester → Liverpool
= 29 + 69 + 43 + 34 = 175

Liverpool → Manchester → Preston → Leeds → Liverpool
= 34 + 32 + 69 + 72 = 207

Liverpool → Preston → Manchester → Leeds → Liverpool
= 29 + 32 + 43 + 72 = 176

Hence the first route is the shortest.

Investigation D

Does it make any difference in Example 13 if the headquarters is in
Manchester rather than Liverpool? Which town is the best location for
the headquarters?

EXERCISE **7.11**

Find the minimum distance to visit each of the centres
indicated, returning to headquarters on each occasion.

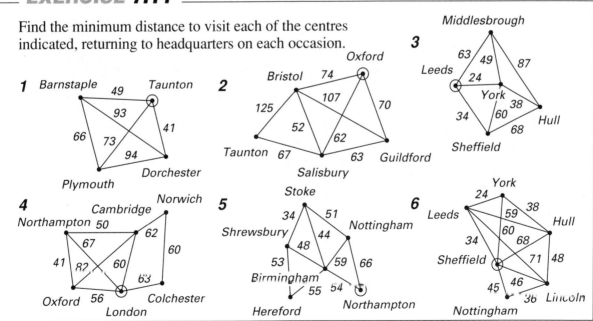

Traversable networks

A network is said to be **traversable** if all arcs in the network can be passed along just once in tracing out that network. It is *not* necessary to start and finish at the same point. Traversability is considered quite important for local services, like refuse collection and road sweeping, where the vehicles have to pass down every road.

This network is traversable:

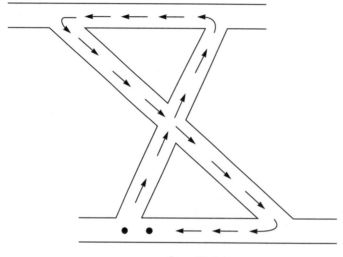

Start Finish

This network is *not* traversable:

EXERCISE 7.12

1 Which of the following networks are traversable:

(a)
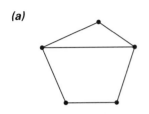

(b)
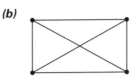

(c)

(d)

(e)
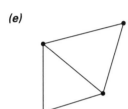

(f)
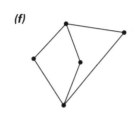

(g)
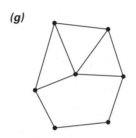

(h)
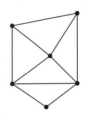

2 Which of the networks in Exercise 7.11 are traversable?

Investigation E

Use a local map of your area and plan a route for the refuse collectors.

Drinking and driving

Following much publicity most people are aware of the dangers of drinking and driving, though unfortunately there is still a minority of people who continue to drink and drive.

EXERCISE 7.13

1 How many people were killed or injured in the year shown in the pie chart?

2 Draw another pie chart and express each of the figures as a percentage of the total.

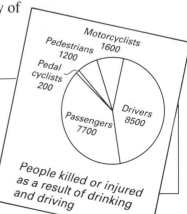

People killed or injured as a result of drinking and driving

3 The figures in the pie chart on p.181 have been rounded to the nearest hundred. What is (*a*) the maximum (*b*) the minimum number of drivers indicated by the pie chart?

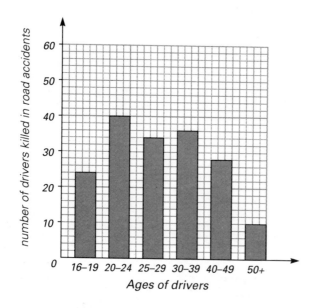

4 State the age ranges of drivers with alcohol above the legal limit who are most commonly killed in road accidents.

5 What percentage of drivers killed were in the age range (*a*) 16–19 (*b*) 25–29?

6 What age range had a percentage of about half that of the 16–19 age range?

7 What was the percentage reduction between the 30–39 and 40–49 age ranges?

The legal blood alcohol limit of 80 mg per 100 ml of blood is roughly equivalent to 5 units of alcohol for a man, and 3 units of alcohol for a woman (bearing in mind the considerable variation between individuals). It takes 2 hours for 1 unit of alcohol to be processed by the body, and for the effects of each unit to disappear.

Effect	Man		Woman	
	Units	Blood alcohol conc.	Units	Blood alcohol conc.
Enhanced sense of well being	2	32	1	25
Mild loss of inhibition; judgement impaired, increased risk of accidents	4	63	2	50
Physical coordination reduced. Noticeably under the influence.	5	79	3	74
Clumsiness; loss of control; extreme responses; over the legal limit.	7	110	4	99
Slurred speech; loss of memory	10	158	6	149
Sleepiness; loss of consciousness	24	378	14	347
Coma and possible death	33	520	20	496

One unit

¹/₂ pint of medium strength beer   ¹/₃ pint of strong beer   A single sherry, Martini, etc   A single spirit   A glass of wine

EXERCISE **7.14**

Each of the following describes a person's drinking habits. Investigate the alcohol in their blood over the period of time. If it is the case that the level exceeds the legal limit, state the time over which this happens. You could consider drawing a graph to help you.

1 Joe has 2 pints of beer at 11 a.m., followed by another at 11.30 a.m., and a fourth at 12 noon. He then drives home.

2 Barbara has two glasses of wine with her lunch at 1 p.m., followed by a sherry at 2 p.m., and another at 2.30 p.m., then drives back to work

3 Jerry has a pint of beer at 6 p.m., another at 6.30 p.m., and another before he leaves the pub at 7 p.m. He drives home, and has a spirit before going out again at 8 p.m.

4 Jackie goes to a wedding. She has two sherries upon her arrival at the reception at 3 p.m., and two glasses of wine with her meal at about 4 p.m. At 5 p.m. she has a spirit before driving home.

5 Mark has three pints of strong beer between 3 p.m. and 4 p.m. At 5 p.m. he also has two spirits. (*a*) At what time does his alcohol level fall below the legal limit? (*b*) At what time will his blood be completely free of alcohol?

6 Martin arrives at a function at 2 p.m., and has two sherries. He expects to have two glasses of wine with his meal at 4 p.m. What quantity of beer could he drink before 6 p.m. if he wants to leave at 10 p.m. with no alcohol in his blood?

Hiring vehicles

Moving house? Need another car in an emergency? There are many companies who specialise in hiring out cars, lorries, or vans.

EXERCISE 7.15

	NO MILEAGE CHARGE	
	DAILY	**WEEKLY***
FORD FIESTA 1100L VOLKSWAGEN POLO	23.90	125.00
FORD ESCORT 1400L FORD ORION 1400L VOLKSWAGEN GOLF	28.25	149.00
FORD SIERRA 1600L FORD SIERRA SAPPHIRE 1600L	33.50	176.00
VOLKSWAGEN GOLF GTi FORD SIERRA ESTATE 1600L	39.90	216.00
FORD GRANADA 2.0i GL Automatic	57.50	341.00

*ADDITIONAL DAYS OVER ONE WEEK CHARGED AT ONLY 1/7th OF WEEKLY RATE

Calculate the rental rates for the following:

1 An Orion for 7 days

2 A Sierra 1600L for 4 days

3 A Granada for 2 days

4 A Fiesta for 6 days

5 A Golf GTi for 1 week

6 A Polo for 10 days

7 A Sierra Estate for 5 days

8 An Orion for 18 days

OPEN TRUCKS		PER DAY £	PER WEEK £
	35cwt. 3.5 GVW*	30	150
	3/4 ton. 7.5 GVW*	45	235
	6/8 ton. 12.5 ton GVW	52	270
	9/10 ton. 16 ton. GVW	65	340
	16 ton. 24 ton. GVW	75	410
TIPPERS	35 cwt. 3.5 GVW*	32	160
	3 ton. 7.5 GVW*	50	270
TAIL LIFT VANS OR DROPSIDES	3 ton. Tail lift 7.5 ton. GVW*	50	265
	9/10 ton. Tail lift 16 ton. GVW	68	360
TRACTOR UNITS	32 ton. Unit Volvo/DAF/Merc and others	78	390
	38 ton. DAF/Merc/Scania or Volvo	84	420
	38 ton. 6 Wheeler Units	98	490

* HGV licence not needed

Calculate the rental rates for the following:

9 A 35 cwt open truck for 3 days

10 A 3 ton Tail Lift for 6 days

11 A 38 ton DAF Tractor Unit for 1 week

12 A 35 cwt Tipper for 4 days

13 A 16 ton open truck for 4 weeks

14 A 38 ton 6-wheeled tractor unit for 2 weeks

15 A 3 ton tipper for 5 days

16 A 3/4 ton open truck for 14 days.

17 A man is quoted a rental rate of £25 per day plus 80p per mile. How much will he be charged for an estimated 80 miles during 2 days?

18 A rental rate for a car is £18 per day plus 10p/mile. What would be the charge for (*a*) 120 miles during 2 days (*b*) 300 miles during 5 days?

19 Jenny completes a mileage of 180 miles over 3 days in a rented car. Calculate the charge if the rental rate is 12.3p per mile plus £26 per day.

20 Find the cost of hiring a truck at a rate of £51 per day plus 18.5p per mile, if it is needed for an estimated 90 miles over a 5-day period.

Investigation F

Quick Car Rentals offers a car rental rate of £15 per day plus 9p per mile. At Transport Hire the rate quoted for the same model of car is £24.90 per day with no mileage charge. Can you find the mileage at which the firms quote the same hire charge over (*a*) one day (*b*) two days (*c*) three days? (*d*) Can you find a formula for *n* days?

Travelling expenses

Example 13

Dawn can claim travelling expenses of 18.5p per mile up to 150 miles, and 12p per mile for any additional mileage. How much can she claim for a journey of 180 miles?

First 150 miles: $150 \times 18.5 = 2775p = £27.75$

Remaining 30 miles: $30 \times 12 = 360p = £3.60$

Total claimed $= £31.35$

EXERCISE 7.16

In each question calculate the expenses due according to the stated travelling rate.

1 A rate of 17p per mile for the first 120 miles, and 10p per mile thereafter. (*a*) 40 miles (*b*) 100 miles (*c*) 150 miles.

2 A rate of 18.9p per mile for the first 100 miles, and 15p per mile thereafter. (*a*) 50 miles (*b*) 75 miles (*c*) 120 miles.

3 A rate of 16.5p per mile for the first 80 miles, and 12p per mile thereafter. (*a*) 50 miles (*b*) 90 miles (*c*) 140 miles.

4 A rate of 23p per mile for the first 100 miles, and 16.5p per mile thereafter. (*a*) 73 miles (*b*) 100 miles (*c*) 180 miles.

5 A rate of 18.7p per mile for the first 150 miles, and 12.8p per mile thereafter. (*a*) 100 miles (*b*) 180 miles (*c*) 322 miles.

8. Sport

To a greater or lesser extent, most sports involve some mathematical calculations at some stage. Discus throwing requires a distance to be measured, whereas the judging of diving involves consideration of the level of difficulty of dive (tariff) as well as the opinion of the judges.

First, we look at times, distances, weights and speeds in a variety of sports.

Timings

1 In an 800 m race, the winner took 58.7 s to cover the first 400 m, and 53.6 s for the last 400 m. What was the winner's time for the race?

2 In a medley relay race the times of the four swimmers were 12.5 s, 14.1 s, 12.4 s and 11.8 s. What was their total time for the race?

3 Each round in a boxing match lasts for three minutes. In one boxing match the referee stopped the fight after 2 min 13 s of the sixth round. For how long were the contestants boxing?

4 Elizabeth is practising, in order to try to beat the 1000 m record at her cycling club, which stands at 1 min 28.6 s. In her attempt she times herself taking 93.4 s. How many seconds faster will she have to be to break the record?

5 Wendy wins a 200 m race in 28.9 s, Chris is second in 29.3 s and Della is third in 30.8 s.

(*a*) How many seconds was Wendy faster than Chris?

(*b*) By how many seconds was Della slower than Wendy?

6 Lee was 6.8 s behind Ray, who won the 3000 m race in 8 min 12.4 s.

    (*a*) What was Lee's time for the race?

    (*b*) If Melvin was 13.2 s behind Lee, what was Melvin's time?

7 In a freestyle swimming race over three lengths of the pool, Dorothy finished in 1 min 14.6 s. If she swam the first length in 24.3 s and the second in 26.5 s, how long did she take to swim the last length?

8 Michael's time for a 10-mile road race was 1 hour and 17 minutes. If the race started at 2.47 p.m., at what time in the afternoon did Michael cross the finishing line?

9 In a cricket match David went in to bat at 3.08 p.m. He scored his 50th run at 3.44 p.m., and was out, caught, 27 minutes later, when he had scored 99 runs.

    (*a*) How long did it take him to score 50?

    (*b*) At what time was he out?

    (*c*) How long did his innings last?

10 The current school record time for running the 1500 m is 4 min 10.3 s. Robert knows that he can run the last lap in 58 s. In the race, he is leading as he begins the last lap, having taken 3 min 11.5 s so far. Can Robert beat the record?

EXERCISE 8.2

In a 200 m backstroke race of six swimmers, the time taken, in seconds, to swim each length is given in the table opposite.

1 Who swam the first length fastest?

2 Was he still in the lead after two lengths?

EXERCISE 8.2

	1st length	2nd length	3rd length	4th length
Henry	42.1	44.0	43.4	42.8
John	40.9	41.8	41.3	40.5
Philip	41.6	42.7	42.4	40.9
Alvin	39.8	41.2	43.7	40.4
Chi	40.5	42.8	41.7	41.1
Thomas	40.9	42.2	42.2	42.0

3 One of the swimmers swam two of his lengths in exactly the same time. Who was it?

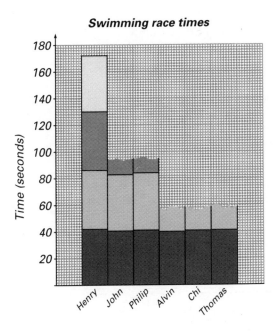

4 Make a column of total times for each swimmer in the race.

5 (*a*) Who won, and what was his time? (*b*) By how many seconds did Chi beat Henry?

6 Copy, and complete the bar graph on p.187, showing the times of each swimmer after each length.

7 Using this graph, find out (*a*) who was last after two lengths (*b*) who was third after three lengths.

8 List the swimmers in order of finishing.

9 What was Philip's average time for one length?

10 Henry, John and Philip are in Green house, and Alvin, Chi and Thomas are in Blue house. Work out which house had the faster total time.

Investigation A

Choose a race (sprint, middle or long-distance) and find out, using a sporting reference book, the last eight world record times for men. Draw a bar graph of these times. Who beat the previous record by the greatest margin?

On the same diagram, draw the bar graph for the same race, by women. When do you think the current men's record will be beaten by a woman?

Distances

EXERCISE 8.3

1 The last three holes on a golf course have lengths of 183 yards, 452 yards and 277 yards. How long are these three holes altogether?

2 In a regatta, the first boat was 4 lengths ahead of the second. If a length is 3.4 m, by what distance did the first boat win?

3 World swimming records can be made only in pools of length 50 m. How many lengths will be swum in a race of (*a*) 400 m (*b*) 1500 m?

4 The distance of the first hole from the tee on Jane's home golf course is 346 yards. She drives her ball 185 yards from the tee towards the hole. How much further does Jane have to hit her ball to reach the hole?

5 With only one throw remaining in a javelin contest, the leading distance is 53. 58 m. With his last throw, Howard wins by 4.92 m. How far was Howard's last throw?

6 In 1989 the world record high jump reached 8 feet. How high is this in metres? (1 m = 39.4 inches, 12 inches = 1 foot.)

7 Bill lines up six golf balls and hits them one after the other with his 5-iron. The distances travelled, in metres, before landing were 87.4, 80.3, 78.6, 84.5, 91.3 and 88.5. What is the average distance that Bill hit a golf ball with his 5-iron?

8 The diagram represents a tennis court. The nine lines are marked with white tape. What is the total length of tape required?

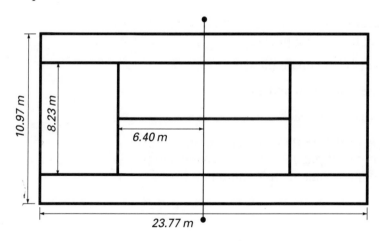

9 It is proposed to surround the tennis court with a rectangular fence, leaving 7.5 m between the fence and the base and side lines. What length of fencing is required?

10 The diagram represents a running track. The total distance round the track is 400 m. If the radius of the two semicircular ends is 27 m, how long is the straight section? Give your answer to the nearest 0.1 m.

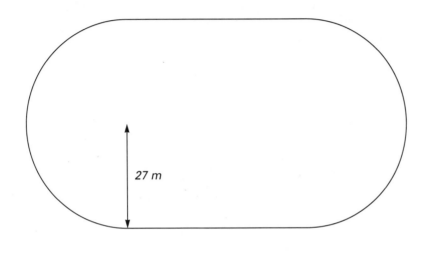

27 m

Investigation B

As manager of a new sports centre, you have the task of planning where to arrange various pitches on the sport's field shown in the diagram opposite.
Your instructions are:

(*a*) include at least three soccer pitches, two rugby pitches, a hockey pitch, and two all-weather five-a-side pitches,

(*b*) do not encroach on to the cricket square (shown),

(*c*) leave at least 10 m between one pitch and another,

(*d*) put the all-weather pitches close to each other.

By making a scale drawing of the sports field, and cutting out rectangles representing each type of pitch, show how you would plan out your field. Try to include more than the minimum number of pitches.

Use the following information:

Soccer pitch:	length 100 m – 110 m	width 65 m – 80 m
Rugby pitch:	length 100 m – 120 m	width 60 m – 65 m
Hockey pitch:	length 85 m – 95 m	width 50 m – 60 m
All-weather pitch:	length 25 m	width 15 m

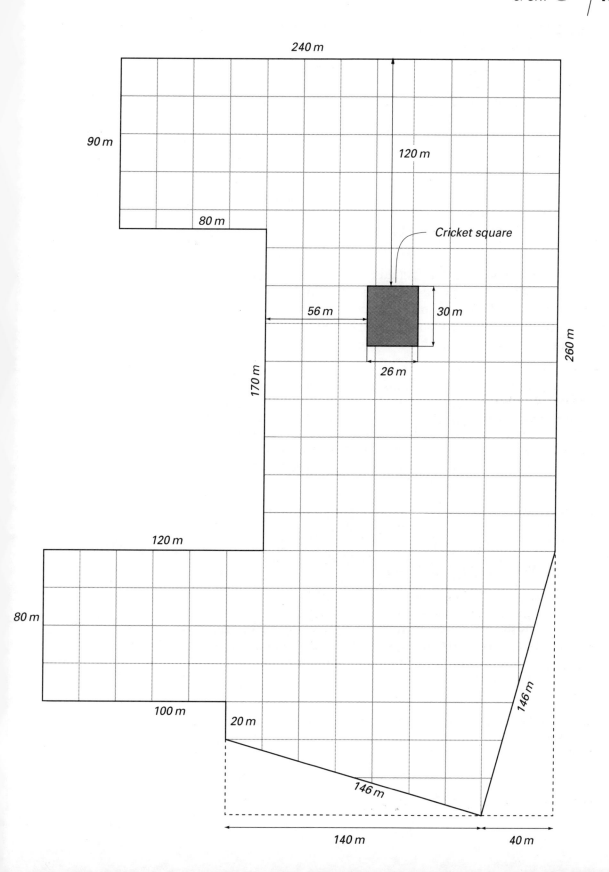

240 m

90 m

120 m

80 m

Cricket square

56 m

30 m

26 m

170 m

260 m

120 m

80 m

146 m

100 m

20 m

146 m

140 m

40 m

Weights

EXERCISE 8.4

1 In 1952 Richard Walker, an angler from Hertfordshire, caught a carp weighing 44 lb. How heavy is this in kilograms? (1 kg = 2.2 lb)

2 A weightlifter has just lifted 94.75 kg. Two weights, each of 3.75 kg, are added, one to each end of the bar. What is the weight that has now to be lifted?

3 The heaviest weight permitted for a middleweight boxer is 11 stones and 11 pounds. Brian hopes to fight at middleweight next month. If he now weighs 12 stones and 4 pounds, how many pounds weight will he need to lose? (There are 14 pounds in one stone.)

4 (a) The weights, in kilograms, of the eight oarsmen in a boat are 90.4, 88.5, 94.0, 91.1, 89.7, 96.5, 82.4 and 86.7. What is the average weight of these oarsmen?

   (b) The average weight of the oarsmen in a second boat of eight rowers is 88.5 kg. Which boat carries the greater weight, and by how much?

5 A weightlifter lifted three weights of 102.3 kg, 103.4 kg and 104.8 kg in a competition.

   (a) What was the total weight lifted?

   (b) What was the average weight per lift?

   (c) The next competitor lifted 101.5 kg and 103.1 kg on his first two lifts. What is the minimum weight that he will have to lift in order to beat the previous competitor?

6 A batsman has been using a cricket bat weighing 1.22 kg. He decides to try a bat which is 10% lighter. (a) How heavy is this lighter bat? (b) What is the minimum percentage of 1.22 kg which will make the new bat weigh less than 1 kg?

7 In an angling competition, the winner caught seven fish,
weighing 375 g, 620 g, 260 g, 830 g, 705 g, 320 g and 390 g.

    (*a*) Draw a bar graph of the weights, starting with the
lightest fish.

    (*b*) Work out the median weight, and the mean weight.

Speeds

EXERCISE 8.5

1 Edward wins the 400 metres hurdles in 50 seconds. What is
his average speed (*a*) in metres per second (*b*) in kilometres
per hour?

2 In the 3 km steeplechase, Jeremy finishes in 9 minutes and
14 seconds. Work out his average speed (*a*) in metres per
second (*b*) in kilometres per hour. Give your answers
rounded to two decimal places.

3 An ice skater recorded a time of 43.7 s in a 500 m race.
What was his average speed in (*a*) metres per second
(*b*) kilometres per hour?

4 How long will it take Sofia to swim the 1280 m across a
lake, if she can swim at an average speed of 40 metres per
minute?

5 In a Manx TT race, each lap of the circuit is 60.72 km.
A motor cyclist takes 2 hours 25 minutes to complete a six-
lap race. Work out his average speed, in kilometres per
hour, to the nearest km/h.

6 Melissa can maintain a brisk walking pace of 8 km/h.
At this rate, (*a*) how many metres will she walk in one
minute (*b*) how long will it take her to walk 2 km (*c*) can
she reach her friend's house, 5.4 km away, in 40 minutes?

7 A fast bowler can bowl a cricket ball at 36 km per hour. How many seconds will it take the ball to travel the 19.2 m from his hand to the stumps?

8 The distance of the marathon race is 26 miles and 385 yards. What average speed, in kilometres per hour, would be required in order to run the marathon in 2 hours? (1 mile = 1.61 km, 1 mile = 1760 yards)

9 In a 200 m race, Saeed wins in 24.5 s. Angus finishes last in a time of 28.0 s.

(*a*) How many seconds is Saeed ahead of Angus?

(*b*) On graph paper, draw a horizontal scale up to 30 seconds and a vertical scale up to 200 metres. Assuming that each boy ran at a steady speed, draw two lines, one for each boy, beginning at the origin, to represent each boy's run.

(*c*) From your graph, work out (i) how many metres Saeed was ahead of Angus when Saeed crossed the finishing line (ii) Saeed's average speed.

10 The diagram opposite represents the journeys made by Sam on his bicycle, and his mother in the family car, from their home to their caravan site, on Friday evening.

(*a*) At what time did Sam leave home?

(*b*) At what time did Sam first stop for half-an-hour's rest?

(*c*) How far away from home was Sam then?

(*d*) At what time did Sam's mother pass him?

(*e*) Was Sam resting or cycling at this time?

(*f*) Work out Sam's average speed over the whole journey.

(*g*) What was Sam's mother's average speed?

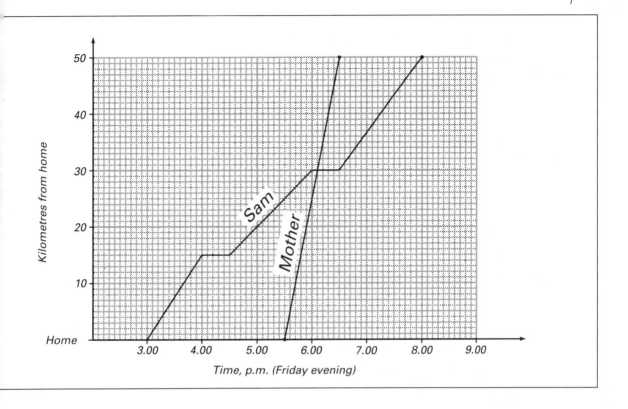

Darts

There are many opportunities to practise arithmetic, especially subtraction, in a game of darts. Although many games can be played, the usual game is to score 501 before your opponent does. At each turn you throw three darts at the dartboard, add up your score and take the total from 501. Your opponent then does the same, and you alternate, each of you taking your total away from your remaining score. To win the game you must finish by throwing a 'double', the outermost ring on the board.

If, for example, you have to score 51, then one way is to score 11, then double 20 (sometimes called 'double top' for obvious reasons).

Work out another way of scoring 51, assuming that you have already thrown one of your three darts.

This example shows the scoring in a game so far.

Example 1

(*a*) What was Len's first total?

(*b*) Joe's first score was 100. How is he most likely to have scored this total?

(*c*) Which player scored 120?

(*d*) What is Len's lowest score?

(*e*) Len can score 74 with two darts. Show one way of doing so.

(*f*) Can Joe win with two darts? If so, show how. If not, explain why not.

Len	Joe
501	501
441	401
400	356
280	311
254	231
154	171
74	121

(*a*) Len's first total was 60.

(*b*) 20, 20 and treble 20 (in any order).

(*c*) Len, in going from 400 to 280.

(*d*) From 280 to 254 is 26.

(*e*) Treble 14, and double 16 is one way.

(*f*) Joe must score an *odd* number with his first dart in order to leave a double on which to finish. The highest odd number with one dart is treble 19, or 57. This would leave 64, which is impossible with one dart, as the highest double is 40. [In fact, the centre ring, or 'bull's eye', counts as a double (double 25 = 50).] Hence Joe cannot win with two darts.

EXERCISE **8.6**

1 Why do you think darts' players often aim to get down to 32, which is double 16?

2 The highest score obtainable with three darts is 180 (treble 20 three times). What is the next highest possible score with three darts?

3 The maximum score on which you can finish is 170 (two treble 20s and the 'bull', counting as double 25). List all possible totals less than 170 on which you *cannot* finish with three darts.

4 It is possible to score 501 in nine darts. Show one way in which this can be done.

5 I score three separate adjacent doubles (e.g. 1, 18 and 4). What is the highest possible score that I could make with three adjacent doubles?

6 Lucy wins a game by scoring 117 with three darts. If her first dart was a 20, what did the second dart score? And the third?

7 John's total score over five games was 1769. If he threw 117 darts during the five games, what was his average score (*a*) for each dart (*b*) for three darts?

8 If I needed 36 to finish a game, I could score a single 6, then a treble 6 and then a double 6. Which scores greater than 100 could I get in a similar way (i.e. a single, double and treble of the same number)?

9 Eric, who needs 42 to finish, throws his three darts into the same double. Which double?

10 'Round the board' means hitting a single 1, then 2, then 3, etc. up to 20, then a 25 and finally a 'bull'. What is the total score?

Scatter graphs

In the long jump, you would expect that a tall person would be able to jump farther than someone smaller. Other factors (e.g. fitness, weight, running speed) affect long jumping ability; we can more easily see if there is some connection between height and how far you can jump by means of a **scatter graph.**

Example 2

The table shows the heights of the nine competitors in a long jump event, and the actual distances that each managed to achieve during the competition. All lengths are in metres, correct to two decimal places.

Competitor	A	B	C	D	E	F	G	H	I
Height (m)	1.62	1.70	1.75	1.69	1.57	1.81	1.77	1.75	1.74
Distance jumped (m)	4.23	5.33	5.81	5.00	4.31	6.00	5.95	6.08	5.72

(a) Each distance has been measured to the nearest _____. What should be put in place of the '_____'?

(b) Draw a scatter graph. From your graph, would you say that taller people can jump farther than shorter people?

(c) Draw in a 'trend line' as accurately as you can.

(d) A tenth competitor, 1.72 m tall, was injured. Had he been able to take part, about how far would you estimate that he would have jumped?

(a) In any number, the second decimal place stands for hundredths. As there are 100 centimetres in a metre, the distances have been measured to the nearest *centimetre*.

(b) and (c) The graph is shown on the next page.

As there is a clear trend upwards on the graph, then in general the taller competitors jump farther than the smaller ones.

(d) From the trend line, we can estimate that he would have jumped about 5.52 m.

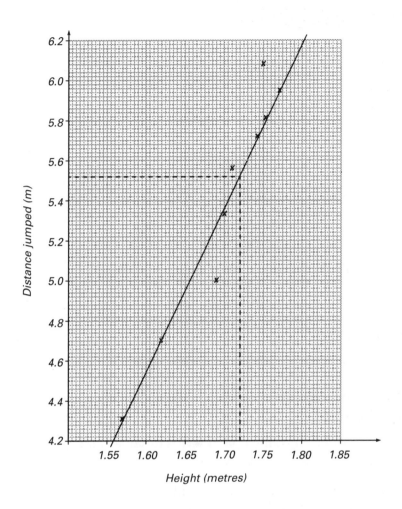

1 In the shot-put event, the distances reached by seven competitors, together with their weights, are given in the table.

Shot-putter	1	2	3	4	5	6	7
Weight (kg)	88.5	82.3	94.3	80.7	90.5	86.0	87.9
Distance (m)	12.41	11.68	13.13	11.14	12.62	12.60	12.16

Draw a scatter graph, and if there is a trend, draw in the trend line. Which competitor do you think is the strongest?

2 The table shows the heights of 8 runners in a 400 m race, together with their finishing times.

No. on runner's vest	287	978	333	254	803	161	842	554
Height (m)	1.69	1.74	1.67	1.63	1.76	1.75	1.70	1.71
Finishing time (s)	60.4	58.1	61.8	55.7	55.5	61.8	56.0	57.6

Draw a scatter graph. What conclusion can you draw from your diagram?

3 'The taller you are, the higher you can jump.'
From the figures in the table, draw a scatter graph. If there is a trend line, draw it in. (You need to take extra care in drawing the graph because the heights of the competitors, and the heights jumped, are measured in the same units, and are fairly close to each other.)

Competitor	P	Q	R	S	T	U	V	W	X
Height of competitor (m)	1.68	1.66	1.80	1.53	1.70	1.72	1.85	1.57	1.77
Height jumped (m)	1.28	1.38	1.45	1.16	1.48	1.21	1.55	1.28	1.37

Does your graph tend to agree with the statement 'the taller you are, the higher you can jump'?

Averages

To work out your batting average in cricket, the total number of runs you have scored is divided by the number of times you have been out (bowled, caught, run out, etc.).

Example 3
Geoffrey has scored 58, 3, and 41 in his last three innings. Each time he was out, caught. What is his batting average?

Total runs scored = 58 + 3 + 41 = 102

Geoffrey's batting average is $\frac{102}{3} = 34$ runs per innings.

A bowling average is worked out by dividing the total number of runs that have been scored from your bowling by the number of batsmen you have dismissed (i.e. the number of wickets that you have taken).

Example 4

When bowling in these last three games, Geoffrey has managed to dismiss 8 batsmen, while having a total of 68 runs scored when he was bowling. What is his bowling average?

Geoffrey's bowling average is $\frac{68}{8} = 8.5$ runs per wicket.

Example 5

The results of our first five basketball matches are given below.

Match number	1	2	3	4	5
Our team (points)	67	48	45	52	77
Opponents (points)	56	51	46	30	59

(a) How many matches have we won?

(b) What is our average points score per match, so far?

(c) What is the average number of points per match scored against us?

(a) We have won three matches.

(b) Average *for* is $\frac{67 + 48 + 45 + 52 + 77}{5} = \frac{289}{5} = 57.8$

(c) Average *against* is $\frac{56 + 51 + 46 + 30 + 59}{5} = \frac{242}{5} = 48.4$

EXERCISE 8.8

1   Last year our netball team scored 186 goals in 12 games. What was the average number of goals per game?

2   Norman caught seven fish in a competition. Their total weight was 315 g. What was the average weight of the fish in Norman's catch?

3 In November 1966, Roger Taylor beat Wieslaw Gasiorek in a tennis match. They played 126 games in three sets. What was the average number of games per set? (The set scores were 27–29, 31–29, 6–4.)

4 Christopher hits five golf balls with his 7-iron. The distances reached are 85 m, 91 m, 82 m, 85 m and 87 m. What is the average distance reached by Christopher with his 7-iron?

5 David and Peter are the opening batsmen for the local cricket team. Their scores for the first eight games are given below.

David	17	4	36	12	68	42	0	14
Peter	14	72	10	49	20	3	2	39

Who has the better batting average? (Both were out eight times.)

6 Sandra played fourteen rounds of golf on a golfing holiday. Her scores were: 85, 84, 91, 89, 95, 86, 87, 86, 82, 83, 86, 81, 83, 84. What was her average score for a round? Give your answer to the nearest whole number of shots.

7 The Harlem Globetrotters' basketball team played 8756 games in 39 seasons up to 1965. What is the average number of games played in a season?

8 The average number of goals per game scored by Michael during a football season was 1.6. If Michael played in 40 games, how many goals did he score?

9 A relay race involves four swimmers, each covering 100 m, one after the other. The first three swimmers took 2 minutes 57 seconds altogether to complete 300 m. How fast will the fourth swimmer have to swim the last 100 m if the average time for a 100 m length is to be 58 seconds?

10 In a marbles championship the Toucan Terribles cleared the ring of 49 marbles at an average rate of one marble per 4.37 seconds. How long, to the nearest second, did it take them to clear the ring?

This final exercise includes general questions to do with sport; the questions require a variety of approaches and methods, sometimes bringing in two or three different areas of mathematics within one problem.

EXERCISE **8.9**

1 How much further, in metres, do athletes run in a mile race compared with a 1500 m race? (1 mile = 1.61 km.)

2 A yacht reached a speed of 13.5 knots during a race. How fast is this, in km/h? (1 knot = 1 nautical mile per hour, 1 nautical mile = 6080 feet, 1 foot = 0.305 m.)

3 There are seven judges in a county diving competition. They each give a mark out of 10 for every dive. To work out the score, the highest and lowest marks are ignored, and the average of the remaining five marks is the score awarded to that dive.

(*a*) Work out the scores for these six divers.

Judge	A	B	C	D	E	F	G
Cheryl	4.8	5.6	5.7	5.0	5.3	6.0	5.6
Aileen	6.7	7.3	7.8	6.5	6.6	7.4	7.4
Anita	5.7	6.9	5.9	6.3	6.3	7.0	6.7
Kathleen	8.7	7.2	7.8	6.2	7.3	8.0	7.8
Laura	5.2	6.0	4.9	5.3	6.0	5.8	6.0
Jenny	6.1	6.3	6.9	8.3	7.7	6.9	7.2

(*b*) Who won?

4 Fred, one of the bowlers on our cricket team, has had 284 runs hit from his bowling, and has taken 21 wickets. Another bowler, Brian, has taken 27 wickets, but has had 392 runs scored from his bowling. Who has the better bowling average?

5 A rowing crew covered the 3.6 kilometres of a race in 12 minutes and 53 seconds. What was the average rowing speed, in km/h?

6 Adrian has 700 mm wheels on his bicycle. (The diameter of the wheels is 700 mm.)

(a) When the wheel makes one complete revolution, how far forward does the bicycle travel?

(b) How many revolutions will the wheels make when the bicycle is ridden a distance of 100 metres?

7 The attendances at our town's last three home soccer matches were 23 852, 14 072 and 17 192.

(a) What was the total attendance for the three games?

(b) Work out the average attendance per match.

(c) Write down each of the three attendances (i) to the nearest 1000 (ii) to the nearest 100.

(d) If the entrance fee is £2.40, work out the total takings for the three matches, to the nearest £1000.

(e) If the team plays 24 home matches throughout the season, use your answers to (b) and (d) to estimate the total amount of money taken, giving your answer to the nearest £1000.

8 The diagram opposite shows the height of the hammer above ground level during the time it is in the air after it has been thrown by a competitor in the hammer-throwing event.

(a) At what height above the ground was the hammer at the instant it left the thrower's hands?

(b) What was the maximum height reached by the hammer?

(c) For how long was the hammer in the air?

(d) If the hammer had a horizontal speed of 13.63 m/s, how long was the throw?

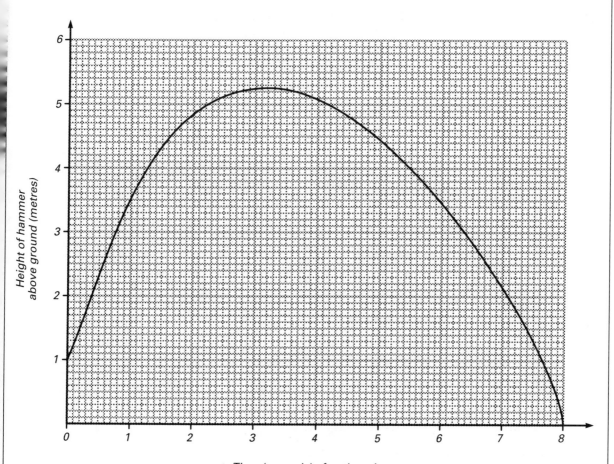

Height of hammer above ground (metres)

Time (seconds) after throwing

9 The diagram on page 206 represents an 18-hole golf course. Use whatever method you choose to estimate the area of land that the golf course covers. Give your answer in hectares. (1 hectare = 10 000 square metres.)

10 In our pool league you get two points for a win, one for a draw and none if you lose. One team, the Potty Potters, have 22 points, and their rivals, the Q-Kings, have 20 points. Both teams have played 14 games.

(*a*) The Potty Potters have lost one game. How many have they won?

(*b*) List all the possible ways that the Q-Kings could have scored their 20 points.

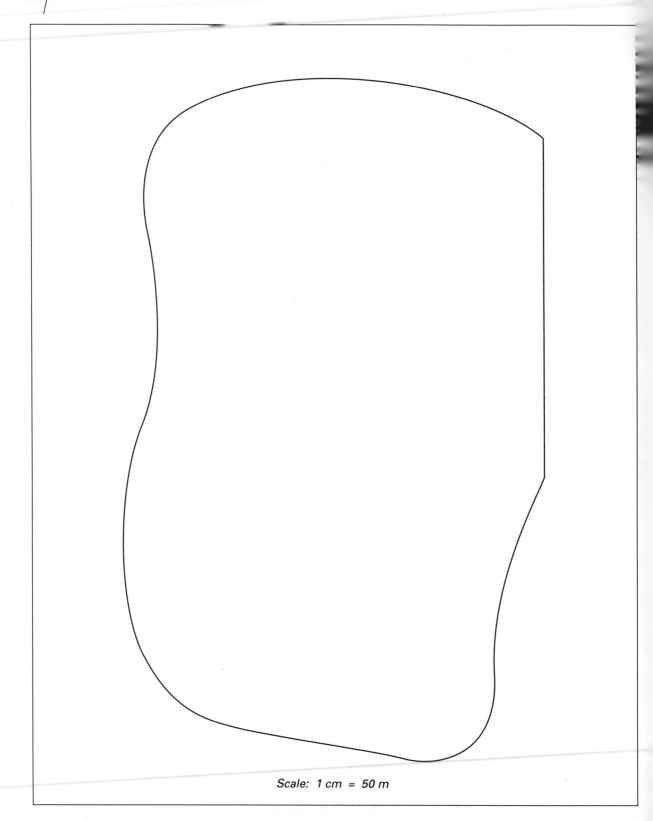

Scale: 1 cm = 50 m

9. Hobbies

Many of us have hobbies or leisure activities which we pursue in our spare time. Without us realising it, mathematics is used when following many of these activities. In this chapter a number of these activities are examined in detail.

Knitting

Knitting is one of the oldest crafts known, and is still practised in many homes today. The first simple technique in knitting is to check the tension in a piece of knitting. The size of knitting needles determines the tension, and, sometimes, the needles suggested in the pattern are not the correct size for the wool being used. The sizes of knitting needles available are shown in the table below.

Metric	10 mm	9 mm	8 mm	$7\frac{1}{2}$ mm	7 mm	$6\frac{1}{2}$ mm	6 mm	$5\frac{1}{2}$ mm
British	000	00	0	1	2	3	4	5
Metric	5 mm	$4\frac{1}{2}$ mm	4 mm	$3\frac{3}{4}$ mm	$3\frac{1}{2}$ mm	$3\frac{1}{4}$ mm	3 mm	
British	6	7	8	9	–	10	11	

Example 1

'28 stitches and 42 rows to 10 cm on $4\frac{1}{2}$ mm needles' is a typical knitting instruction, and by knitting 42 rows across and 28 stitches on size $4\frac{1}{2}$ mm needles you should knit a square of side 10 cm. If the square turns out to be of side 11 cm, the needles are too big for the wool, and you need a smaller pair of needles, 4 mm say.

(a) If the square is 11 cm, find the percentage error. (b) Find the total number of stitches, in the square.

(a) The error is 1 cm, so the percentage error is $\dfrac{1 \text{ cm}}{10 \text{ cm}} \times 100 = 10\%$.

(b) 28 stitches for 42 rows is $28 \times 42 = 1176$ stitches in the square.

EXERCISE **9.1**

For each square find (*a*) the correct size of needle (*b*) the percentage error (*c*) the total number of stitches.

1 20 stitches and 24 rows to 10 cm on $4\frac{1}{2}$ mm needles, which actually gives an 11 cm square.

2 20 stitches and 28 rows to 10 cm on 4 mm needles, which actually gives an 11 cm square.

3 22 stitches and 26 rows to 10 cm on $11\frac{1}{2}$ cm square. actually gives an $11\frac{1}{2}$ cm square.

4 30 stitches and 32 rows to 10 cm on $3\frac{1}{4}$ mm needles, which actually gives a 9 cm square.

5 27 stitches and 36 rows to 10 cm on 6 mm needles, which actually gives an 11 cm square.

6 28 stitches and 28 rows to 10 cm on $3\frac{3}{4}$ mm needles, which actually gives a 9.1 cm square.

7 32 stitches and 28 rows to 10 cm on 5 mm needles, which actually gives a 10.9 cm square.

8 26 stitches and 34 rows to 10 cm on $4\frac{1}{2}$ mm needles, which actually gives a 10.8 cm square.

9 Metric sizes of needles continue down to the smallest size of 2 mm. What are the sizes between 3 mm and 2 mm?

10 Write down what you think would be the British equivalents to the metric sizes from 3 mm to 2 mm, if 2 mm is equivalent to size 14.

11 What would be an alternative way to represent sizes 00 and 000?

12 Why do you think 00 and 000 are used in preference to any other suggestion?

Enlargement

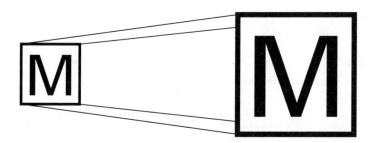

In embroidery, and many other handicrafts, it is sometimes necessary to enlarge a picture to the size needed for a template or a pattern. The most common way to do this is by using squared paper or graph paper.

Example 2

Produce an enlargement of scale factor 2 of the picture for a template. What is the area scale factor?

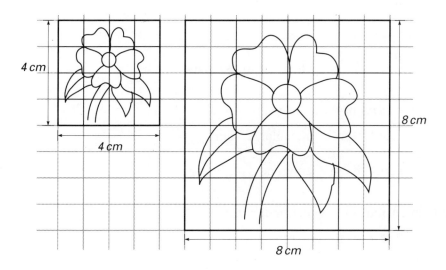

Each square should be drawn to twice its size, and the lines of the drawing increased proportionately. The new dimensions of the picture are 8 cm × 8 cm. The area of the old picture is 16 cm^2; the area of the enlarged picture is 64 cm^2, so the area scale factor is 4.

EXERCISE 9.2

Produce an enlargement of each of the drawings to the scale factor stated:

1

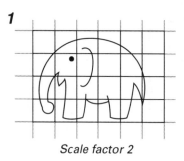

Scale factor 2

2

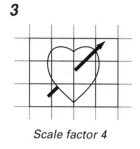

Scale factor 3

3

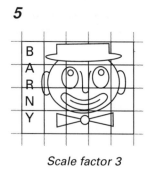

Scale factor 4

4

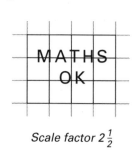

Scale factor 2

5

Scale factor 3

6

Scale factor $2\frac{1}{2}$

7 A picture measuring 7 cm × 8 cm is enlarged to twice its size (scale factor 2).

    (*a*) What are the dimensions of the enlarged picture?

    (*b*) What is the area scale factor for the enlargement?

8 A picture measuring 4 cm × 8 cm is enlarged by a factor of 3.

    (*a*) What are the dimensions of the enlarged picture?

    (*b*) What is the scale factor for the enlargement?

9 A picture measuring 3 cm × 3 cm is enlarged by a factor of $2\frac{1}{2}$.

    (*a*) What are the dimensions of the enlarged picture?

    (*b*) What is the area scale factor for the enlargement?

10   A picture measuring 5 cm × 10 cm is enlarged by a factor of $1\frac{1}{2}$.

  (*a*) What are the dimensions of the enlarged picture?

  (*b*) What is the area scale factor for the enlargement?

11   Describe the relationship between the scale factor of enlargement and the area scale factor of enlargement.

In each of the following questions a square picture is to be embroidered using a circular frame. Find (*a*) the radius *r* (*b*) the circumference of the frame needed. (The circumference *C* of a circle radius *r* is calculated using the formula $C = 2\pi r$.)

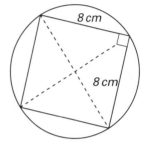

Write your answers correct to the nearest $\frac{1}{10}$ cm (to one decimal place).

12   8 cm wide   **13**   5 cm wide   **14**   7 cm wide

15 $6\frac{1}{2}$ cm wide   **16** $10\frac{1}{2}$ cm wide

Reflection and pattern

Coloured patterns can be used to brighten up knitted jumpers. Diagrams are given in knitting patterns to help explain what is required in the knitting.

  This pattern has been reflected about the dotted line to create a symmetrical picture for knitting into the front of a jumper.

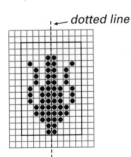

dotted line

8th row: 5 w., 1 r., * 5 w., 1 r., 1 n., 2 w., 1 n., 5 w., 1 r.; repeat from * until 5 sts. remain, 5 w.
9th row: All w.
10th row: 1 n., 2 w., 1 n., 3 w., 1 n., 2 w., * 1 n., 2 w., 1 r., 1 w., 1 r., 2 w., 1 n., 2 w., 1 n., 3 w., 1 n., 2 w.; repeat from * until 1 st. remains, 1 n.
11th row: 1 w., 2 n., 5 w., 2 n., * 2 w., 2 r., 1 w., 2 r., 2 w., 2 n., 5 w., 2 n.; repeat from * until 1 st. remains, 1 w.
12th row: 11 w., * 7 r., 11 w.; repeat from * to end.
  These 12 rows form the repeat of the pattern. Pattern a further 74 rows.
  Mark each end of the last row to denote end of side seams. **
  Pattern a further 62 rows.
  Cast off for shoulders and back neck, marking centre 45 (49) (53) sts. for centre back neck.

THE FRONT: Work as back to **. Pattern a further 41 rows.
  To divide for neck: Next row: Pattern 46 (53) (60) and leave these sts. on a spare needle for right front neck, cast off next 27

EXERCISE 9.3

Copy and complete these patterns by drawing in a reflection about the dotted line:

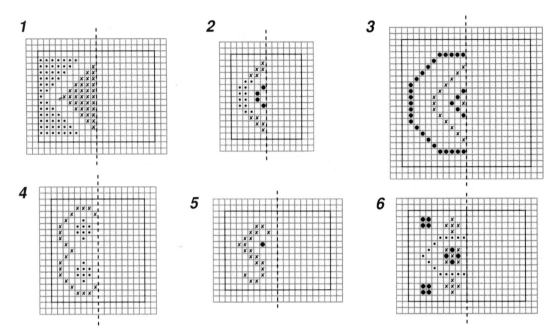

Reflect into each quadrant to make a complete pattern:

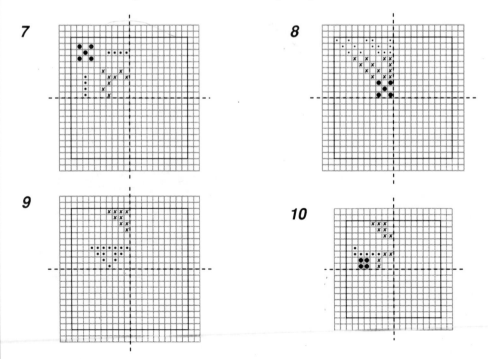

HOBBIES 9 213

Continue each of the patterns:

11

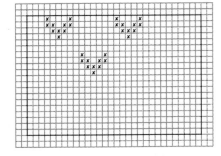

12

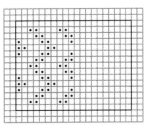

13

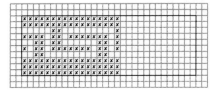

14

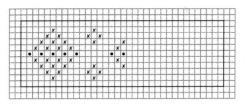

15

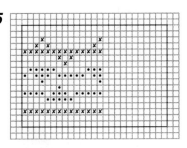

16

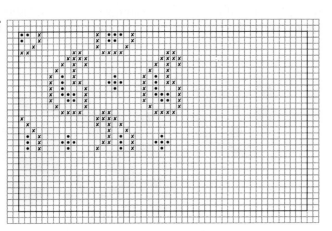

Investigation A

Produce some of your own diagrams for knitting patterns which involve reflections.

Investigation B

It is important sometimes to produce a pattern which 'fits together' or **tessellates.** Which shapes can you use to produce diagrams which do fit together and can be outlined? Invent some of your own diagrams which tessellate.

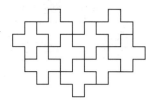

Crosswords and rotation

Solving crosswords is a popular way of passing the time and testing knowledge of words, but mathematics is also involved since the pattern of each crossword is based on symmetry of order 2 (180°) or order 4 (90°). Words are numbered, and the position of the number is decided by the pattern: consecutive numbers are inserted at the position where each word (across or down) starts.

Example 3

Use the shape as a pattern, to be rotated through 90° about the point shown, to create a crossword to be numbered.

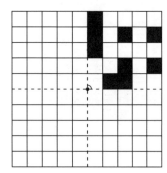

EXERCISE **9.4**

Copy and number these crossword puzzles:

1

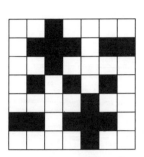

2

3

4

5 What order of rotational symmetry are the crossword puzzles in questions 1–4?

Rotate these patterns about the point shown to create a crossword puzzle, which should then be numbered.

6 **7** **8** **9**

  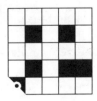 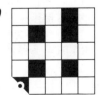

10 Draw a crossword puzzle of your own.

Investigation C

Examine some of the crossword puzzles in either newspapers or puzzle books. Try to identify the type of rotational symmetry on which each of them is based.

Fishing

Fishing is still one of the most popular of participation sports or hobbies. Much of the mathematics in fishing involves calculating weight, which is still largely done in imperial units.

16 ounces (oz) = 1 pound (lb)

14 pounds (lb) = 1 stone (st)

Example 4

Change (*a*) 30 oz into lb and oz (*b*) $4\frac{1}{2}$ lb into oz.

(*a*) 30 oz = 16 oz + 14 oz = 1 lb 14 oz.

(*b*) $4\frac{1}{2}$ lb = $4\frac{1}{2} \times 16$ oz = 72 oz.

EXERCISE 9.5

Change the following into pounds and ounces:

1 20 oz   **2** 35 oz   **3** 42 oz   **4** 60 oz   **5** 52 oz

Change the following into ounces:

6 1 lb 1oz   **7** 3 lb   **8** $2\frac{1}{2}$ lb   **9** $3\frac{1}{4}$ lb   **10** 5 lb

11 $4\frac{3}{4}$ lb   **12** 4 lb 9 oz   **13** 6 lb   **14** $3\frac{1}{2}$ lb   **15** $\frac{1}{8}$ lb

Change the following into stones and pounds:

16 180 lb   **17** 125 lb   **18** 83 lb   **19** 140 lb   **20** 138 lb

Change the following into pounds:

21 $10\frac{1}{2}$ st   **22** 9 st 3 lb   **23** 8 st 10 lb   **24** 6 st 13 lb

25 7 st 7 lb   **26** 8 st 4 lb

27 The longest fish recorded was a 6 ft Nile perch weighing 416 lb. What weight is this in stones and pounds?

28 The heaviest freshwater fish landed was an 834 lb sturgeon in 1981. What weight is this in stones and pounds?

Adding imperial units

In adding such weights we cannot use calculators, which have been designed to handle decimals only.

Example 5

Find the total of: 3 lb 2 oz, 2 lb 10 oz, 1 lb 8 oz.

lb	oz
3	2
2	10
1ᵢ	8
7	4

$(2 + 10 + 8)$ oz = 20 oz = 1 lb 4 oz
i.e. carry 1 and 4 down.

Example 6

5 oz, 8 oz, 8 oz, 11 oz, 13 oz are the weights of several fish caught.

Find the (*a*) mean weight (*b*) modal weight (*c*) median weight.

(*a*) Mean weight = $\dfrac{5 + 8 + 8 + 11 + 13}{5} = \dfrac{45}{5} = 9$ oz.

(*b*) Modal weight (weight occurring most often) = 8 oz.

(*c*) Median weight (middle one): 5, 8, <u>8</u>, 11, 13, which is 8 oz.

EXERCISE 9.6

Calculate:

1 2 lb 4 oz + 3 lb 2 oz + 1 lb 6oz

2 1 lb 3 oz + 10 oz + 2 lb 4 oz

3 3 lb 10 oz + 2 lb 2 oz + 1 lb 9 oz

4 2 lb 11 oz + 13 oz + 4 lb 1 oz

5 5 lb 7 oz + 3 lb 5 oz + 1 lb 4 oz

6 4 lb 13 oz + 4 lb 9 oz + 2 lb 2 oz

7 13 oz + 11 oz + 2 lb 10 oz

8 3 lb 1 oz + 1 lb 5 oz + 4 lb 9 oz + 2 lb 8 oz

9 2 lb 3 oz + 4 lb 8 oz + 1 lb 7 oz + 9 oz

10 10 oz + 3 lb 11 oz + 2 lb 13 oz + 4 lb 10 oz

For each of the following find, where possible, (*a*) the mean weight (*b*) the modal weight (*c*) the median weight.

11 3 lb 2oz, $2\frac{1}{2}$ lb, 2 lb 13 oz, 3 lb, 2 lb 10 oz

12 $2\frac{3}{4}$ lb, $2\frac{1}{4}$ lb, 2 lb 9 oz, $2\frac{1}{4}$ lb, 3 lb

13 $3\frac{1}{2}$ lb, 2 lb 6 oz, 2 lb 10 oz, $3\frac{1}{4}$ lb, 3 lb, 3 lb 4 oz

14 10 oz, 1 lb, $1\frac{1}{2}$ lb, 13 oz, 1 lb 3 oz, 1 lb, 15 oz, $1\frac{1}{4}$ lb, 1 lb

15 $2\frac{3}{4}$ lb, 1 lb 9 oz, $1\frac{3}{4}$ lb, 1 lb 13 oz, 2 lb 6 oz, $2\frac{1}{2}$ lb, 1 lb 11 oz

EXERCISE 9.7

The following questions each list the total weight of several catches of fish. Place the lists in order, starting with the largest catch first.

1 $3\frac{1}{2}$ lb, 2 lb 2 oz, 3 lb 9 oz, 1 lb 10 oz, $3\frac{1}{4}$ lb, 3 lb 5 oz

2 2 lb 11 oz, $3\frac{1}{4}$ lb, 3 lb 3 oz, $2\frac{3}{4}$ lb, 2 lb, 2 lb 13 oz

3 $1\frac{1}{2}$ lb, 1 lb 5 oz, $2\frac{1}{4}$ lb, 1 lb 10 oz, 2 lb 3 oz, $2\frac{1}{2}$ lb

4 3 lb, $2\frac{3}{4}$ lb, 2 lb 13 oz, 2 lb 7 oz, $2\frac{1}{2}$ lb, 2 lb 10 oz

5 $4\frac{1}{4}$ lb, 4 lb 2 oz, $3\frac{3}{4}$ lb, 3 lb 5 oz, 3 lb 15 oz, 3 lb 10 oz

The following lists include some weights in kg (1 kg = 2.2 lb = 35.2 oz = 2 lb 3.2 oz). Again place all weights in order, with the largest first.

6   3 lb 2 oz, 1 kg, $2\frac{1}{2}$ lb, 2 lb 13 oz, 1.5 kg, $2\frac{3}{4}$ lb, 2 lb 10 oz

7   2 lb 11 oz, 2 kg, 3 lb, $2\frac{1}{2}$ lb, 2 lb 12 oz, 3 lb 3 oz, $2\frac{3}{4}$ lb

8   4 lb 5 oz, 3 lb 7 oz, 1.8 kg, 3 lb 1 oz, 1 kg, $3\frac{1}{2}$ lb

9 $2\frac{3}{4}$ lb, 3 lb 2 oz, 3 lb 9 oz, 1.6 kg, 4 lb 1 oz, 3 lb 12 oz, 1.2 kg

10   Draw a conversion graph to change weights up to 5 kg into lb.

EXERCISE **9.8**

The table describes the specifications of two different types of fishing line.

	Gut			Monofil	
	Diameter	Breaking strain		Diameter	Breaking strain
(a)	0.010 inch	3.5 lb	(e)	0.010 inch	6 lb
(b)	0.009 inch	2.7 lb	(f)	0.009 inch	5 lb
(c)	0.008 inch	2 lb	(g)	0.008 inch	4 lb
(d)	0.007 inch	1.5 lb	(h)	0.007 inch	3 lb

Rewrite the tables, expressing the decimal diameters as fractions of an inch. Change the breaking strains to ounces, written to the nearest ounce. For each diameter, calculate the circumference of the line, in inches.

Write down which of the lines is nearest to these weights of
fish, and yet strong enough to land the fish (i.e. the most
suitable line):

1 $3\frac{1}{4}$ lb   **2** $4\frac{1}{2}$ lb   **3** $1\frac{3}{4}$ lb   **4** $2\frac{3}{4}$ lb

5 $2\frac{1}{2}$ lb   **6** $5\frac{1}{2}$ lb   **7** $3\frac{3}{4}$ lb   **8** $2\frac{1}{4}$ lb

9 3 lb 7 oz   **10** 2 lb 13 oz

Cookery

In cooking we spend a lot of time measuring quantities, temperatures,
capacities, time, etc. We also have to be flexible enough to use recipes
or equipment marked out in imperial or metric units.

Example 7

To convert temperatures written in °F to °C we use the formula:

$$°C = \frac{(°F - 32) \times 5}{9}$$

What is 190°F in °C?

$$°C = \frac{(190 - 32) \times 5}{9} = \frac{158 \times 5}{9} = 87.77°C$$

$$= 88°C \text{ to the nearest degree.}$$

Example 8

This is a conversion graph to help us change between millilitres (ml)
and fluid ounces (fl. oz). Convert 5 fl.oz into ml.

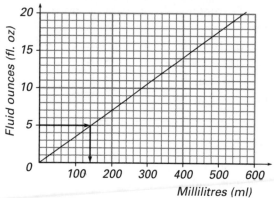

As indicated on the graph, 5 fl.oz is 140 ml.

EXERCISE **9.9**

Use the formula $°C = \dfrac{(°F - 32) \times 5}{9}$ to convert these

temperatures into °C, to the nearest degree.

1 320°F   **2** 450°F   **3** 340°F   **4** 400°F

5 375°F   **6** 350°F

Use the formula $°F = \left(\dfrac{°C \times 9}{5}\right) + 32$ to convert these temperatures
into °F.

7 150°C   **8** 190°C   **9** 175°C   **10** 250°C

11 215°C   **12** 160°C

Use the conversion graph in Example 8 to change these quantities
into ml.

13 8 fl.oz   **14** 13 fl.oz   **15** 4 fl.oz   **16** 10 fl.oz

17 17 fl.oz   **18** 14 fl.oz

Use the conversion graph in Example 8 to change these quantities
into fluid ounces (fl. oz).

19 100 ml   **20** 450 ml   **21** 150 ml   **22** 200 ml

23 225 ml   **24** 475 ml

Write down the quantities as indicated on each of the following
scales, taken from items of kitchen equipment:

25

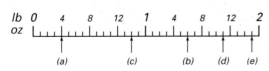

26

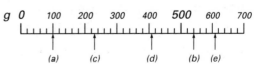

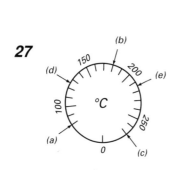

28

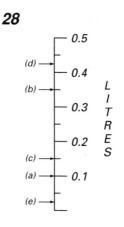

29

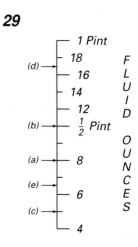

Example 9

To make shortcrust pastry, take margarine and flour in the ratio of 1 : 2. How much flour would be needed for 300 g of pastry?

1 : 2 represents 3 parts altogether, so 1 part is 300 ÷ 3 = 100 g.

Flour is 2 parts = 2 × 100 g = 200 g of flour for 300 g of pastry.

Example 10

Here is a biscuit recipe for 30 biscuits:

  230 g self-raising flour
  150 g butter
  100 g caster sugar
    1   beaten egg

What quantities would you need for 45 biscuits?

45 biscuits is half as much again:

  230 + 115   = 345 g self-raising flour
  150 + 75   = 225 g butter
  100 + 50   = 150 g caster sugar
    $1 + \frac{1}{2}$ = $1\frac{1}{2}$ or 2 beaten eggs

Since eggs cannot be divided we round upwards.

_ EXERCISE **9.10** _____

1 A recipe for a basic steamed pudding to serve four people is: 160 g self-raising flour, 80 g butter, 80 g caster sugar, 1 beaten egg, 80 ml milk. Write out a recipe to make a pudding for (*a*) 2 (*b*) 8 (*c*) 10 people.

2 A biscuit crust is made using biscuits and butter in the ratio of 2 : 1.

(*a*) Calculate the weight of biscuit needed to make 675 g of crust.

(*b*) How much crust could be made using 400 g of biscuit?

(*c*) How much crust could be made using $\frac{2}{5}$ of a 250 g packet of butter?

3 The label of this can reads 'Dilute one part evaporated milk with $1\frac{1}{2}$ parts of water to obtain the equivalent of full cream milk'.

(*a*) How much water is needed to dilute the contents of the can?

(*b*) How much milk will you have?

4 A recipe for a loaf of bread is: 25 g fresh yeast, 450 ml water, 675 g flour, 15 ml salt. What quantities should a local baker use to make 20 loaves?

5 A recipe for 10 coconut buns is: 50 g self-raising flour, 25 g desiccated coconut, 25 g glacé cherries, 50 g margarine, 50 g sugar, 1 egg. What quantities would you need to make 25 buns for a party?

6 A recipe suggests a pot stew is made using quantities of meat, potatoes and vegetables in the ratios 4 : 7 : 8.

(*a*) How much potato and vegetable will be needed if there is 2 kg of meat?

(*b*) How much meat and vegetable would be needed for $3\frac{1}{2}$ kg of potatoes?

(*c*) What would be the total weight of a stew made with $3\frac{1}{2}$ kg of potatoes?

(*d*) Calculate, to the nearest gram, the weight of meat and potatoes you would use for 500 g of vegetables.

7   A recipe for macaroni cheese is: 100 g macaroni, 150 g cheese, 40 g margarine, 40 g flour, 500 ml milk. Write the quantities as ratios expressed in their lowest terms.

8   Lamb and chick-pea ragoût for four: 175 g chick peas, 30 ml oil, 1 kg neck of lamb, 30 g flour, 450 ml chicken stock, 300 ml apple juice, 225 g carrots. What quantities would you use for a family of six?

9   A pizza mix for two people consists of: 275 g white bread, 6 tomatoes, 30 ml tomato purée, 60 ml oil, 75 g garlic sausage, 175 g cheese. What quantities would you use to make sufficient pizzas for nine people?

10   Potted fish: 350 g haddock, 150 ml single cream, 50 g butter. These amounts are sufficient for a family of four, that is, two full portions for adults and two half portions for children. What quantities will you need for a family of three adults and three children?

Investigation D

Imagine you are about to do some baking for your whole class, perhaps for a party. Create your own recipe for the things you want to bake, and write the recipe in the correct quantities you would need for the entire class.

Roasting

Cooking times for roasting meat and fowl at a temperature of 190–200°C are shown in the table:

Meat	Cooking time
Beef	30 min per $\frac{1}{2}$ kg plus 25 min
Beef, boned	30 min per $\frac{1}{2}$ kg plus 30 min
Mutton and lamb	30 min per $\frac{1}{2}$ kg plus 35 min
Pork and veal	35 min per $\frac{1}{2}$ kg plus 35 min
Ham	35 min per $\frac{1}{2}$ kg plus 35 min
Chicken	20 min per $\frac{1}{2}$ kg plus 20 min
Duck	30 min per $\frac{1}{2}$ kg plus 25 min
Turkey	20 min per $\frac{1}{2}$ kg up to $3\frac{1}{2}$ kg then 10 min per $\frac{1}{2}$ kg

Example 11

How long would it take to cook a piece of beef of weight $1\frac{1}{2}$ kg?

$1\frac{1}{2}$ kg $\div$ $\frac{1}{2}$ kg $= 3$, so the timing is $(3 \times 30 \text{ min}) + 25 \text{ min}$

$\qquad\qquad\qquad\qquad\qquad\quad = 115 \text{ min} = 1 \text{ h } 55 \text{ min.}$

EXERCISE 9.11

Find the cooking time for the following:

1 $1\frac{1}{2}$ kg of boned beef   **2** 2 kg of pork   **3** $2\frac{1}{2}$ kg of beef

4 A turkey of weight 3 kg   **5** A duck of weight 2 kg   **6** $1\frac{1}{2}$ kg of mutton

7 A chicken of weight $1\frac{1}{2}$ kg   **8** A turkey of weight $4\frac{1}{2}$ kg   **9** $2\frac{1}{2}$ kg of ham

10 A joint of lamb of weight 2 kg

11 Julie has a joint of beef of weight 2 kg, and wants it cooked by 4.30 p.m. At what time should she put it in the oven?

12 Bill will arrive home at 5.30 p.m., and would like his 1 kg of lamb cooked by then. At what time should he set his 24-hour cooker timer to switch (*a*) on and (*b*) off?

13 Shaima would like her chicken, of weight $1\frac{3}{4}$ kg, cooked half an hour before the meal she has planned to start at 7.15 p.m. At what time should she put the chicken in the oven?

14 Alan is cooking a Christmas turkey of weight 5 kg. The family would like Christmas dinner at 2.15 p.m., and he needs to allow quarter of an hour to set out the meal after the turkey is cooked. At what time should he put it in the oven?

15 Ann is cooking for a party. She needs to prepare a ham joint first, of weight $1\frac{1}{2}$ g, followed by a joint of beef of weight 2 kg, to be ready for 8 p.m. At what time should she (*a*) put the ham in the oven (*b*) exchange the beef for the ham?

Keeping in shape

Ideal weight (women)				Ideal weight (men)			
Height ft in	Small frame st lb	Medium frame st lb	Large frame st lb	Height ft in	Small frame st lb	Medium frame st lb	Large frame st lb
4 11	7 10	8 1	8 10	5 2	8 9	9 3	9 9
5 0	7 13	8 3	8 13	5 3	8 11	9 6	9 13
5 1	8 2	8 7	9 2	5 4	9 1	9 9	10 3
5 2	8 5	8 10	9 5	5 5	9 4	9 13	10 7
5 3	8 7	8 13	9 8	5 6	9 8	10 2	10 11
5 4	8 11	9 2	9 11	5 7	9 12	10 6	11 1
5 5	8 13	9 5	10 2	5 8	10 1	10 11	11 5
5 6	9 3	9 9	10 6	5 9	10 5	11 0	11 8
5 7	9 6	9 13	10 9	5 10	10 9	11 4	11 10
5 8	9 9	10 3	10 12	5 11	11 0	11 9	12 4
5 9	9 12	10 7	11 3	6 0	11 4	11 12	12 9
5 10	10 3	10 12	11 7	6 1	11 8	12 4	13 2
5 11	10 6	11 2	11 11	6 2	12 1	12 9	13 7
				6 3	12 6	13 0	13 12

(12 in = 1 ft; 14 lb = 1 st)

'Ideal weight' is an indication of how height and shape might relate to
a person's weight. Such tables are not clinically accurate, but are used
by fitness clubs and enthusiasts to help people keep in shape.

EXERCISE 9.12

Find the ideal weight for these people:

1 A woman of height 5 ft 5 in and medium frame.

2 A man of height 5 ft 11 in and medium frame.

3 A man of height 5 ft 8 in and large frame.

4 A woman of height 5 ft 2 in and small frame.

5 A woman of height 5 ft 5 in and large frame.

6 A man of height 6 ft 2 in and medium frame.

7 A woman of height 5 ft 10 in and medium frame.

8 Jerry is 5 ft 10 in tall and has a medium frame, and weighs $11\frac{1}{2}$ st. How much weight does the table suggest he should try to lose?

9 Louise is 5 ft 7 in tall, is 11 st in weight with a large frame. How overweight does the table suggest she might be?

10 Susie is 5 ft 9 in tall with a medium frame, was 11 st in weight, but is now 10 st 10 lb. How much weight has she (*a*) already lost (*b*) yet to lose?

11 William has returned home after a period of illness in hospital. He is 5 ft 8 in tall, of normally large frame, and weighs $10\frac{1}{2}$ st. How much weight can he safely put back on?

12 Draw three graphs on the same axes to compare height and weight for each of the three frame sizes for women, and three similar graphs on another pair of axes for men.

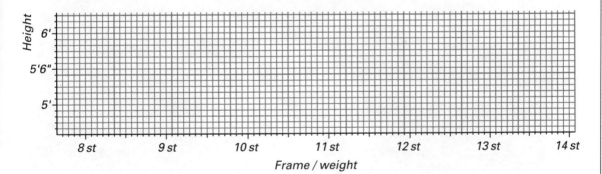

Star gazing

A hobby which gained in popularity with the return of Halley's comet in 1985 is star-gazing, or astronomy, and with it came a demand for more knowledge of our own solar system. The table lists some statistics of the principal planets in our solar system.

Planet	Average distance from the sun (millions of miles)	Diameter (miles)	Orbit time
Mercury	36	3032	88 days
Venus	67	7519	224.7 days
Earth	93	7926	365.25 days
Mars	142	4217	687 days
Jupiter	484	88700	11.9 yrs
Saturn	887	74600	29.5 yrs
Uranus	1784	32200	84 yrs
Neptune	2794	30800	164.8 yrs
Pluto	3674	3700	247.7 yrs

As astronomical distances can be so great it is inconvenient to write such large numbers. We use *standard form* as a shorter way to represent these numbers.

Example 12

Write in standard form (*a*) 35 million (*b*) 0.0012.
Also write (*c*) 4.28×10^5 as an ordinary number.

(*a*) 35 million = 35 000 000 = $3.5, \times 10^7$

(*b*) $0.0012 = 1.2 \times 10^{-3}$

(*c*) $4.28 \times 10^5 = 428\ 000$

EXERCISE 9.13

Write the following numbers in standard form:

1 400	**2** 23	**3** 4210	**4** 50 000	**5** 27 612
6 5 421 000	**7** 4 000 000	**8** 1 million	**9** 0.04	**10** 0.000 56
11 0.14	**12** 12	**13** 0.513	**14** 0.0421	**15** 1.34

Write the following as ordinary numbers:

16 5.2×10^3	**17** 4.9×10^5	**18** 2.39×10^2	**19** 7.96×10^7	**20** 5.542×10^4
21 1.243×10^3	**22** 9.87×10^{-1}	**23** 4.0×10^{-4}	**24** 7.83×10^{-3}	**25** 2.441×10^1

26 Write the distances of the nine planets from the sun in standard form. Remember that the table gives these distances in millions of miles.

Example 13

Calculate the time it would take Concorde to circumnavigate the earth at a speed of 1400 m.p.h.

Circumference $= \pi \times D = 3.14 \times 7926 = 24\ 890$ miles (to 4 sig.figs.).

$$\text{Time} = \frac{\text{distance}}{\text{velocity}} = \frac{24887.64}{1400} = 17.777 \text{ hours}$$

but $0.777 \times 60 = 50$ min (to the nearest 10 minutes), so time is 17 h 50 min.

Example 14

How long does light take to travel from the sun to the earth at a speed of 186 000 miles per second?

$$\text{Time} = \frac{\text{distance}}{\text{velocity}} = \frac{93\ 000\ \cancel{000}}{186\ \cancel{000}} = \frac{93\ 000}{186} = 500 \text{ s} = 8 \text{ min } 20 \text{ s.}$$

EXERCISE 9.14

1 Calculate the times it would take Concorde to circumnavigate each of the other planets in the solar system, to the nearest 10 minutes.

2 Find the times it takes for light from the sun to reach the other planets of the solar system.

3 The formula to find the volume of a spherical planet is

$$\text{volume} = \frac{4 \times \pi \times (\text{radius})^3}{3}$$

Calculate the volume of each planet in cubic miles, writing your answer in standard form to three decimal places.

4 Which planet comes nearest to the earth, and how far away is it at its closest approach?

5 Which planet is of a similar size to the earth?

6 Find how long it would take a radio message to travel at the speed of light from a spacecraft near each of the following planets back to earth: (*a*) mars (*b*) venus (*c*) jupiter (*d*) saturn (*e*) uranus (*f*) neptune. (Assume in each case that the planet is at its nearest approach to the earth.)

7 How far will light travel in a year (365 days)?

8 The star Alpha Centaurus is 4.3 light years away. How far is this in miles? (A light year is the time it takes light to travel in one year.)

9 How long will it take a radio message to travel at the speed of light to the moon, 250 000 miles away, and back to earth?

10 A star is 800 light years away. How far is this in miles?

Mathematical puzzles

Professional mathematicians define a sequence by giving a formula for the general term, and some rule by which the terms of the sequence can be calculated. Such mathematical puzzles are a popular pastime. Some of the simplest are number sequences.

Example 15

Find what you think are the next three terms in this series of numbers: 1, 4, 11, 22, 37, . . ., . . ., ...

Each number is different from the next: $1_{+3} = 4_{+7} = 11_{+11} = 22_{+15} = 37$

So the difference between each of the given terms forms another sequence increasing by 4. We therefore expect the next three terms to be 56, 79, 106.

EXERCISE 9.15

Find the next three terms of these sequences:

1 1, 6, 12, 19, 27, . . .

2 5, 7, 11, 19, . . .

3 2, 6, 12, 20, . . .

4 1, 7, 19, 37, 61, . . .

5 0, 9, 16, 21, 24, 25, 24, . . .

6 1, 2, 6, 24, . . .

7 2, 6, 18, 54, . . .

8 1, 5, 14, 30, 55, . . .

9 A group of part-time football teams meet to play a knock-out tournament.
How many games will have to be played if there are
(*a*) 20 teams (*b*) 28 teams (*c*) 40 teams?

10 Six coins are arranged in a row as shown. What is the minimum number of moves needed to rearrange the coins with the 5p coins and 10p coins together, if the only move you can make is to swap adjacent coins?

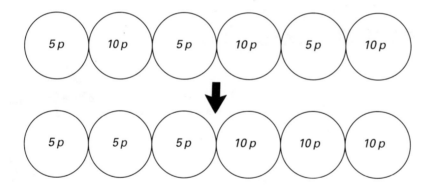

11 Martin begins working on Monday 1st for five consecutive nights as a computer operator, followed by three nights off in rotation. Martha works four nights during the week as a nurse, plus one night at the weekend, but she can request her nights off, in order to spend as much time as possible with Martin. Write out her off-duty requests for the first four weeks.

12 Crack the code if the letters A–Z are represented by the numbers 1–26.

   13131391212114131208192151519

13 A number of 2p and 5p coins add up to 43p. How many 2p and 5p coins are there? Give all the possible answers.

14 How many direct routes can you take from A to B in each of these diagrams?

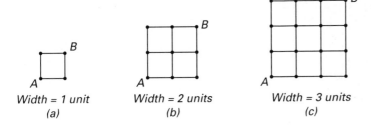

Width = 1 unit   Width = 2 units   Width = 3 units
     (a)   (b)   (c)

15 A series of columns has been built using matchsticks.

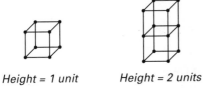

Height = 1 unit   Height = 2 units

How many matchsticks go to make columns of these heights: (*a*) 1 unit (*b*) 2 units (*c*) 3 units (*d*) 5 units (*e*) 15 units (*f*) 20 units?

EXERCISE 9.16

The square template on this square of numbers is called a
'template based on 13', since the first and lowest number over
which it is positioned is a 13.

1	2	3	4	5	6	7	8	9	10
11	12	13	14	15	16	17	18	19	20
21	22	23	24	25	26	27	28	29	30
31	32	33	34	35	36	37	38	39	40
41	42	43	44	45	46	47	48	49	50
51	52	53	54	55	56	57	58	59	60
61	62	63	64	65	66	67	68	69	70
71	72	73	74	75	76	77	78	79	80
81	82	83	84	85	86	87	88	89	90
91	92	93	94	95	96	97	98	99	100

1   (*a*) What is the total of the numbers in a template based on
(i) 16 (ii) 65 (iii) 84 (iv) 37?

(*b*) Using terms from algebra, draw a template and its
contents if the template is based on the number x.

(*c*) Write down and simplify the total of the terms used in
part (*b*).

(*d*) Can you find the number on which a template of total
85 is based? Give an explanation with your answer.

2 Repeat question 1 with a template of shape:

3 Repeat question 1 with a template of shape:

4 Repeat question 1 with a template of shape:

5 Repeat question 1 with a template of shape:

EXERCISE **9.17**

Number sequences can be generated by the use of flow charts.
Work through the following flow charts, answering the
questions for each one.

1 What does the flow chart do?

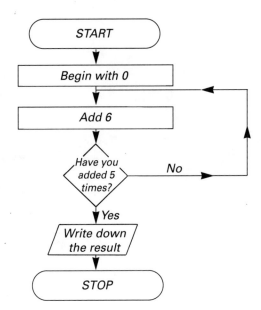

2 (*a*) How many times was 6 taken away?

(*b*) What does the flow chart do?

(*c*) What would happen if we tried to divide 57 by 8 on the flow chart?

(*d*) What could you put in the question box so that we could divide 57 by 8?

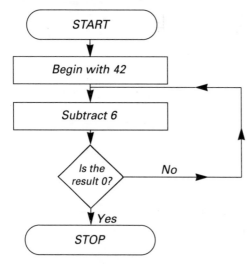

3 Write down the results of working through this flow chart.

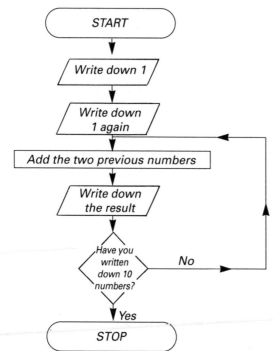

4 Work through the flow chart and write down the results.

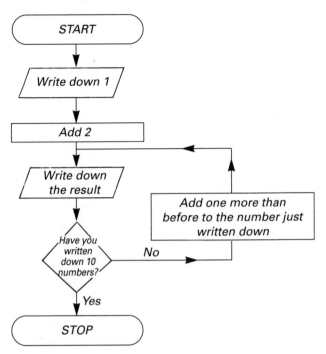

5 Work through the flow chart and write down the results.

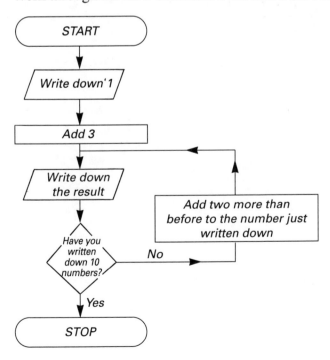

6 Work through the flow chart using the numbers 164, 167, 161, 165, 163.

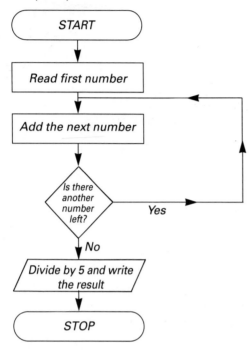

(*a*) What is the result? (*b*) What does the flow chart do?

10. Household planning

Do-It-Yourself (DIY) used to be considered as merely a hobby. Nowadays, for many, it is more than a pastime. In order to save money, many people have decided to do their own house repairs. DIY superstores have increased in number, and now sell many products designed to make it easy for the unskilled to do tasks around the house.

There are some important things to remember when doing work in your own house:

Safety is most important. Read all instructions carefully when using tools or products; some tasks should be left to the experts.
Planning. Decide the order in which the operations of a job should be done. Make sure you have all the tools and materials needed to complete it before you start. Be sure you understand what needs to be done.
Budgeting. Be aware of the pitfalls of buying cheap products which may be lacking in quality. Shop around for the materials needed to find the best price. If the job is not a necessary repair, ask yourself if you can afford to do it.

If all the necessary planning has been done before a job is started, you will understand exactly what needs to be done, and will find it easier to finish the work once it is started. This applies to all tasks in the home, whether it is gardening, decorating, fitting furniture or building an extension!

Remi and Louise are both keen on DIY. They not only do all the jobs on their own house, but help other people with work in their homes also. In the last year they worked on twelve different rooms, for each of which they started with a plan:

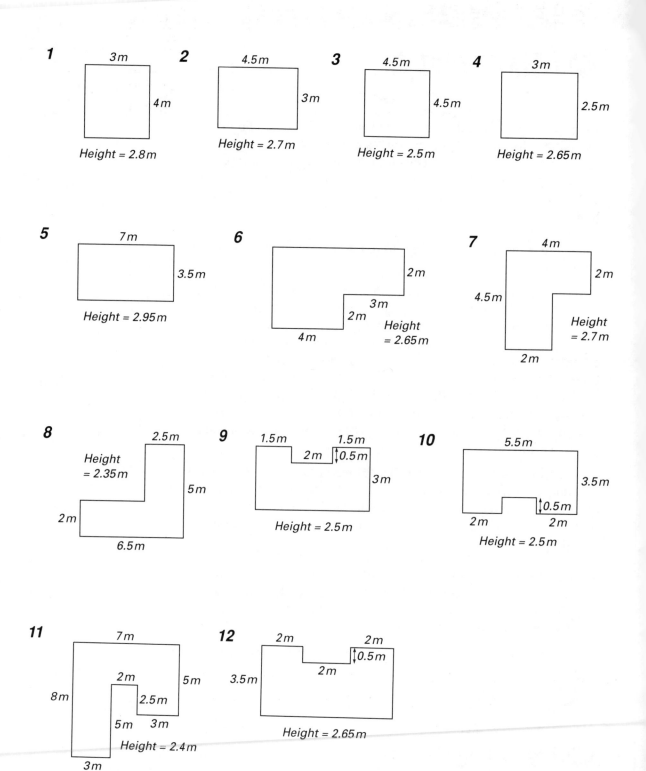

240

1

3m

4m

Height = 2.8m

2

4.5m

3m

Height = 2.7m

3

4.5m

4.5m

Height = 2.5m

4

3m

2.5m

Height = 2.65m

5

7m

3.5m

Height = 2.95m

6

2m

3m

2m

4m

Height = 2.65m

7

4m

2m

4.5m

2m

Height = 2.7m

8

2.5m

Height = 2.35m

5m

2m

6.5m

9

1.5m   1.5m

2m   0.5m

3m

Height = 2.5m

10

5.5m

3.5m

0.5m

2m   2m

Height = 2.5m

11

7m

2m

5m

8m

2.5m

5m   3m

3m

Height = 2.4m

12

2m   2m

0.5m

2m

3.5m

Height = 2.65m

Decorating

Rollage Calculation Chart

WALLS Height from skirting feet	metres	feet 30 / metres 9.1	34 / 10.4	38 / 11.6	42 / 12.8	46 / 14.0	50 / 15.2	54 / 16.5	58 / 17.7	62 / 18.9	66 / 20.1	70 / 21.3	74 / 22.6	78 / 23.9
7-7½	2.15-2.30													
7½-8	2.30-2.45	4	5	5	6	6	7	7	8	8	9	9	10	10
8-8½	2.45-2.60	5	5	6	6	7	7	8	8	9	9	10	10	11
8½-9	2.60-2.75	5	5	6	7	7	8	9	9	10	10	11	12	12
9-9½	2.75-2.90	5	5	6	7	7	8	9	9	10	10	11	12	12
9½-10½	2.90-3.05	6	6	7	7	8	9	9	10	10	11	12	12	13
10-10½	3.05-3.20	6	6	7	8	8	9	10	10	11	12	12	13	14
		6	7	8	8	9	10	10	11	12	12	13	14	15
CEILINGS		2	2	2	3	3	4	4	4	5	5	6	7	7

Measurement round walls, including doors and windows

Number of rolls required

Example 1

For this room plan find (*a*) the number of rolls of wallpaper needed for the walls (*b*) the total cost, if the price of each roll is £6.99.

Perimeter = 5 + 2 + 3 + 4 + 2 + 6 = 22 m.
The nearest perimeter *above* 22 m in the table is 22.6 m. For a height between 2.30 m and 2.45 m and perimeter 22.6 m the table indicates that 10 rolls are needed. Cost of 10 rolls = 10 × £6.99 = £69.90.

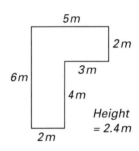

EXERCISE 10.1

For each of the twelve rooms worked on by Remi and Louise, calculate (*a*) the number of rolls of wallpaper (*b*) the cost according to the following details, showing what is to be papered, and the price of the wallpaper in each case:

1 Walls only at £6.99 per roll

2 Walls only at £7.99 per roll

3 Walls only at £3.49 per roll

4 Walls and ceiling at £3.99 per roll

5 Walls and ceiling at £4.99 per roll

6 Walls only at £5.99 per roll

7 Walls and ceiling at £2.79 per roll

8 Walls and ceiling at £4.59 per roll

9 Walls only at £3.86 per roll

10 Walls only at £7.42 per roll

11 Walls and ceiling at £6.19 per roll

12 Walls and ceiling at £5.49 per roll

Areas of walls and ceilings

The area of a wall is easily found as it is normally a rectangle.

Area = 5 m × 2.5 m = 12.5 m²

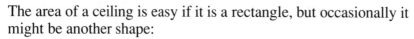

The area of a ceiling is easy if it is a rectangle, but occasionally it might be another shape:

Area of large rectangle = 5 m × 4 m = 20 m²
Area of small rectangle = 2 m × 0.5 m = 1 m²
Area of ceiling = 20 m² − 1 m² = 19 m²

Area of rectangle A = 4 m × 2 m = 8 m²
Area of rectangle B = 3 m × 2 m = 6 m²
Total area of ceiling = 14 m²

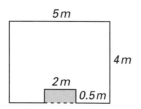
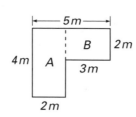

EXERCISE 10.2

Find the areas of these ceilings:

1
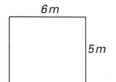

2
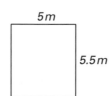

3
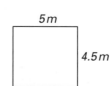

4
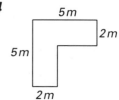

5
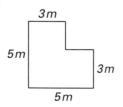

6
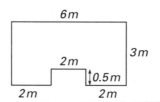

7
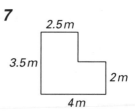

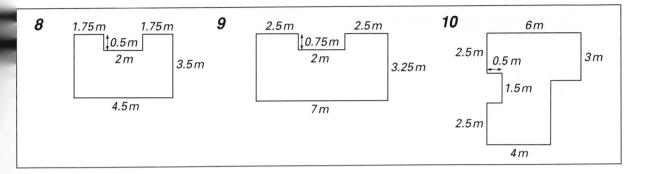

Painting

It is rather difficult to calculate the amount of gloss paint needed for window frames, skirting boards, doors, etc., and we have to rely on our own estimates. However, when using emulsion paint on walls and ceilings, the areas we need to paint are much bigger and easier to work out. The table below indicates the coverage expected per tin of emulsion paint:

Emulsion paint coverage	
Capacity of tin	Expected coverage
3 litres	40 m²
6 litres	78 m²
10 litres	130 m²

Example 2

The walls of this room need painting. The windows and doors take up an estimated 20% of the area of the walls. Calculate the number of tins needed.

The walls of the room can be 'opened out' like a net to help us find the area:

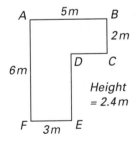

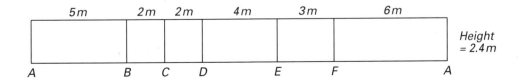

Total area of the walls = $(5 + 2 + 2 + 4 + 3 + 6) \times 2.4$
$$= 22 \text{ m} \times 2.4 \text{ m} = 52.8 \text{ m}^2.$$

20% of this area we do not need to paint: $\frac{20}{100} \times 52.8 \text{ m}^2 = 10.56 \text{ m}^2.$

Area we need to paint = $52.8 \text{ m}^2 - 10.56 \text{ m}^2 = 42.24 \text{ m}^2.$

As a 3-litre tin would only cover 40 m², we need one 6-litre tin.

Investigation A

Can you find an easier way of working out the total surface area of
the walls of a room? It might have something to do with the work we
did in Exercise 10.1.

EXERCISE 10.3

Using the room plans prepared by Remi and Louise, and the
emulsion paint coverage table, calculate what size tins of paint
are needed for each room plan, given the following deductions
for windows and doors:

1 5 m²   **2** 4.5 m²   **3** 10%   **4** 15%   **5** 10%   **6** 4 m²

7 10%   **8** 15%   **9** 5 m²   **10** 10%   **11** 5%   **12** 10%

Floor coverings

When buying carpets and other floor coverings, we buy them from a
roll of a certain width. The standard width for carpets is 4 m. The
price is calculated on the *area* of carpet you buy, for example, £8.50
per m².

Example 3

We need a 4 m length of this carpet. Find how much this will cost.

Area = $4 \text{ m} \times 4 \text{ m} = 16 \text{ m}^2$, cost = $16 \times £8.50 = £136.00.$

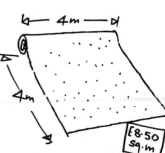

EXERCISE **10.4**

Each of these carpets has a width of 4 m. Calculate the cost of
the length required:

1 4 m at £4.99 per m^2 **2** 8 m at £6.59 per m^2 **3** 7 m at £7.99 per m^2

4 5 m at £5.32 per m^2 **5** 7 m at £10.99 per m^2 **6** 6 m at £14.20 per m^2

7 8 m at £5.99 per m^2 **8** 9 m at £15.30 per m^2 **9** 7 m at £13.99 per m^2

10 9 m at £11.50 per m^2

"COLOROLL" MODERN TONAL

The latest addition to our "Coloroll" collection – five year wear guarantee

8^{95} FITTED FREE

'AVANT GARDE' COLLECTION

Exceptionally hardwearing – choice of modern tonal and graphic designs

9^{95} FITTED FREE

80/20 QUALITY AXMINSTER

80% Wool 20%Nylon woven quality – beautiful designs.

15^{95} FITTED FREE

LIVING ROOM DESIGNS

Economical range of leaf and chintz designs – built-in foam underlay

2^{95}

NEW AXMINSTER DESIGNS

Choose from a range of superb new designs – seven year wear guarantee

6^{95} FITTED FREE

"RUSTIC CHARMS" BERBER

Hardwearing fine loop pile – selection of beautifully natural country tones

7^{95} FITTED FREE

SCULPTURED ELEGANCE

Sumptuous, carved stain resistant pile – seven year wear guarantee

11 **45** FITTED FREE

FINE QUALITY VELOUR

Soft, smooth velvet pile for anywhere in your home – super plain shades

4^{95}

---

11 8 m of the New Axminster   **12** 6 m of the 'Rustic Charms'

13 7 m of the Quality Axminster   **14** 7 m of the economical Living Room

15 9 m of the 'Coloroll'   **16** 8 m of the 'Avante Garde'

Investigation D

When you buy carpets through home shopping catalogues, the price is given per metre length rather than per square metre. What would be the equivalent cost in m² of a carpet advertised at 4 m wide and £24 per 1 m length?

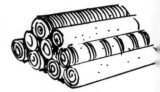

Unfortunately rooms are not made to fit carpet sizes, and we have to decide how to lay the carpet. Careful planning can sometimes make a difference to the cost. We try to reduce the amount of carpet left over, for which we have to pay even though it is not needed.

Example 4

Find the minimum cost to carpet this room when the carpet chosen has a price of £7.99 per m².

There are two ways of laying the carpet:

Method 1
The total length of carpet needed is 6 m + 3 m = 9 m

The cost of the carpet is therefore $\underset{\text{area}}{9 \text{ m} \times 4 \text{ m}} \times \underset{\text{price}}{£7.99} = £287.64$

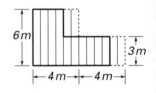

Method 2
The total length of carpet needed is

   3 m + 7.5 m = 10.5 m ≈ 11 m (if we need to buy whole metre lengths of carpet).

The cost of the carpet is therefore $\underset{\text{area}}{11 \text{ m} \times 4 \text{ m}} \times \underset{\text{price}}{£7.99} = £351.56$

The first method is the cheapest, at a cost of £287.64.

It might not be necessary for us to work out two methods for each room plan, as sometimes it is obvious which is the best method. Remember total lengths of carpets which include a fraction of a metre should be rounded up before pricing.

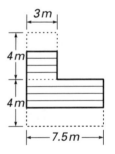

EXERCISE 10.5

Calculate the minimum cost for Remi and Louise to carpet the rooms represented by their plans. The prices of the 4 m wide carpets chosen are as follows:

1   £5.99 per m²   *2* £7.50 per m²   *3* £10.20 per m²   *4* £9.99 per m²

5   £13.90 per m²   *6* £4.99 per m²   *7* £8.23 per m²   *8* £7.49 per m²

9   £14.50 per m²   *10* £10.90 per m²   *11* £15.05 per m²   *12* £19.99 per m²

Investigation C

Remi and Louise find that some firms fit the carpets free of charge. 'Discount Carpets' offer free fitting for all carpets costing more than £10 per m². 'Total Warehouses' will fit the carpets free of charge if the cost of the carpet exceeds £100. Copy the axes and shade in the region on the graph for which free fitting would be offered by (*a*) Discount Carpets (*b*) Total Warehouses.

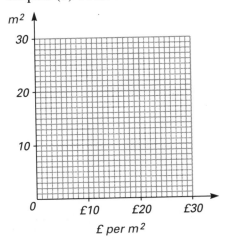

Vinyl flooring

An alternative to laying carpets is to lay vinyl flooring. Easier to clean and considerably cheaper than carpet, this can be bought from rolls of varying widths, and can also be bought using the imperial measurement of feet.

Example 5

Calculate the cost of vinyl flooring for this room:
One sheet of vinyl of width 3 m and length 6 m:
$6 \times 3.28 = 19.68$ ft ≈ 20 ft.
One sheet of vinyl of width 2 m and length 2m:
$2 \times 3.28 = 6.56$ ft ≈ 7 ft.
Cost = $(20 \times £5.25) + (7 \times £3.50) = £105.00 + £24.50 = £129.50.$

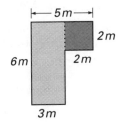

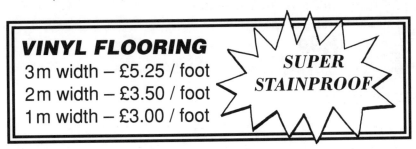

VINYL FLOORING
3 m width – £5.25 / foot
2 m width – £3.50 / foot
1 m width – £3.00 / foot

SUPER STAINPROOF

EXENOISE 10.6

Using the table in Example 5, calculate the minimum cost of laying vinyl flooring in each of Remi and Louise's twelve room plans. If at all possible the vinyl should be laid in a single sheet with no joins.

Tiles

Tiles come in all shapes and sizes, in different patterns, and in different quantities. Tiles can be cut into smaller pieces, which can then be used on the wall.

Example 6

How many Geometric red 20 cm × 20 cm tiles would be needed for this wall?

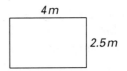

Area of wall = 2.5 m × 4 m = 250 cm × 400 cm = 100 000 cm²
Area of a tile = 20 cm × 20 cm = 400 cm²
Number of tiles needed = 100 000 cm² ÷ 400 cm² = 250 tiles.
The tiles are sold in boxes of 12.
250 ÷ 12 = 20.8 ≈ 21 boxes at £14.95 = £313.95
Some tiles will need to be cut in half.

EXERCISE 10.7

Calculate the cost of tiling the walls:

1 Plain Travertino 20 cm × 30 cm.

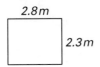

2 White gloss 15 cm × 15 cm wall tiles.

3 Marino blue 20 cm × 7 cm wall tiles.

4 White gloss 15 cm × 15 cm wall tiles.

5 Amapola white plain 15 cm × 25 cm wall tiles.

6 15 cm × 15 cm co-ordinated tiles.

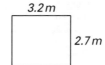

7 15 cm × 15 cm Waldorf range tiles.

8 15 cm × 15 cm Mexican sand tiles.

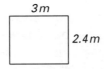

EXERCISE 10.8

Find the cost of tiling the walls in Example 6 with the pattern indicated.

1 20 cm × 20 cm plain white gloss with 20 cm × 20 cm geometric black.

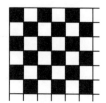

2 15 cm × 15 cm plain kitchen harmony with 15 cm × 15 cm patterns.

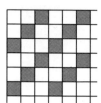

3 15 cm × 15 cm white gloss with 15 cm × 15 cm grey borders.

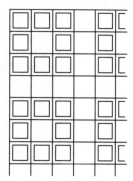

4 15 cm × 25 cm plain wall tiles with 15 cm × 25 cm flower set tiles.

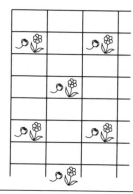

Investigation D

A regular tessellation is made by repeating the same shape to make a continuous pattern. Tiles can be bought of various shapes to produce tessellations. Produce your own tessellations. You might like to consider which of the common polygons tessellate.

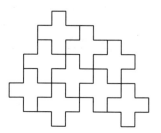

Investigation E

It may be possible to mix rectangular tiles of two or more different sizes. Can you produce some patterns from the tile sizes you have used in Exercise 10.7?

Gardening

Just as with indoor DIY, gardens involve planning, particularly where growing plants are concerned. Planting is a critical stage in the growth of any plant, and the guidance given about spacing should be followed.

Outdoor vegetables

Vegetable	Sow	Plant	Spacing (cm) between plants	Spacing (cm) between rows	Harvest
Beetroot	Apr.–Jun.		10	30	Aug.–Oct.
Carrot	Mar.–Jun.		8	30	Jul.–Oct.
Cauliflower	Apr.–May		50	50	Aug.–Dec.
Leek		Apr.–Jun.	15	35	Sep.–Mar.
Lettuce	Mar.–Jun.	Apr.–Jul.	23	30	May–Oct.
Marrow		May–Jun.	60	75	Aug.–Sep.
Onion		Mar.–Apr.	10	30	Jul.–Sep.
Potato		Apr.	30	60	Jul.–Aug.
Radish	Mar.–Sep.		13	25	Apr.–Oct.
Runner bean	May	Jun.	30	40	Aug.–Oct.
Spinach	Feb.–May		23	30	May–Nov.
Spring cabbage	Jul.–Aug.	Mar.–May	30	45	Mar.–May
Sprout	Mar.–Apr.	May–Jun.	75	75	Sep.–Mar.
Summer cabbage	Mar.–Apr.	Apr.–May	45	50	Jun.–Sep.

Example 7

Linda has a plot of garden land 3 m × 2 m surrounded by a brick wall.
How many lettuces can she plant?

3 m = 300 cm, 2 m = 200 cm

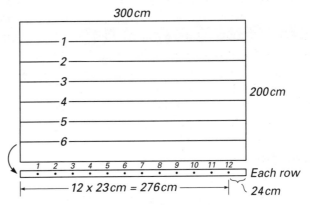

The chart indicates lettuce need 23 cm between each plant and 30 cm between each row, which can be organised as in the diagram. With only 24 cm at the end of each row there is not enough room for another plant, as this would mean that it would be planted 1 cm away from the wall. So the total number of plants is:

6 rows × 12 plants = 72 plants.

Investigation F

Using the information given in Example 7, how much space needs to be left around *each* plant? Why in the table do you think the spacing between each row is always greater than the spacing between each plant?

EXERCISE 10.9

Calculate the number of plants needed for planting in the following plots of land:

1 3 m × 2 m to grow cauliflower   **2** 3 m × 2 m to grow radish

3 3 m × 2 m to grow carrots   **4** 4 m × 2 m to grow marrows

5 3.5 m × 2 m to grow runner beans   **6** 2.5 m × 2 m to grow sprouts

7 3 m × 2.5 m to grow spinach   **8** 3.5 m × 1 m to grow lettuce

9 2 m × 1 m to be equally divided between beetroot and leeks

10 2.5 m × 1 m to be equally divided between potatoes and carrots.

Garden fencing

The lengths of a fence around either lawns or flower beds may need to be estimated. For rectangular lawns or flower beds we need to calculate the perimeter, while for circular plots the circumference is calculated by using the formula C = π × diameter.

Example 8

A trellis fence costs £13.99 for 4 m. How much will it cost for fencing to go around (*a*) a rectangular lawn 10 m × 6 m (*b*) a circular flower bed of radius 1.5 m?

(*a*) Perimeter = 10 + 6 + 10 + 6 = 32 m.
    32 ÷ 4 = 8 sections of fencing at £13.99 = £13.99 × 8 = £111.92

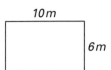

10m

6m

(*b*) Radius = 1.5 m, so the diameter is 1.5 m × 2 = 3 m.
    Circumference = π × 3 = 9.42 m.
    So 3 sections of fencing are needed at £13.99 each = £41.97.

1.5m

EXERCISE 10.10

Find the cost of fencing in each case:

1 A redwood trellis fence for a 10 m × 8 m lawn at £10.99 for
    2 m.

2 A PVC border fence for a circular flower bed of diameter
    4 m costing £13.50 for 10 m.

3 A chain-link fence costing £26.50 per 10 m for a lawn of
    dimensions 8 m × 5 m.

4 A fence costing £21.00 for 10 m for a lawn of dimensions
    7 m × 4.5 m.

5 A fence costing £9.99 per 5 m for a circular flower bed of
    radius 1.2 m.

6 Wire netting costing £16.99 per 16 m for a lawn of
    dimensions 8 m × 4.5 m.

7 A trellis fence costing £12.99 for 4 m for a circular flower
    bed of diameter 1.2 m.

8 Wire netting costing £20.99 per 16 m for the lawn:

9 PVC fencing at £16.99 for 3 m:

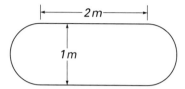

10 Border fencing at £23.99 for 10 m:

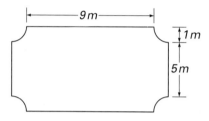

Lawns

To keep a lawn in good condition it needs fertilizer and possibly lawn seed for patches which sometimes appear during the summer months. Both lawn seed and fertilizer are bought according to the area of lawn to be covered.

The area of a rectangular lawn is length × breadth.

The area of a circular lawn is $\pi \times (\text{radius})^2$.

Example 9

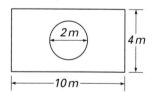

The lawn has a flower bed in the middle. Calculate the amount of lawn seed and fertilizer needed for the lawn if the recommended coverage is

lawn seed: 1 kg bag for 20 m²; fertilizer: 10 litres for 15 m²

Area of grass = area of rectangle – area of flower bed
$$= 10 \text{ m} \times 4 \text{ m} - \pi \times 1 \text{ m} \times 1 \text{ m}$$
$$= 40 \text{ m}^2 - 3.142 \text{ m}^2 = 36.86 \text{ m}^2$$

So we need two 1 kg bags of lawn seed and 30 litres of fertilizer.

EXERCISE 10.11

For each of the lawns, find the quantity of (*a*) lawn seed
(*b*) fertilizer needed, given a recommended coverage of 1 kg
bag of lawn seed for 20 m² and 10 litres of fertilizer for 15 m².

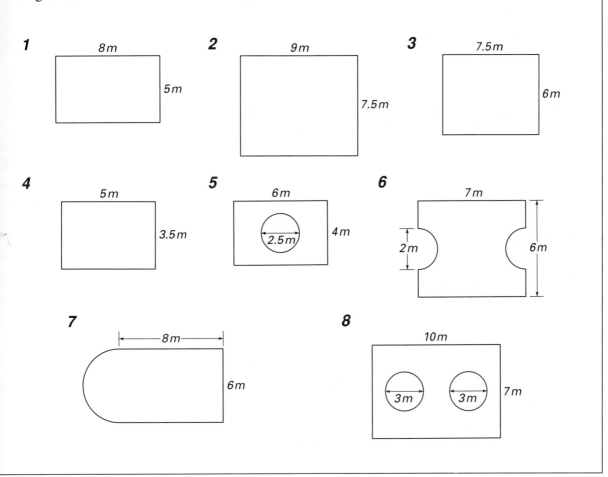

Investigation G

There are different sizes of lawn mowers, usually 12", 14", 15", 16" or 18" in width. Calculate the total length you would have to walk, in feet, with each size of mower for the lawn shown (12" = 1 ft).

Can you describe a method to help find the total length for any size of (*a*) lawnmower (*b*) lawn?

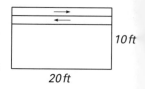

10 ft

20 ft

Investigation H

Extend Investigation G to consider circular lawns of different radii.

Geometrical drawings

When planning work in the home or in the garden it is useful to be able to draw an accurate diagram to help in planning the operation. Production of these drawings is made easier by using basic geometry.

A full circle is 360°

A half circle (semicircle)
is 180°

Angles in a triangle
add up to 180°

Angles in a quadrilateral
add up to 360°

Computer work

Much of this work in drawing diagrams can also be done on computer. You might like to use the MOVE & DRAW instructions on some computers, or LOGO, to help you construct some of these diagrams on the computer screen.

EXERCISE **10.12**

Find the missing angles indicated by letters in each diagram:

1

125°
x

2

x 34°

3

132°
x

4

135°
a
b

5

c
d
75°

6

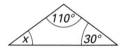

110°
x 30°

7

70° 50°
x

8

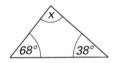

x
68° 38°

9

x
45°
76°

10

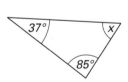

37° x
85°

11

110° 88°
92° x

12

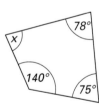

78°
x
140° 75°

13

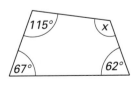

115° x
67° 62°

14

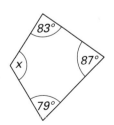

83°
x 87°
79°

15

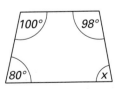

100° 98°
80° x

Special triangles

The **isosceles** triangle has two sides of equal length; the two angles opposite these two sides are also equal.

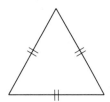

The **equilateral** triangle has all three sides equal, and hence all three angles are also equal, and each must be 60°.

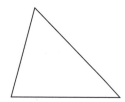

An **acute angled** triangle has all its angles less than 90°.

An **obtuse angled** triangle has one angle greater than 90°.

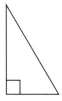

A **right angled** triangle has one angle equal to 90°.

EXERCISE **10.13**

For each diagram (a) find the missing angle marked with a
letter (b) name the type of triangle.

1

2

3

4

5

6

7

8
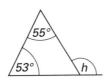

9

10
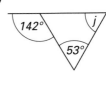

11
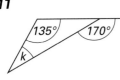

12
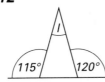

13
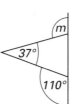

14
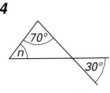

15
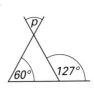

16

17

18

19
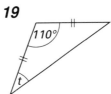

20
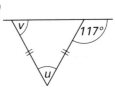

Parallel lines

Alternate angles are equal.

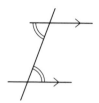

Corresponding angles are equal.

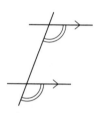

EXERCISE 10.14

Find the missing angles indicated by letters in each diagram.

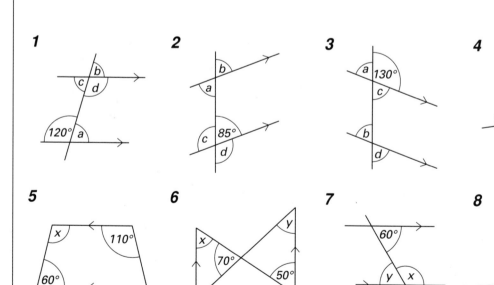

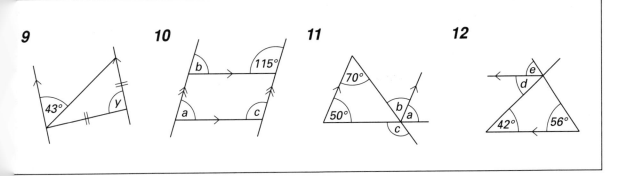

9 10 11 12

Accurate drawings

In producing accurate drawings you will need protractor, ruler and a pair of compasses.

EXERCISE 10.15

Draw the following diagrams accurately.

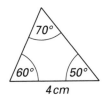

1

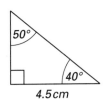

2

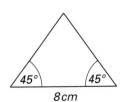

3

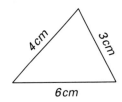

4

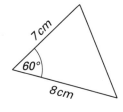

5

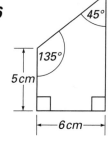

6

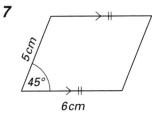

7

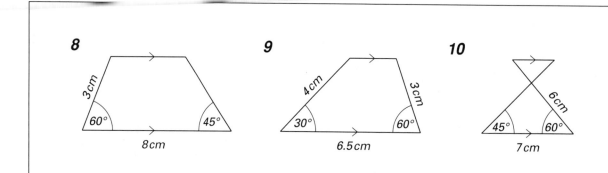

8

9

10

Constructions

A construction is a method of drawing an accurate diagram without the aid of a protractor. Some simple constructions follow.

To draw a 60° angle, construct an equilateral triangle.

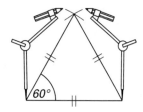

To draw a 30° angle, bisect a previously drawn 60° angle.

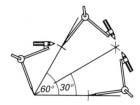

To draw a 90° angle, construct a perpendicular line.

To draw a 45° angle, bisect the 90° angle.

To bisect a line, follow the diagram.

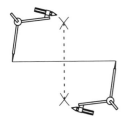

EXERCISE 10.16

Draw the diagrams in Exercise 10.15 accurately, using only a
ruler and compasses.

Scale diagrams

Scale diagrams can help us in solving problems and in planning.

Example 10
On a lawn of dimensions 30 m by 20 m, a goat is tethered in the centre
(the intersection of the diagonals) by a rope 8 m long. On a diagram
show the part of the lawn that the goat can eat.

Scale: 1 cm = 5 m. So 20 m = 4 cm, and 30 m = 6 cm.

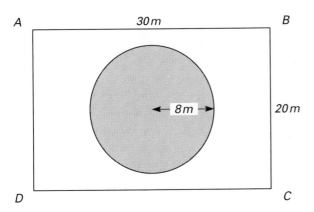

EXERCISE 10.17

Copy the outline of the 30 m × 20 m lawn from Example 10 for each question.

1 A goat is tethered in turn to each of the four corners of the lawn on a rope of length 5 m. Show what region of the lawn can be eaten by the goat.

2 A dog runs at not more than 5 metres from the fence AB. Shade the region in which the dog runs on the lawn.

3 A new path of width 1 metre is to be an equal distance from fences AB and BC. Draw the path on your plan of the lawn.

4 A garden sprinkler is positioned so as to be an equal distance from AB and DC. Indicate all possible positions for the sprinkler.

5 An apple tree 15 m from A and 15 m from D drops apples within 2.5 m of its trunk. Shade in the region in which apples are expected to fall.

Copy this room plan for each of the following questions.

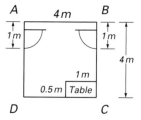

6 People passing directly though the room walk within a metre of wall AB. Indicate the area of most wear on the carpet.

7 A wall light half way between A and D illuminates a circle of radius 1.5 m. Show the area of brightness on your plan.

8 Crumbs are normally dropped within 0.5 m of the edge of the table. Shade in the part of the carpet where you would expect most crumbs.

9 A light in the centre of the ceiling illuminates a circle of radius 2 m. Show on the plan the area which is *not* illuminated.

10 A chair is put in the room so that it is the same distance from walls AD and DC. Indicate all possible positions for the chair.

Planning permission

If you need more living space, rather than move to a bigger house, many of you could consider building an extension to your house. If so, it is more than likely that Planning Permission will be needed from your local council under the Town and Country Planning Act. Planning permission is not needed if the extension does not increase the overall volume of the original house by whichever is the greater of these two methods:

	Semi-detached and detached	Terraced
Method 1	15% of the volume of the original house up to a maximum of 115 cubic metres	10% of the volume of the original house up to a maximum of 115 cubic metres.
Method 2	70 cubic metres	50 cubic metres

Note: if the house already has an extension and a further extension is to be built, then the volume upon which calculations are based is the original house *only*. Any new extension is counted together with the volume of the existing extension.

Example 11

Calculate the maximum volume permitted in an extension before planning permission is needed if the dimensions of a semi-detached house are 8 m × 6 m × 6 m.

Volume of house is $8 \times 6 \times 6 = 288$ m³.

Method 1: 15% of $288 = \dfrac{15}{100} \times 288 = 43.2$ m³.

Method 2: the volume is 70 m³.

From the two methods the greater volume is 70 m³, which is therefore the maximum volume permitted for an extension without planning permission.

EXERCISE **10.18**

Calculate the maximum permitted volume for an extension, if possible, before planning permission is needed for the following houses.

1   A semi-detached house of dimensions 7 m × 6 m × 6.5 m.

2   A terraced property of dimensions 10 m × 6 m × 7 m.

3   A terraced property of dimensions 9 m × 7 m × 10 m.

4   A detached property of dimensions 10 m × 12 m × 6.5 m.

5   A semi-detached property of dimensions 9 m × 7 m × 6 m.

6   A detached property of dimensions 8 m × 8 m × 6.5 m, which already has an extension measuring 4 m × 8 m × 2.5 m.

7   A terraced property of dimensions 8.5 m × 6.5 m × 9 m, which already has an extension of volume 60 m³.

8   A semi-detached property of dimensions 7 m × 6 m × 6 m, which already has an extension measuring 3 m × 4 m × 3 m.

9   A terraced property of dimensions 7 m × 4.5 m × 6 m, which already has an extension measuring 3 m × 2 m × 2.5 m.

10   A detached property of dimensions 15 m × 12 m × 6.5 m, which already has an extension measuring 6 m × 4 m × 6 m.

Kitchen planning

When planning to fit a kitchen, it is essential that the whole operation is planned before any work is done and units ordered. You need to ensure that:

(i)   certain appliances, such as washing machines, sink units, go on outside walls
(ii) sufficient space is left for other appliances, such as fridges, and for doors to open
(iii) wall units and base units are fitted so as to provide sufficient storage space, and for doors to be opened.

Kitchen designers usually draw their plans on graph paper using a suitable scale: 1000 mm = 1 m, so each small square on the graph paper represents 100 mm. Hence the cupboard shown is 500 mm deep and 600 mm wide, reproduced to scale.

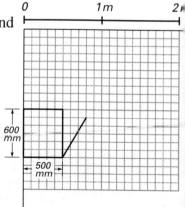

KITCHENS

Wickes kitchen range —

Full Door Base Units

	300mm	500mm	600mm	1000mm	1200mm	1100mm Corner using 500mm Door	1100mm Corner using 600mm Door
MG	30.40	31.40	32.40	39.95	43.95	49.50	50.50
C	37.80	38.80	41.30	54.75	61.75	56.90	59.40
SG	40.40	41.40	45.40	59.95	69.95	59.50	63.50
M	47.80	48.80	52.80	74.75	84.75	66.90	70.90
W	48.80	49.80	54.40	76.75	87.95	67.90	72.50
AP	50.40	51.40	56.40	79.95	91.95	69.50	74.50

Door & Drawer Base Units

	500mm	600mm	1000mm	1200mm	1100mm Corner using 500mm Door	1100mm Corner using 600mm Door
MG	40.90	42.30	58.95	63.75	59.00	60.40
C	51.70	54.80	80.55	88.75	69.80	72.90
SG	56.30	61.30	89.75	101.75	74.40	79.40
M	65.30	69.70	107.75	118.55	83.40	87.80
W	66.70	71.90	110.55	122.95	84.80	90.00
AP	68.30	73.90	113.75	126.95	86.40	92.00

720mm high Wall Units

	300mm	500mm	600mm	1000mm	1200mm	600mm Corner	600 × 350mm Hob Wall
MG	29.40	29.40	30.40	40.95	43.95	34.40	36.90
C	36.80	36.80	39.30	55.75	61.75	41.80	44.30
SG	39.40	39.40	43.40	60.95	69.95	44.40	46.90
M	46.80	46.80	50.80	75.75	84.75	51.80	54.30
W	47.80	47.80	52.40	77.75	87.95	52.80	55.30
AP	49.40	49.40	54.40	80.95	91.95	54.40	56.90

4 Drawer Unit / 3 Drawer Unit / 2 Drawer Unit

	4 Drawer 500mm	4 Drawer 600mm	3 Drawer Unit 600mm	2 Drawer Unit 600mm
MG	58.85	60.45	72.70	84.95
C	72.45	74.85	87.30	99.75
SG	80.45	84.45	94.70	104.95
M	86.85	88.45	104.10	119.75
W	88.45	90.85	106.30	121.75
AP	88.45	90.85	107.90	124.95

Larder Unit / Single Oven Unit / Double Oven Unit

	Larder 500mm	Larder 600mm	Single Oven Unit 600mm	Double Oven Unit 600mm
MG	93.65	96.65	90.65	113.10
C	115.85	123.35	111.45	127.90
SG	123.65	135.65	123.05	133.10
M	145.85	157.85	137.85	147.90
W	148.95	162.65	141.65	149.90
AP	153.65	168.65	145.65	153.10

720mm high Glass Wall Unit / Open End Wall Unit / Under Oven Base Unit

	Glass Wall 500mm	Glass Wall 1000mm	720mm high Open End Wall Unit	Under Oven Base Unit 600mm
MG	65.40	112.95	Honey 34.95	25.40
C	77.40	136.95		28.40
SG	82.40	146.95		31.80
M	83.40	148.95		31.80
W	85.40	152.95		32.40
AP				32.40

Accessories

Decorative End Panels Wall Unit from	5.59
Oven/Larder Unit	31.18
Pine Knobs pkt of 10	6.50
Westminster Door Handles pkt of 10	10.95
Drawer Handles pkt of 2	2.75

MG = Mica Grey SG = Slate Grey AP = Antique Pine
C = Country W = Westminster M = Maple

N.B.
Wall units are 720mm high.
Base units are 900mm high including 28mm worktop or 910mm high including white or maple 38mm worktop.
The Hob Wall unit is 350mm high and the Larder and Oven units are 2130mm high. All drawer base prices include appropriate drawer box.

All prices exclude handles

EXERCISE **10.19**

Using the details shown on p. 267, produce a scale diagram of a
kitchen design. Choose the units you want to use, which are all
500 mm deep. A 1000 mm full door base unit can be used to
house a sink. Choose the style you want for each kitchen, and
also produce a costing for each kitchen planned.

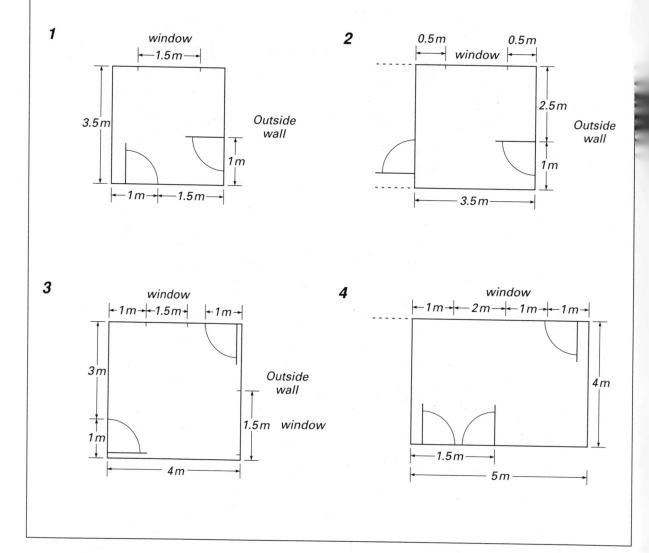

Investigation I

Measure your own kitchen, and from your local DIY superstore or
furniture centre obtain the details of the kitchen units for sale. Plan
your own kitchen and the necessary costing. Could you afford the
kitchen? How much would it cost you to take out a loan to cover the
cost?

Central heating

Heat output is measured in BTUs. When planning to install central heating radiators they should be of a size to give the correct output of heat to maintain the temperature in the room in the range 65°F to 70°F. Rooms that are constantly lived in (lounge, kitchen, hall, etc.) are usually kept at 70°F, while other rooms (bedrooms, bathroom) are kept at 65°F.

Example 12

A radiator of height 600 mm is needed for a bedroom of dimensions 17 ft × 10 ft on the first floor of a house. Which radiator should be used?

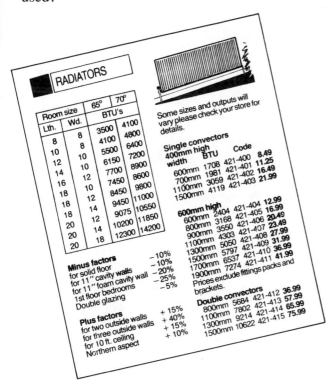

The next largest dimension in the table is 18 ft × 10 ft, which is 7450 BTUs for 65°F in the bedroom.

For a first floor bedroom we reduce the BTU requirement by 25%:

$$\frac{25}{100} \times 7450 = 1862.50,$$ so the BTU requirement is $7450 - 1862.50 = 5587.50$

The radiator which will provide this requirement is the 1500 mm for £31.99 (actually 5797 BTUs).

EXERCISE 10.20

Find (*a*) the BTU requirement (*b*) the size and the cost of the most suitable radiator for the following rooms. Assume all rooms have just one outside wall and preferably need a 600 mm high radiator, unless otherwise stated.

1 A 14 ft × 10 ft living room.

2 A 12 ft × 10 ft bedroom on the ground floor of a bungalow.

3 A kitchen of dimensions 10 ft × 8 ft with a solid floor and two outside walls.

4 An 18 ft × 14 ft living room with double glazing.

5 A 12 ft × 8 ft hall with a solid floor and a 10 ft ceiling.

6 An 8 ft × 8 ft bathroom with 11" cavity walls, and a northern aspect. There is only room for a 400 mm high radiator.

7 A 16 ft × 10 ft bedroom on the first floor with double glazing.

8 A 20 ft × 15 ft living room with double glazing and a northern aspect. Double convector radiators are required.

9 A dining room of dimensions 18 ft × 13 ft with two outside walls.

10 A kitchen of dimensions 12 ft × 11 ft, solid floor, three outside walls but 11" foam cavity walls.

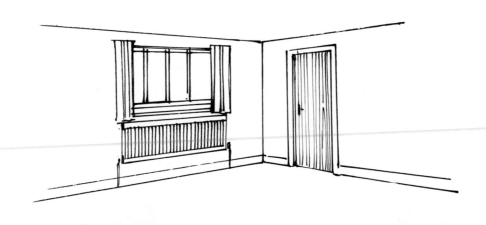

EXERCISE **10.21**

Calculate the total BTU requirement for fitting radiators to each room (excluding the garage and the landing) of this detached house:

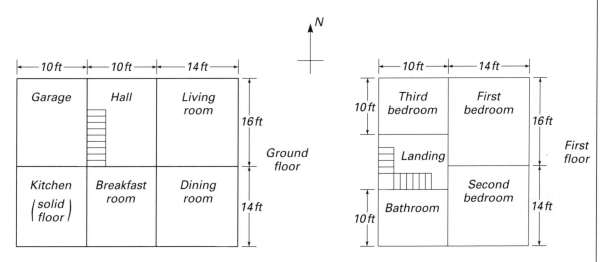

What total BTU output will be needed from the boiler to run the central heating system for the whole house?

Investigation J

Measure the dimensions of your own house, or part of your school. Calculate the total BTU requirement and the radiators needed. Alternatively, check that the radiators already in place are sufficient for the requirements of the rooms.

11. Household finance

A main expense of many households is paying for the house, either (i) by renting from a landlord or (ii) by buying, with a mortgage from a building society, insurance company or bank. Both of these expenses have been considered in Chapter 3.

Initially, in this chapter, we look at other essential demands on household finances in order that you can exist as comfortably as possible. These include heating, lighting, food and clothing, together with other items such as the community charge, often called the poll tax.

Gas

Gas is circulated around the country by means of pipes (sometimes called gas mains) under the ground which are connected to most houses. (There is a small number of areas which are still unconnected to the mains system.) When you use gas, for heating or cooking, a meter in your house counts the volume of gas used (typically in cubic feet). This volume is converted into **therms**, which is a measure of the heating power of the gas you have used. Once every three months a representative from the gas board calls to read the meter, after which you receive a bill for the gas used since the meter was last read. (Sometimes the gas board estimates how much gas you have used.)

Gerry Mason's typical gas bill will have figures like this:

Date of reading	Meter reading		Gas supplied		Charges
	present	previous	Cubic feet (100's)	Therms	
14 AUG	0858	0730	128	133.8	53.25
				Standing Charge	8.70
Tariff – 39.8p per therm				Total Amount Due	61.95

(Note that the meter readings are in 100's of cubic feet.)
You can check that:
(i)   (present reading) – (previous reading) = 0858 – 0730 = 128
(ii) Therms used × cost per therm = 133.8 × 39.8 = 5325.24p =
£53.25
(iii) £53.25 + £8.70 standing charge = £61.95
The conversion factor which changes cubic feet (100's) into therms
can be worked out from the figures given.
If c is the conversion factor, then $128 \times c = 133.8$

Hence $c = \dfrac{133.8}{128} = 1.045$ (to 3 decimal places).

So in order to change cubic feet (100's) into therms, multiply by
1.045.

Example 1

Gerry Mason's next meter reading, on 12th November, is 1034.
Assuming the same standing charge and conversion factor, copy and
complete the missing figures from his next gas bill.

Date of	Meter reading		Gas supplied		Charges
reading	present	previous	Cubic feet (100's)	Therms	
12 NOV	p	0858	d	q	r
				Standing Charge	s
Tariff – 39.8p per therm				Total Amount Due	t

p is 1034, so d is $1034 - 0858 = 176$.

q is therefore $1.045 \times d = 1.045 \times 176$
$\qquad\qquad = 183.92 = 184$ (to the nearest therm).

r is $q \times 39.8\text{p} = 184 \times 39.8$
$\qquad\qquad = 7323.2\text{p} = £73.23$ (to the nearest penny).

s is the same: £8.70.

Hence t is $r + s = £73.23 + £8.70 = £81.93$.

EXERCISE 11.1

1 Continuing with the example above, the next meter reading for Mr Mason, on 12th February, is 1297.
   Make out a bill, just like those in the examples, to work out how much he has to pay for gas during this quarter of the year.

2 During the next quarter, Mr Mason's bill was £108.20. Work out: (*a*) the actual charge for gas used (*b*) the number of therms used (*c*) the number of cubic feet (100's) used (*d*) the meter reading on 13th May.

3 Mr Mason's next-door neighbour, Colin Sands, had gas bills of £75.89, £98.35, £162.42 and £159.30 during last year.

   (*a*) How much was Mr Sand's total bill for gas during the year?

   (*b*) Mr Sands pays for his gas by twelve equal monthly payments of £40. Work out whether he paid more or less than he needed, and by how much.

4 A special offer on a new gas cooker costing £224.50, allows you to pay 10% deposit, followed by eight equal payments over the next two years, added on to your normal gas bill. How much will each payment be, correct to the nearest penny?

GAS BOARD

For quarter ending 13 Oct 88

Mr. D. Lal,
17, Smith Street,
Newtown

Date of reading	Meter reading		Gas supplied		Charges
	present	previous	Cubic feet (100's)	Therms	
			c	d	e
12 Oct	3182	2984			9.30
			STANDING CHARGE		
TARIFF — 39 8p per therm			TOTAL AMOUNT DUE		f

5 Last year Michelle Wells paid a total of £347.71 in gas bills. Gas prices will rise by 8% this year.

   (*a*) If Michelle uses the same amount of gas, what will be this year's total gas bill?

   (*b*) How much per month will she need to save (to the nearest £) in order to cover this year's gas bills?

6 Work out the missing figures *c, d, e* and *f* on Mr Lal's gas bill on page 279.

7 If Mr Lal pays £45.00 a month starting from now, after how many months will he be in 'credit'?

Electricity

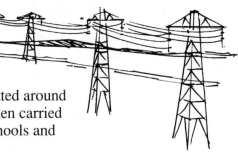

Electricity is generated in power stations, and is transmitted around the country by overhead cables carried on pylons. It is then carried under the ground in built-up areas, and into factories, schools and houses.

As with gas, a representative from the electricity company reads your electric meter each quarter or half year, after which a bill, similar to a gas bill, arrives through the post.

Like the gas board, the electricity company often estimates how much electricity you have used.

Example 2

Gerry's electricity meter is of the dial type. What is the reading on this meter?

10,000	1,000	100	10	1 kWh per div
				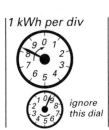

ignore this dial

Some of the dials are numbered clockwise, some anticlockwise. It is easy to find the reading by taking the *lower* of the two numbers between which each pointer lies.

The first figure is therefore 1, as the pointer is between 1 and 2.
The other figures are 4, 7, 5 and 8.
The reading is therefore 14758 units.
(A **unit** is a kilowatt-hour, a measure of electrical energy.)

EXERCISE 11.2

Work out the reading on each of these electricity meters:

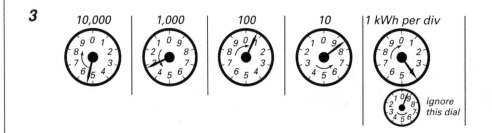

1

2

3

4

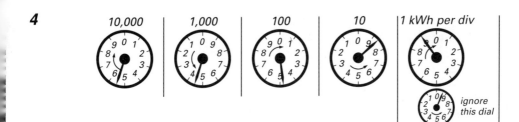

5

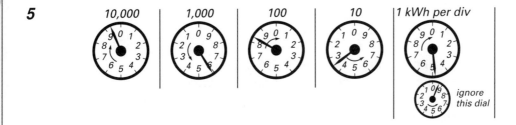

6

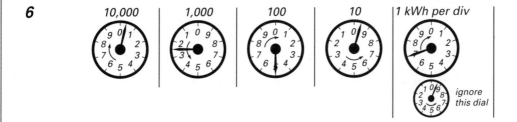

7 The diagram shows the meter reading a week before the electricity board representative read my meter as 37041. How many units have I used in the week?

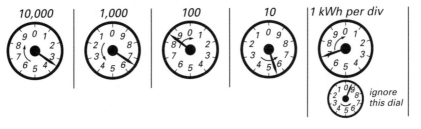

8 Mr Thompson's last electricity bill reading was 42754.
Today his meter dials show the following:

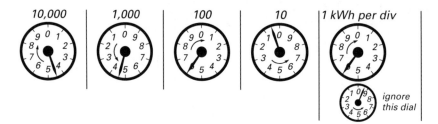

How many units has he used since the last reading?

9 Tim says that the reading on their meter is 32075. Sarah
says that he is wrong, as it should be 31975. Who is correct?

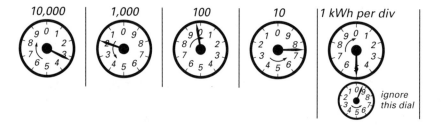

10 I read my meter each Sunday for the last three weeks. The
diagram shows the dials.

(a)

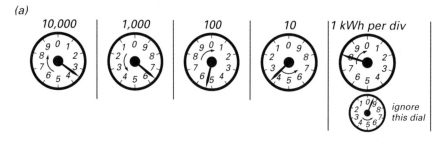

(b)

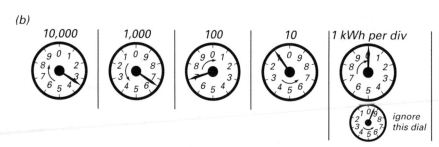

(c)

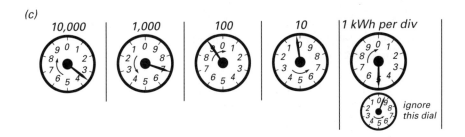

| 10,000 | 1,000 | 100 | 10 | 1 kWh per div |

(a) Work out whether I used more electricity during the first week or the second.

(b) How many units did I use during the fortnight?

Example 3

One of Gerry Mason's recent electricity bills contains these figures:

Tariff	Meter readings		Units	Units	Unit	Amount
	present	previous	used	charged	price p	£ p
			Quarterly Charge			9.10
D1	56102	53629	2473	2473	5.25	129.83
	Electricity charges this quarter					138.93

Reading date : 11 April

Check that (a) the number of units used is correct, and (b) the charge for those units is correct.

EXERCISE 11.3

1 Continuing with Example 3, Gerry's next meter reading was 57956. Assuming the same quarterly charge and unit price, work out the charges for this quarter.

2 During the next quarter he used 1497 units. Work out the missing figures in this bill (again, no change in quarterly charge or unit price):

Tariff	Meter readings		Units	Units	Unit	Amount
						Reading date : 11 October
	present	previous	used	charged	price p	£ p
			Quarterly Charge			*
D1	*	57956	*	*	5.25	*
	Electricity charges this quarter					*

3 Gerry's sister Amanda lives in an area where the quarterly charge is £9.50 and the unit price is 5.82p. What will be her total electricity charges in the next quarter, in which she uses 1850 units?

4 At the end of the quarter, her bill was actually £129.57. How many units had she used?

5 (a) If Amanda used 2473 units during one quarter, how much would these units cost her?

   (b) What would be her electricity charges for this quarter?

   (c) Gerry's charges for 2473 units were £129.83, as in Example 3 above. Work out as a percentage how much more these electricity charges are for Amanda than for Gerry.

6 How many units would Gerry have used if his bill came to £129.57 (assuming a quarterly charge of £9.10 and unit price of 5.25p)?

7 Last year Colin Sands agreed to pay £12 per week throughout the year for electricity. His first three bills during the year were for £172.05, £241.83 and £114.62. A letter with the fourth bill says that he owes the electricity company £3.48. For how much was his last bill?

8 Work out the missing figures on this electricity bill:

ELECTRICITY BOARD

Reading date: *25 June*

Tariff	Meter readings		Units used	Units charged	Unit price p	Amount £ p
	present	previous				
				Quarterly Charge		10.28
D1	37801	*	*	2106	5.25	*
				Electricity charges this quarter		*

Council Tax

Before the council tax, local authorities obtained money from (i) government grant and (ii) local rates. The rates that a householder paid were based upon the *rateable value* of the house, so that people in larger houses paid more, as did those who lived in towns rather than in country areas.

Example 4

All adults (i.e. over 18 years old) are due to pay council tax of £348 in a particular area. Gerry Mason, his wife Jean, and their three children Wendy (19), Matthew (16) and Lisa (14), live in this area.

(*a*) How much council tax is due, per year, from their household?

(b) Council tax can be paid by 12 equal instalments. How much will each instalment be for Gerry's household?

(c) Wendy starts a full-time course at the local College of Higher Education. She is therefore a student, which means that she has to pay only 20% of the council tax. Work out the new monthly instalment due from Mr Mason's house.

(d) What is the percentage reduction in council tax payments, now that Wendy is a student?

(a) Council tax due
$= £348 \times 3$
$= £1044$

(b) Each instalment
$= \dfrac{£1044}{12}$
$= £87$

(c) Wendy now will pay 20% of £348
$= £69.60$

Total council tax
$= £348 + £348 + £69.60$
$= £765.60$

New monthly instalment
$= \dfrac{£765.60}{12}$
$= £63.80$

(d) Original instalment
$= £87$
Reduction in instalment
$= £87 - £63.80 = £23.20$

Percentage reduction
$= \dfrac{£23.20}{£87} \times 100$
$= 26.7\%$

Part (d) could have been worked out using total annual figures:

Reduction
$= £1044 - £765.60$
$= £278.40$

Percentage reduction
$= \dfrac{£278.40}{£1044} \times 100$
$= 26.7\%$

Telephone

The advance of technology has enabled more and more people to use telephones. Recent improvements include extension 'phones upstairs, in-car 'phones, or even rechargeable cordless 'phones for taking down to the bottom of the garden which eliminate having to come all the way back to the house to answer a wrong number!

The method of paying a telephone bill is similar to that for a gas or electricity bill; you receive a statement each quarter, on which is printed the amount you have to pay for using the telephone system. Although British Telecom do not have meter readers who come to your house, each telephone line is automatically metered, so that all calls made are registered. There are different rates of charge, depending on whether you are making a local call, or a call to another district, or, indeed, to another country. From most private telephones you can call directly to most countries in the world.

Telephone bills are usually charged under four headings: rental-system, rental-apparatus, metered calls and operator calls.

Example 5

Work out the total charge for metered units on this telephone bill. What will be the total amount due, if VAT at 15% is to be added on to the total of all the charges?

Rental-System Charge	1st May to 31st July		14.65
Rental-Apparatus Charge	1st May to 31st July		0.95
Metered Calls			
Date	Meter reading	Gross units	Cost per unit
7th MAY	38825		
6th FEB	36886	1939	5.06p
		Total Charge For Metered Units	m
		Total Charge For Operator Calls	5.40
		Total of Current Charges (excl. VAT)	c
		Value Added Tax at 15%	v
		Total of Current Charges (incl. VAT)	t

Total charge for metered units, $m = 1939 \times 5.06\text{p}$
$= 9811.34\text{p}$
$m = £98.11$ (to the nearest penny).

Total of current charges, $c = £14.65 + £0.95 + £98.11 + £5.40$
$c = £119.11$

VAT, $v = 15\%$ of £119.11; $v = £17.87$ (to the nearest penny).

Total of current charges (incl. VAT) $= £119.11 + £17.87$
$t = £136.98$

EXERCISE 11.4

1 Five students agree to share the cost of a telephone. How much will each pay, over the year, if the four quarterly 'phone bills are £87.93, £70.66, £105.72 and £81.44?

2 I estimate that, for next year, my 'phone bills will be about £125 per quarter. About how much should I save, per month, to cover the cost of my bills?

3 By removing the extension telephone from my son's bedroom, my 'phone bill has dropped from £136.85 to £114.95 for the quarter.
   (a) What percentage decrease is this? (Give your answer to the nearest whole number.)
   (b) How much per week have I saved by taking out the extension 'phone? (Assume that a quarter is of length 13 weeks and give your answer to the nearest penny.)

4 Work out Gerry Mason's total telephone bill for this quarter.

Rental-System Charge	1st Feb to 30th April			14.65
Rental-Apparatus Charge	1st Feb to 30th April			2.03
Metered Calls				
Date	Meter reading	Gross units	Cost per unit	
7th FEB	71402			
8th NOV	69633	*	5.06p	
		Total Charge For Metered Units		*
		Total Charge For Operator Calls		12.97
		Total of Current Charges (excl. VAT)		*
		Value Added Tax at 15%		*
		Total of Current Charges (incl. VAT)		*

5 (*a*) Work out my total bill, including VAT, if the charge
excluding VAT is £116.47.
(*b*) My last bill came to a total, including VAT, of £140.30.
What was the charge without VAT?

Charge bands and rates

In the UK there are three main charge bands: **L** for *local calls*, **a** for
calls up to 56 km, and **b** for *calls over 56 km*.
There are also three rates of charge, depending upon the time of day:

peak rate (*P*), from 9.00 a.m. until 1.00 p.m. Monday to Friday,

standard rate (*S*), from 8.00 a.m. until 9.00 a.m. and from 1.00 p.m.
until 6.00 p.m. Monday to Friday, and

cheap rate (*C*) at all other times.

The table gives the length of time, in seconds, that you could have telephoned for 5.06p, in 1989.

Charge band	L	a	b
Cheap rate (C)	360	100	45
Standard rate (S)	90	34.3	24
Peak rate (P)	60	25.7	18

For example, if you rang the local post office on a Tuesday afternoon then you would be on the standard rate, and the local charge band. Therefore you would be charged 5.06p for a call lasting anything up to a minute-and-a-half (90 seconds). A little longer, and you would be charged 10.12p. If your call lasted just longer than three minutes, it would cost you another 5.06p, making 15.18p.

Example 6

Work out the cost of an 80-second call in charge band **a,** for each of the three rates.

At the *cheap rate*, I can have up to 100 s for 5.06p. Hence 80 s will cost the same, 5.06p.

At the *standard rate*, 34.3 s cost 5.06p, so up to 68.6 s will cost 10.12p, and up to 102.9 s will cost 15.18p. Hence 80 s will cost 15.18p.

At the *peak rate*, $\frac{80}{25.7}$ = 3.1128 . . ., which means I am into the fourth set of 25.7 s, which will cost me $4 \times 5.06p = 20.24p$.

EXERCISE 11.5

Using the table above, answer these questions.

1 Jamie rings his friend Walter one evening to discuss some maths homework. He is on the 'phone for $3\frac{1}{2}$ minutes. How much will this local call have cost?

2 At 8.30 a.m. the next morning, Walter telephones Jamie to check his homework. His call lasts 5 minutes. How much will it cost?

3 I have a recipe to pass on to my cousin which will take about 5 minutes to explain over the 'phone. How much would I save if I rang in the afternoon (*S* rate) rather than in the morning (*P* rate)? My cousin lives 250 km away, so the charge band is **b**.

4 Mandy told her friend: 'Last night Mum was on the 'phone to my Aunt Sheila for half-an-hour. It must have cost over £1.' If calls to Aunt Sheila are in charge band **a**, was Mandy correct?

5 One morning Savinder made three telephone calls. The two local calls lasted for $2\frac{1}{2}$ minutes and 6 minutes, and the call to London lasted 7 minutes. If the London call is charged at band **b**, work out the cost of the three 'phone calls.

6 How much would Savinder, in question 5, have saved if she had made her three calls in the afternoon (*S* rate) instead of in the morning?

7 Glyn is trying to reduce his 'phone bill. He needs to telephone Simon, and is allowing himself to spend £1.50 at most on the call. Simon lives quite a distance from Glyn, in charge band **b**.

(*a*) How long could Glyn's 'phone call last, at the cheap rate?

(*b*) If he can 'phone Simon only at 3.15 p.m. on a Thursday, how long can this call last?

(*c*) How much time would Glyn have, at the peak rate, for £1.50?

8 Work out the cost of a five-minute call for each of the rates and bands and then copy and complete the table.

Cost of a five-minute call (pence)			
Charge band	**L**	**a**	**b**
Cheap rate	5.06	*	*
Standard rate	*	*	65.78
Peak rate	*	60.72	*

Water

In many regions rain water is collected in large reservoirs, where it is filtered and cleaned by a Water Company, before being piped through water mains to homes, offices, factories, etc. A typical water company may charge householders for three items:
(i)   supplying water to the house
(ii)   sewerage services
(iii) environmental services (pollution control, fisheries, nature conservation, etc.)

A domestic bill for water rates usually comes once a year; you can sometimes arrange to pay your bill by eight instalments.

Here is an example of a bill for water services:

		Instalments	
		Date	Amount
Water Rate	73.02		
		1 MAY	19.40
Sewerage Services	79.77	1 JUN	19.28
		1 JUL	19.28
Environmental Services	1.57	1 AUG	19.28
		1 SEP	19.28
Total Amount Due	154.36	1 OCT	19.28
		1 NOV	19.28
		1 DEC	19.28

Check that the total of the instalments comes to £154.36.

EXERCISE 11.6

1 My water rates are £113.78, and after the first payment I pay seven instalments of £14.20. How much is my first instalment?

2 My next-door neighbour's bill is £127.43, and his first instalment is £16.13. How much is each of the seven remaining instalments?

3 Complete this water bill:

		Instalments	
Water Rate	87.36	Date	Amount
		1 MAY	*
Sewerage Services	96.03	1 JUN	23.50
		1 JUL	23.50
Environmental Services	4.74	1 AUG	23.50
		1 SEP	23.50
Total Amount Due	*	1 OCT	23.50
		1 NOV	23.50
		1 DEC	23.50

4 Basil's water rate bill requires a first instalment of £17.23, followed by seven instalments of £17.07. Basil would prefer to pay seven instalments of £17, and to increase the first instalment, so that the total payment is the same.

(*a*) What is Basil's total charge for water?

(*b*) What will be the new first instalment?

5 Mr Hall, a pensioner living on his own, has a water meter installed in his house. He has worked out that it will be cheaper to pay for water actually used than to pay the standard rate. Without a meter his water supply charge would have been £73.52. The meter has registered 1136

Budgeting

The process of deciding what you can afford to spend from your income, once you have taken into account any regular outgoings, is called **budgeting**. It is a necessary process for all households, so that essential items (rent or mortgage, gas, electricity, food, etc.) can be paid for, leaving money to be allocated for improvements (for example, a new fridge, or a garage extension) or luxuries (for example, a weekend holiday break, or a bar of fruit-and-nut chocolate).

Example 7

Victoria would like to buy a video cassette costing £15.99. She babysits regularly on Wednesdays and Fridays, for which she is paid £3.50 a night. From her money she has to pay 75p a week to a mail-order firm, and she usually spends £1.50 at a disco each Saturday. How many week's babysitting will she need to do in order to be able to afford the video?

Weekly income $\quad\quad\quad\quad = £7.00 \quad (2 \times £3.50)$
Weekly outgoings $\quad\quad\quad = £2.25 \quad (75p + £1.50)$
Total weekly amount left over $= £4.75$
If Victoria does not buy anything else, then after two weeks she will have £9.50, and after three weeks she will have £14.25.
At the end of four weeks she will be able to buy the video and have $(4 \times £4.75) - £15.99 = £19.00 - £15.99 = £3.01$ left over to spend.
We could have divided £15.99 by £4.75, giving 3.366 . . . . This means that it will take *four* weeks to save enough money for the video.

EXERCISE 11.7

1 If my regular outgoings each week are £107.49, and my take-home pay is £133.02, how many weeks will it take me to save up £120?

2 Stella earns £8.35 a week. From this she has to pay £2.78 each week to her sister, £1.83 weekly to a mail-order firm for clothes, and she saves £3.30. How much does she have left over each week?

3 Andrew does a paper round, for which he is paid £7.50 a week. He also works in the local butcher's shop each Saturday and earns £3.40. He pays £3.00 a week to his mother, saves £4.00, and buys a weekly magazine for 95p.

(*a*) How much does he have left over, each week?

(*b*) It costs £0.85 an hour at the snooker club. For how many hours a week, to the nearest half hour, can he afford to play snooker?

4 Frank's take-home pay is £117.45 a week. He lives with his parents and pays his mother £45 for his 'board and lodging'. He pays an insurance premium of £7.81 weekly, and has weekly hire purchase payments on a motor bike and a midi-system of £16.69. His poll tax is £6.15 a week. He estimates that he spends on average £7.50 a week on clothes. How much each week does he have left?

5 The Browns have estimated that their monthly outgoings are as follows:

Item	Cost
Mortgage	322.83
Electricity	65.00
Poll tax	58.00
Water	19.00
Insurance	45.71
Telephone	40.00
Car loan	104.72
HP	58.62
Train/bus	85.00

If the total income to the Brown's household is £1040 per month, how much do they have left for food, clothes and other expenses?

Investigation

Make a list of the things on which you usually spend your money, either each week or each month, whichever you find more convenient. Try to see if there are ways in which you can make savings, or increase your income, so that you have a little more left each week.

Budget accounts

Most banks can offer you a **budget account**. You estimate your regular outgoings for the year, divide by 12, and transfer that amount monthly from your current account into your budget account. You pay for those items in your budget account by a separate budget account cheque book, whenever the bill comes in. It does not matter that the bill makes you 'overdrawn' in one particular month, because the next month or two will probably bring you back into credit. At the end of the year you should be 'all square'.

Example 8

What is the monthly payment for this budget account?

Item	Cost
Mortgage	4200
Poll tax	930
Gas	600
Electricity	750
Water	270
Telephone	540
Car	1000
Total	
+ 10% emergency	
Final cost	

Total = £8290, and 10% of £8290 = £829.
So the final cost = £8290 + £829 = £9119.

The monthly payment will be $\frac{£9119}{12}$ = £759.92.

(You may as well pay £760 a month, as some of the figures are estimates of next year's bills.)

EXERCISE **11.8**

Work out the monthly repayments for these budget accounts.
Remember to add on 10% for emergencies, before calculating
the monthly figure, which you should round up to a suitable
amount.

1

Rent	1267.76
Poll tax	786.00
Electricity	845.00
Water	215.85
Insurances	216.48

2

Mortgage	3216.00
Poll tax	1120.00
Gas	856.50
Electricity	695.00
Water	395.97
Telephone	621.60
Car loan	703.68
Insurances	460.80

3
Mortgage	: £238.51 per month
Poll tax	: £352 × 2, annually
Gas	: £560 a year, approximately
Electricity	: £760 a year, approximately
Water	: £352.91, annually
Car loan	: £93.47 per month

Some of the larger department stores and hypermarket chains run a
budget scheme. You can buy an expensive item and pay for it by regular
monthly payments spread over a year, sometimes longer. Once you have
made a few payments, you can usually buy some other items, adding
them to your budget scheme. You still pay the same monthly instalment,
but now for a longer period of time until you have paid for the items.
There is usually a charge for allowing you to run such a scheme.

EXERCISE **11.9**

1 A supermarket runs a budget scheme, where the charge for
using the scheme is 8% of the cost of the item. After that the
minimum payment is 5% of the total charge. Work out the
budget payments on items costing (*a*) £100 (*b*) £625
(*c*) £462.72 (*d*) £699 (*e*) £237.51.

2 At a supermarket, Nancy decides to buy a patio set, costing £79.99, by means of a budget scheme. The charge for using the scheme is £5.73. If Nancy's repayments are £4.80, after how many payments will she have cleared her account with the supermarket?

3 A table and four chairs costs £349 at a store. After adding the charge of £19.69, the budget payments are 8% of the total. How much is each payment?

4 The total charge for buying a television set and video recorder through a budget scheme is £647.20.

(*a*) The minimum payment is 5% of the total charge. How much is this?

(*b*) Joseph would like the bill cleared in twelve monthly payments. Work out how much each payment would be, to the nearest £.

(*c*) If Joseph can afford to pay £45 per month at most, how many payments must he make before he has paid the total charge?

5 Pru buys a carpet for her lounge. The total bill is £462.71, and her budget payments are £6.38 per week. As soon as she owes less than £200 she can buy curtains, costing £84.26, without having to increase her payments.

(*a*) After how many weekly payments can she have the curtains?

(*b*) How many more weeks will it take to pay for both carpet and curtains?

The Post Office

As well as selling stamps and delivering letters and parcels, post offices perform many other services. At post offices you can buy telephone savings stamps which count as part payment towards your telephone bill, pay gas, electricity, telephone and other bills, and, if qualified to, receive Child Benefit and State Pension payments. One useful facility is a post office National Savings Bank account: a post office is open for longer hours than a bank, and is usually much nearer.

EXERCISE 11.10

1 How much will a sheet of 240 15p stamps cost?

2 I have eight overseas letters to post. Can I post them all, at 39p each, if I have only £3?

3 Mrs Chung collects her pension and allowance of £41.68 each week from her post office. How much will she receive in a year?

4 I have a parcel to post, which I am told at the post office will cost £2.82 to send. If I also buy eight 22p stamps, how much change will I receive from a £5 note?

5 Mrs Blackburn has three young children. She receives Child Benefit of £7.25 per week for each child. One Tuesday she buys three 50p television savings stamps, a £5 telephone stamp, a postal order costing £10.41 and four 22p stamps using the child benefit money. How much will she have left?

Use the table to work out these postage costs.

Non-EEC European letters and postcards					
Not over	£	p	Not over	£	p
20 g		23	450 g	1	91
60 g		39	500 g	2	11
100 g		55	750 g	2	90
150 g		74	1000 g	3	68
200 g		92	1250 g	4	25
250 g	1	10	1500 g	4	83
300 g	1	31	1750 g	5	40
350 g	1	51	2000 g	5	98
400 g	1	71			

6 A letter weighing 150 g.

7 Three postcards weighing 11 g each.

8 A letter weighing 670 g.

9 Two letters, weighing 280 g and 730 g.

10 Five letters, each weighing 267 g.

11 In question 9 above, the two letters were for the same person. If the letters had been sent in one envelope, how much cheaper would it have been?

12 The table gives the 1986 costs for posting a letter in the UK.

Weight not over	1st class	2nd class	Weight not over	1st class	2nd class
60 g	18p	13p	500 g	92p	70p
100 g	26p	20p	600 g	£1.15	85p
150 g	32p	24p	700 g	£1.35	£1.00
200 g	40p	30p	750 g	£1.45	£1.05
250 g	48p	37p	800 g	£1.55	Not
300 g	56p	43p	900 g	£1.70	admissible
350 g	64p	49p	1000 g	£1.85	over 750 g
400 g	72p	55p	Each extra 250 g		
450 g	82p	62p	or part thereof 45p		

(*a*) How much did a second class letter weighing 250 g cost?

(*b*) A letter weighing 382 g was sent first class. How much did the stamp cost?

(*c*) How much cheaper was it to send five letters, each weighing 487 g, by second class than by first class post?

(*d*) A large letter weighed 1.44 kg. How much did it cost to send it by letter post?

(*e*) The secretary of a sport's club sent out information by post to its 134 members. How much was the postage, second class, if each letter weighed 109 g?

13 Parcel post rates during part of 1989 are given in the table.

Weight not over	National rate	Area rate	Weight not over	National rate	Area rate
1 kg	£1.50	£1.30	7 kg	£3.10	£2.90
2 kg	£1.90	£1.70	8 kg	£3.25	£3.05
3 kg	£2.35	£2.15	9 kg	£3.45	£3.25
4 kg	£2.55	£2.35	10 kg	£3.60	£3.40
5 kg	£2.75	£2.55	25 kg	£4.60	£4.40
6 kg	£2.95	£2.75			

(Area rate operates if a parcel is to be sent over a short distance.)

(*a*) Two parcels, weighing 2.3 kg and 4.4 kg, were sent to a school. How much was the national rate postage?

(*b*) How much cheaper would it have been if the two parcels could have been combined into one?

(*c*) What weight was the heaviest parcel that I could have sent, at the area rate, if I was allowed only £2.50 to spend on postage?

Melanie had five books to post. They weighed 820 g, 1.13 kg, 693 g, 1.45 kg and 1.38 kg.

(*d*) How much would it have cost to post them separately?

(*e*) They have to be made up into two parcels before posting. How can this be done least expensively?

12. Mathematical postscript

Simultaneous equations

If five light bulbs cost £3.50, you can easily find the cost of one light bulb, by dividing £3.50 by 5 to give 70p.

We can write this problem in algebraic terms (letters standing for numbers) by letting x be the cost of a light bulb, and *solving the equation* $5 \times x = £3.50$.

This gives $x = \dfrac{£3.50}{5} = £0.70$

The equation $5x = 3.50$ is an example of a *linear* equation in one unknown (x).

Example 1

Three nuts and two bolts cost 37p, and two nuts and a bolt cost 23p. How much does a nut cost?

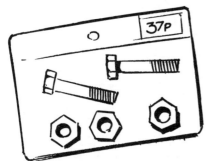 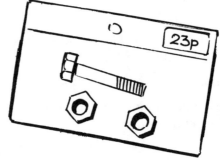

Here we have two unknown prices. If we let the price of a nut be n and the price of a bolt be b, then we can write two algebraic equations:

$$3n + 2b = 37 \quad \text{and} \quad 2n + b = 23$$

(we write b when we have only one b).
In order to find n and b, we **solve the equations simultaneously.**

If two nuts and a bolt cost 23p, then four nuts and two bolts must cost 46p.
We can say that $2n + b = 23$ is equivalent to $4n + 2b = 46$.
(It is also equivalent to $20n + 10b = 230$. As long as we remember to multiply *both* sides of the equation, it will be equivalent to the original, whatever number we multiply it by.)

We now have

$3n + 2b = 37$ and $4n + 2b = 46$

Writing one equation below the other:

$3n + 2b = 37$
$4n + 2b = 46$

If we now take away the top equation from the bottom one, we will be left with

$4n - 3n = 46 - 37$

as the $2b$ terms are equal, and cancel each other out.
This is now $n = 9$
So a nut must cost 9 pence.
We can now work out that, since two nuts and a bolt cost 23p, a bolt must cost $23 - (2 \times 9) = 5p$.
   What we have done is eliminated one of the unknown letters (in this case b), to give us a *linear* equation in *one* unknown, a simple one in this case, $n = 9$.

Example 2

Solve these equations simultaneously:

$4p + q = 15$ and $p + 2q = 16$.

If we double the first equation we will have $8p + 2q = 30$, which contains the same number of q's as the second equation.
Writing one equation below the other,

$8p + 2q = 30$
$p + 2q = 16$

Taking the second equation away from the first

$8p - p = 30 - 16$
i.e. $7p = 14$ (a simple equation in one unknown)
or $p = 2$

Substituting the value of $p = 2$ into one of the original equations will enable us to find the value of q. Choosing the first equation will give

$(4 \times 2) + q = 15$
i.e. $8 + q = 15$
or $q = 7$

We should now *check* that these values for p and q work in the second equation (we often say 'satisfy the equation' rather than 'work in the equation').
$(p + 2q)$ should equal 16; and as $2 + (2 \times 7) = 2 + 14 = 16$, it checks.

EXERCISE 12.1

Solve these equations simultaneously:

1 $a + b = 4$ and $3a + b = 10$ **2** $3x + 2y = 14$ and $x + 2y = 10$

3 $4i + 5j = 23$ and $4i + j = 11$ **4** $4p + 3q = 32$ and $p + 3q = 17$

5 $3x + 2y = 11$ and $2x + y = 7$ **6** $c + 4d = 13$ and $2c + d = 12$

7 $a + b = 7$ and $3a + 2b = 18$ **8** $7x + y = 16$ and $x + 2y = 19$

9 $5x + y = 13$ and $2x + y = 7$ **10** $a + 2b = 12$ and $a + 3b = 12$

Although we have used 'plus' signs in these examples, and the answers are all integers (whole numbers), we can have negative signs in the equations. Later we will look at equations in which the solutions are negative, or fractions or decimals.

Example 3

Solve the equations $3x + 2y = 19$ and $x - y = 3$.

Doubling the second equation gives $2x - 2y = 6$.
Writing this equation below the first one:

$$3x + 2y = 19$$
$$2x - 2y = 6$$

If we now *add* the equations, the '$+2y$' and the '$-2y$' cancel each other out, whatever the value of y. This leaves us with

$$3x + 2x = 19 + 6$$
$$5x = 25$$
$$\text{i.e. } x = 5$$

Substituting this value back into one of the original equations (the second one is simpler), we have $5 - y = 3$,

$$5 - y = 3$$
$$\text{i.e. } y = 2$$

(Check that the first equation does come to 19: $(3 \times 5) + (2 \times 2) = 19$.)

EXERCISE **12.2**

Solve these equations simultaneously:

1 $x + y = 7$ and $x - y = 1$ **2** $p + 2q = 6$ and $3p - 2q = 10$

3 $2a - b = 5$ and $a + b = 4$ **4** $5x - 2y = 1$ and $x + 2y = 5$

5 $10a + b = 53$ and $a - b = 2$ **6** $m + 2n = 14$ and $2m - n = 13$

7 $y + 6z = 34$ and $2y - z = 3$ **8** $3a - b = 28$ and $a + 3b = 16$

9 $4x + 3y = 7$ and $3x - y = 2$ **10** $4c - d = 24$ and $3c + 2d = 18$

In each of the three examples considered so far in this chapter, we have chosen one of the letters and made sure that _both_ equations have the _same number_ of this chosen letter. In Example 3 we added the equations, because we had a '+2y' and a '−2y' which cancelled each other out.

In Examples 1 and 2 we subtracted. In general it causes less chance of error if you _add_ algebraic terms rather than subtract them.
Referring back to Example 1, we had

$$3n + 2b = 37$$
$$\text{and } 4n + 2b = 46$$

Instead of subtracting, we could have multiplied one equation by −1. This has the effect of changing all '+' signs to '−' and all '−' signs to '+'.
The first equation will then become

$$-3n + (-2b) = -37 \text{ or } -3n - 2b = -37$$

If we now _add_ this to the second equation, we will have

$$-3n + 4n - 2b + 2b = -37 + 46$$

which gives $n = 9$, as before.

General strategy for solving simultaneous equations
(i) Choose one letter, and make both equations have the same number of this letter, multiplying each equation by a number, where necessary.
(ii) Make the signs of these equal numbers different (one '+' and the other '−') if they are not different already, by multiplying one equation by −1.
(iii) Add, to eliminate this chosen letter.
(iv) Solve the resulting linear equation, to find one value.
(v) Substitute this value into one of the original equations in order to find the other value.
(vi) _Check_ in the other original equation.

Example 4

Solve the equations $2x - 3y = 13$ and $4x - 5y = 24$.

(i) Choosing y, the first equation will have to be multiplied by 5 and the second by 3, to give $15y$ in both equations

$10x - 15y = 65$ and $12x - 15y = 72$

(ii) As the signs are the same ($-15y$ in both equations), multiply the first one by -1

$-10x + 15y = -65$

(iii) Adding: $-10x + 12x + 15y - 15y = -65 + 72$
which gives $\qquad 2x = 7$
(iv) $\qquad$ i.e. $x = 3.5$
(v) Substituting into the first equation:

$$(2 \times 3.5) - 3y = 13$$
$$\text{i.e. } 7 - 3y = 13$$

Adding $3y$ to each side: $\qquad 7 = 3y + 13$
Subtracting 13 from both sides: $7 - 13 = 3y$
$$-6 = 3y$$
$$\text{i.e. } y = -2$$

(vi) Check in the second equation:
$$4x - 5y = (4 \times 3.5) - (5 \times -2)$$
$$= 14 - (-10)$$
$$= 14 + 10$$
$$= 24, \text{ which is correct.}$$

EXERCISE 12.3

Solve these simultaneous equations. The answers may be fractional, or negative, or both. Although any letters could be used, we use x and y in each question.

1 $x - y = 8, x + y = 14$ $\qquad$ **2** $2x + y = 15, 3x - y = 5$

3 $3x - 2y = 8, 5x + 2y = 16$ $\qquad$ **4** $x + 4y = 12, 3x - 2y = 1$

5 $x + y = 2, 2x - y = 7$ $\qquad$ **6** $3x + y = 3, x + 2y = 16$

7 $x + 4y = 10, 2x + 4y = 17$ $\qquad$ **8** $2x + 3y = 1, 4x - y = 16$

9 $3x + 4y = 1, 5x + 6y = 1$ $\qquad$ **10** $x + y = 1, 6x - 3y = 0$

Solving equations: trial-and-error methods

So far we have seen how to solve linear equations (e.g. $3x + 5 = 11$) and simultaneous equations. For some equations, however, we do not have a straightforward strategy to enable us to find a solution easily. A trial and error method is often a useful approach.

Area
$10cm^2$

x

x

Example 5

Solve the equation $x^2 = 10$

As $(3)^2 = 9$, and $(4)^2 = 16$, an approximate answer is likely to be a little over 3.
Let us try 3.1: $(3.1)^2 = 9.61$
This is still below 10, so try 3.2: $(3.2)^2 = 10.24$
We now have a better answer than $x = 3$: the answer must lie between 3.1 and 3.2.
Repeating the process, let us try 3.15:

$$(3.15)^2 = 9.9225$$

This is quite close, but try 3.16 to see if it is nearer:

$$(3.16)^2 = 9.9856$$

This is even nearer, just let us make sure by trying 3.17:

$$(3.17)^2 = 10.0489$$

Taking each of the last two answers to three significant figures, $(3.16)^2 = 9.99$ (i.e. 0.01 below) and $(3.17)^2 = 10.05$ (0.05 above). Hence, if $x^2 = 10$, then $x = 3.16$, correct to two decimal places. If your calculator has a square root function, then a much more accurate solution can be found ($x = 3.162\ 277\ 7 \ldots$). ($x = -3.162\ 277\ 7 \ldots$ is also a solution of the equation $x^2 = 10$, since $(-x)$ multiplied by $(-x) = +x^2$. In Exercise 12.4 consider only positive solutions.)

If, instead, the equation had been $y^3 = 10$, then your calculator may not have a suitable function for obtaining a solution directly. In this case we may need to use the approximate method already tried. As $2^3 = 8$ and $3^3 = 27$, then a reasonable guess at the value for y might be 2.1.
Trying 2.1: $(2.1)^3 = 9.261$
Trying 2.2: $(2.2)^3 = 10.648$
As 2.2 is rather nearer than 2.1, a better guess at the value of y might be 2.16.

Trying 2.16: $(2.16)^3 = 10.077\ 696$. As this is over 10, it is worth
trying 2.15: $(2.15)^3 = 9.938\ 375$
Both values have about the same error, so try 2.155:

$(2.155)^3 = 10.007\ 874 \ldots$

Check, by trying a value just less, i.e. 2.154:

$(2.154)^3 = 9.993\ 948 \ldots$

We could go on as long as we liked, each time getting a more accurate
answer. For most purposes, three decimal places is adequate.

EXERCISE 12.4

Use trial and error to find a solution to these equations. Work
out your answers to two decimal places. (There may be more
than one solution to some of the equations, just try to find one
solution.)

1 $x^2 = 20$ **2** $2x^2 = 100$

3 $x^2 = 50$ **4** $(x + 2)^2 = 50$

5 $x^2 + x = 13$ **6** $(x - 3)^2 = 35$

7 $x^3 - 4x = 17$ **8** $200 - x^2 = 0$

9 $\dfrac{x^2}{x + 1} = 5$ **10** $x^4 = 1000$

Products of primes

As a reminder, a **prime** number has two different factors only, itself
and 1.

The smallest prime number is therefore 2 (because 1 does not have
two *different* factors).

The next one is 3, but 4 has 2 as a factor, so 4 is not prime. We can
write $4 = 2 \times 2$, expressing 4 as a product of prime numbers only.
(A *product* is the result of *multiplying* numbers together.) Similarly,
$6 = 3 \times 2$; $8 = 4 \times 2 = 2 \times 2 \times 2$, if we wish to use only prime numbers.

Example 6

Write as a product of primes (*a*) 30 (*b*) 98 (*c*) 99 (*d*) 100.

(*a*) $30 = 5 \times 6 = 5 \times 3 \times 2$

(*b*) $98 = 2 \times 49 = 2 \times 7 \times 7 = 2 \times 7^2$

(*c*) $99 = 9 \times 11 = 3 \times 3 \times 11 = 3^2 \times 11$

(*d*) $100 = 10 \times 10 = (5 \times 2) \times (5 \times 2) = 2 \times 2 \times 5 \times 5 = 2^2 \times 5^2$

(Using the power notation can often make the writing shorter.)

It is usual to write the smallest prime number first; the solution to (*a*) in Example 6 will therefore be $30 = 2 \times 3 \times 5$. In working out the prime factors of a large number, beginning with the smallest and working up will usually be the most efficient solution.

Example 7

Express 432 as a product of primes.
As 432 is even, then 2 will be a factor: $432 = 2 \times 216$.
As 216 is even, there will be another factor of 2: $432 = 2 \times 2 \times 108$.
Repeating until we reach an odd number: $432 = 2 \times 2 \times 2 \times 2 \times 27$.
But $27 = 3 \times 9 = 3 \times 3 \times 3$.
Hence $432 = 2 \times 2 \times 2 \times 2 \times 3 \times 3 \times 3 = 2^4 \times 3^3$.

EXERCISE **12.5**

Write these numbers as a product of their prime factors.

1	18	*2*	35	*3*	16	*4*	12
5	42	*6*	90	*7*	72	*8*	100
9	210	*10*	64	*11*	49	*12*	50
13	36	*14*	27	*15*	11	*16*	125
17	14	*18*	216	*19*	1000	*20*	1 000 000

There are occasions when we wish to find the largest number which will divide exactly into two numbers (*highest common factor*), or the least number that two other numbers will divide into exactly (*lowest common multiple*). Using prime factors can simplify these processes.

Example 8

What is the largest number that will divide exactly into (*a*) 18 and 30 (*b*) 20 and 24 (*c*) 48 and 72?

(a) By writing $18 = 2 \times 3 \times 3$ and $30 = 2 \times 3 \times 5$, the factors which are common to both are 2 and 3. The highest common factor is therefore $2 \times 3 = 6$. (Hence there are no other numbers greater than 6 which will divide exactly into both 18 and 30.)

(b) Writing each number as a product of prime factors, $20 = 2 \times 2 \times 5$ and $24 = 2 \times 2 \times 2 \times 3$. The highest common factor is 2×2 i.e. 4.

(c) $48 = 2 \times 2 \times 2 \times 2 \times 3$ and $72 = 2 \times 2 \times 2 \times 3 \times 3$. The highest common factor is $2 \times 2 \times 2 \times 3 = 24$.

Example 9

What is the smallest number into which (a) 4 and 12 (b) 6 and 8 (c) 10 and 12 will divide exactly?

(a) As 4 divides exactly into 12, then 12 is the lowest common multiple. (12 is the least number into which each will divide exactly.)

(b) Using primes: $6 = 2 \times 3$ and $8 = 2 \times 2 \times 2$.
Our answer must have 6 (i.e. 2×3) *and* 8 (i.e. $2 \times 2 \times 2$) as factors. The smallest such number will have prime factors of 2, 2, 2 and 3. Hence the lowest common multiple of 6 and 8 is $2 \times 2 \times 2 \times 3 = 24$.

(c) $10 = 2 \times 5$ and $12 = 2 \times 2 \times 3$. The smallest multiple will have prime factors of $2 \times 2 \times 3 \times 5$, in order to have both 2×5 and $2 \times 2 \times 3$ as factors.
    Hence the lowest common multiple of 10 and 12 is $2 \times 2 \times 3 \times 5 = 60$ (i.e. 60 is the smallest number into which both 10 and 12 can divide exactly.)

EXERCISE 12.6

Find the highest common factor of each pair of numbers.

1	5 and 15	**2**	3 and 12
3	20 and 30	**4**	24 and 36
5	40 and 56	**6**	35 and 50
7	48 and 64	**8**	60 and 100
9	15 and 20	**10**	16 and 18

EXERCISE 12.7

Find the lowest common multiple of each pair of numbers.

1	4 and 8	**2**	5 and 20
3	2 and 5	**4**	6 and 9
5	6 and 10	**6**	12 and 30
7	16 and 20	**8**	100 and 150
9	6 and 7	**10**	24 and 36

Investigation A

Make a flow diagram for deciding whether or not a given number is prime. Test your flow diagram, using the numbers 40, 41, 42, 43, 44, 45, 46, 47, 48 and 49.

Extension

Convert your flow diagram into a computer program, which will print out (*a*) the number, if it is prime, or (*b*) the prime factors of the number, if it is not prime.

Coordinates in three dimensions

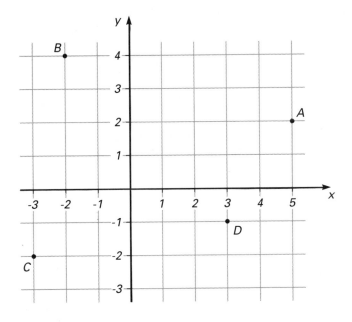

To jog your memory on coordinates, in the diagram the point A is (5,2), B is (–2,4), C is (–3,–2) and D is (3,–1).

So the first number is the *x* **coordinate** and the second number is the *y* **coordinate**.

We can extend the idea of coordinates into three dimensions quite easily, by thinking of the *x* and *y* coordinates as distances east and north of the origin, and introducing a *z* **coordinate** as a measure of the *height* above ground level.

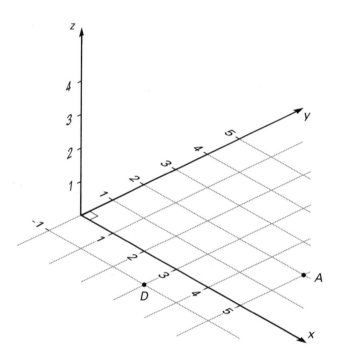

Example 10

Just at the moment when an aeroplane signals to the control tower of an airport, it is 700 m east and 800 m north of the airport, and is flying at a height of 250 m. What are its coordinates, considering the airport as the origin?

The aeroplane's coordinates are (700,800,250).

Example 11

The cube opposite has edges 4 units long. If A is at the point with coordinates (1,2,0), what are the coordinates of B, E, and F?

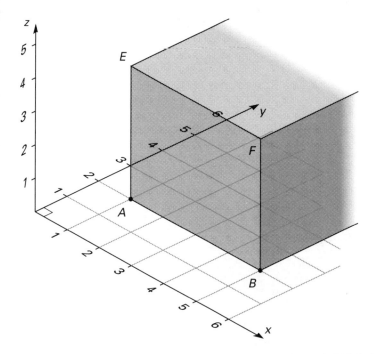

The other corners will be at B(5,2,0), E(1,2,4) and F(5,2,4).

EXERCISE **12.8**

(Triangular 'dotty' paper or isometric paper may help.)

1 A rectangular box has three of the corners of its base at the
points (0,0,0), (7,0,0) and (7,4,0).

   (*a*) What are the coordinates of the fourth corner of the
base?

   (*b*) If the box is 3 cm high, write down the coordinates of
the other four corners.

2 A room is 12 m long, 7 m wide and 3 m high (see overleaf).

   (*a*) If one corner is (0,0,0), what are the coordinates of the
opposite corner on the floor?

   (*b*) Write down the coordinates of the points P, Q and R.

   (*c*) The room can be divided into two by a folding screen,
which is attached to the wall at the points (0,4,0) and
(0,4,3). When the screen is pulled across the room, what
are the coordinates of the top and bottom of the screen
where it reaches the opposite wall?

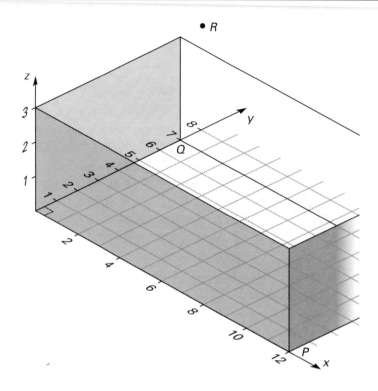

3 F is the midpoint of the line joining E to G. Find the coordinates of:

(*a*) G, if E is (0,0,0) and F is (2,3,4).

(*b*) G, if E is (3,6,5) and F is (5,4,3).

(*c*) F, if E is (2,2,2) and G is (6,6,6).

(*d*) F, if E is (2,0,3) and G is (8,6,3).

4 A box, 8 cm by 6 cm by 5 cm high, has a partition put in diagonally, as shown in the diagram opposite. The partition is 5 cm high.

(*a*) How long is the partition?

(*b*) If the corner 0 is at (0,0,0), what are the coordinates of H, the midpoint of the top of the partition?

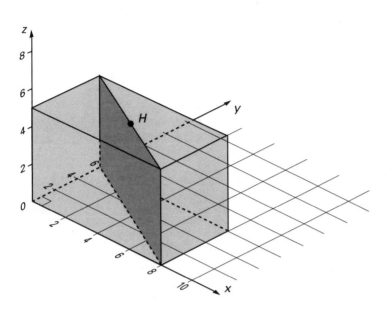

5 I know that the points (1,2,0) and (4,5,3) are the ends of a diagonal of a cube whose faces are parallel to the axes. Work out the coordinates of the other six corners of the cube.

Investigation B

What is the length of the longest straight thin rod which could fit into a box measuring 20 cm by 30 cm by 60 cm?

Triangles

Property

In *any* triangle the three angles always add up to 180°.

Types of triangle

Scalene triangle — all sides and angles different.

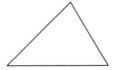

Acute angled triangle – all angles acute (less than 90°).

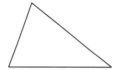

Obtuse angled triangle – one angle obtuse (between 90° and 180°), the other two *must* be acute.

Right angled triangle – one angle is a right angle (90°) (why only one?).

Isosceles triangle – two sides are equal, and the two angles opposite these sides are also equal.

Equilateral triangle – all three sides are equal, and all three angles are equal to 60°.

Quadrilaterals

Property
In *any* quadrilateral the four angles always add up to 360°.

Types of quadrilateral
Scalene — all sides and angles different.

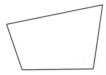

Trapezium — two opposite sides parallel.

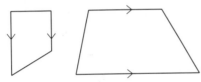

Kite — one pair of opposite angles equal: this means that
    (i) the diagonal joining the equal angles is bisected
        at right angles by the other diagonal
    (ii) the two sides forming an unequal angle are
        equal.

Parallelogram - both pairs of opposite sides parallel: this means that
    (i)   both pairs of opposite sides are equal
    (ii) adjacent angles add up to 180°
    (iii) both pairs of opposite angles are equal
    (iv) diagonals bisect each other.

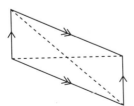
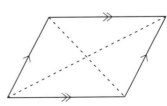

Rhombus   – all four sides equal: this means that
         (i)   adjacent angles add up to 180°
         (ii)   both pairs of opposite angles are equal
         (iii) diagonals bisect each other at right angles.

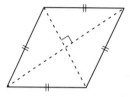

Rectangle   – all four angles are right angles: this means that each
         pair of opposite sides is equal (and parallel).
         (A rectangle is a special type of parallelogram.)

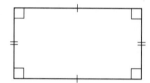

Square   – all four sides equal, all four angles are right angles.

There are two other distinct types of quadrilateral:
(*a*) the 'arrowhead' type, in which there is a reflex angle (greater than
     180°)

(*b*) the 'cross-over' quadrilateral, where two of the sides intersect.

Investigation C

Copy and complete this table, putting a 'tick' in the column if the quadrilateral possesses that property.

	No equal sides	No equal angles	One pair of equal sides	One pair of equal angles	One pair of parallels	Two pairs of equal sides	Two pairs of equal	Two pairs of parallels	4 equal sides	4 equal angles
Square										
Rectangle										
Rhombus										
Parallel-ogram										
Kite										
Trapezium										
Scalene										